Hanna Klien

All Eyes on Shah Rukh!

Filmwissenschaft

herausgegeben von

Privatdozent Mag. Dr. Claus Tieber

Band 14

LIT

Hanna Klien

All Eyes on Shah Rukh!

An Intercultural Approach to the Gaze in Karan Johar's Films

LIT

Cover illustration: Chrish Klose, Wednesday Paper Works
All pictures within the book: © Sony Music India/Dharma Productions

Printed with the support of the Federal Government of Vorarlberg

Vorarlberg
Wissenschaft

Bibliographic information published by the Deutsche Nationalbibliothek
The Deutsche Nationalbibliothek lists this publication in the Deutsche Nationalbibliografie; detailed bibliographic data are available in the Internet at http://dnb.d-nb.de.

ISBN 978-3-643-90371-6

A catalogue record for this book is available from the British Library

©LIT VERLAG GmbH & Co. KG Wien,
Zweigniederlassung Zürich 2013
Klosbachstr. 107
CH-8032 Zürich
Tel. +41 (0) 44-251 75 05
Fax +41 (0) 44-251 75 06
E-Mail: zuerich@lit-verlag.ch
http://www.lit-verlag.ch

LIT VERLAG Dr. W. Hopf
Berlin 2013
Fresnostr. 2
D-48159 Münster
Tel. +49 (0) 2 51-62 03 20
Fax +49 (0) 2 51-23 19 72
E-Mail: lit@lit-verlag.de
http://www.lit-verlag.de

Distribution:
In Germany: LIT Verlag Fresnostr. 2, D-48159 Münster
Tel. +49 (0) 2 51-620 32 22, Fax +49 (0) 2 51-922 60 99, E-mail: vertrieb@lit-verlag.de

In Austria: Medienlogistik Pichler-ÖBZ, e-mail: mlo@medien-logistik.at
In Switzerland: B + M Buch- und Medienvertrieb, e-mail: order@buch-medien.ch
In the UK: Global Book Marketing, e-mail: mo@centralbooks.com
In North America: International Specialized Book Services, e-mail: orders@isbs.com
e-books are available at www.litwebshop.de

Contents

3. Gazing in Song and Dance Sequences

To my sisters Katja and Vera,

For our desires, our loves, our passions

Acknowledgments

First and foremost, I would like to thank my parents, who supported my academic work in multiple ways. Special thanks go to my mother, who introduced me and my sisters to Indian films. Our shared experiences and ideas related to Bollywood as well as many discussions with friends, colleagues and fans have inspired me to investigate the attractions of Karan Johar's films. I have focused on one particular aspect that I consider fundamental to Johar's great popularity across the world and especially in Western Europe: the gaze. The manuscript developed alongside many changes in my life and at the date of its publication I think I am one step closer to understand why these films that are often described as reflecting conservative, patriarchal ideologies, can give us a liberating and comforting feeling.

Furthermore, I am grateful to my professors and lecturers at the University of Vienna. I gained a lot of insights into Cultural Studies as well as anthropological approaches to film from my professors Monika Seidl and Elke Mader. In the field of Hindi cinema and Film Studies in general, Claus Tieber has contributed much to my understanding of theoretical and methodological approaches. I want to thank him, in particular, for supporting me with valuable and helpful feedback on the manuscript as well as with encouraging words. Moreover, my thanks go to Patric Kment for his continuous support throughout the years.

The publication of the manuscript would not have been possible without the support of the provincial government of Vorarlberg. I am grateful for the generous sponsorship the department for science and education of the state granted.

Introduction

In recent times Bollywood has become a global buzzword and even in Western discourses it seems to have reached mainstream status: soprano singer Natalie Dessay in an interview for "Live in HD" promises a "Bollywood-like" production of Giulio Cesare at the Metropolitan Opera; the established German magazine DER SPIEGEL reports on the promotion of an Indian top bank manager in an article entitled "Bollywood in Frankfurt"; and in Vienna's MQ (MuseumsQuartier Wien) dance performers organize a Bollywood Flashmob. All this indicates that Bollywood has become a floating signifier in global imaginaries. It is the result of an intense process of globalization that has not left the cinema culture based in Mumbai untouched. What used to be seen as a derogatory term alluding to the dominant cinema culture of Hollywood is now embraced and used to refer to cultural forms beyond Hindi cinema. Ashish Rajadhyaksha, the author of "Encyclopedia of Indian Cinema" (1999) calls this phenomenon the 'Bollywoodization' of Hindi film (2008). Within the culture industry, Bollywood films in Hindi language are produced that now more than ever incorporate and transform elements of Hollywood. This results in aesthetics in which filmic conventions and codes of various cinematic cultures are negotiated. A leading figure in this process is Karan Johar, whose work as a director and screenwriter has contributed much to the contemporary image of Bollywood all over the world. Various blockbusters in the 90s and 2000s bear his trademark and have been milestones in the assertion of Bollywood as a globally acknowledged cultural form.

However, when discussing this recent development, the fact that Hindi cinema has always interacted with styles and trends in other film as well as media cultures in- and outside India should not be ignored. Generally, films should thus be seen as hybrid media products. The incorporation of elements from other cultural forms is a highly complex process, as they are always negotiated in the context of Hindi film aesthetics. Ravi Vasudevan refers to this process as a mixing of codes, which he describes in the context of the 40s and 50s films labeling them as a "transitional cinema" (Vasudevan 2000b). As my approach to contemporary Hindi films starts out from the perspective of globalization processes, it is essential to discuss the term mixing or hybridization in this context. Criticizing essentialist notions of culture, Homi Bhabha uses the concept of hybridity to point out the ambivalence of colonial discourse. In the presence of the hybrid, he states, "the difference of cultures can no longer be identified or evaluated as objects of epistemological or moral contemplation: they are not simply there to be seen or appropriated" (1985: 156). Hybridity thus signifies moving away from fixed and essentialist notions of culture, which ultimately can also break down "the symmetry and duality of self/Other, inside/outside" (158).

The contestation of this duality is at the core of my research study and is encountered here at different levels of investigation: the general perspective on Hindi cinema in the context of film studies; the negotiation and deconstruction of the two major theoretical approaches; and the analysis of the filmic texts. In the following I will give an overview of all three. Firstly, Hindi cinema is considered here as an inherently hybrid media product. Its hybridity can be seen as a major reason for its global attractiveness. The adaptation of Hollywood style, primarily of the realist mode and continuity editing, might be perceived by Western viewers as a rapprochement of a universal norm. This reflects a Eurocentric perspective on media cultures. As in any other filmic tradition, Hollywood's styles and practices have evolved as a norm in a specific historical and cultural setting. Due to the hegemony of Western media in the world it has spread globally. Consequently, it has to be seen as one of many forms of representation that rely on "maps of meaning" (Hall 1997: 29), shared by us due to our socialization in a specific cultural and social group. Thus, as film recipients and especially as analysts, we are obligated to reflect on our viewing practices, which are shaped by our own social conventions and habituation.

Even in film studies this is a critical issue as can be seen in the discussion around early American cinema. As Tom Gunning points out, early cinema has often been seen as primitive and underdeveloped. In contradiction to this widespread opinion he considers it as a "cinema of attractions". It is exhibitionist in so far that it does not comply with the realist illusion predominating later on (Gunning 1990: 64). The realist mode, which is a crucial marker of contemporary Hollywood, creates the illusion in the spectator that films portray a "hermetically sealed world" (Mulvey 2009 [1975]: 17). Gunning argues that early films have been seen as inferior because they were assessed from a normative point of view with the narrative function as paramount criterion. But the films in question originated in a period when the display and exhibitionism were attractions in their own right (1990: 66). This example shows that even within the American film tradition there is a great deal of variety and that the acknowledged norm in Hollywood productions is by no means 'natural', but conventional.

The aim of this study is to identify a pool of filmic devices that have been established in the recent globalization process as well as in the negotiations of Western forms of representation in Hindi cinema. Primarily, the focus lies on Karan Johar's style and specific forms of representations in his films. Yet there are no clear-cut borders, as other filmmakers have used and continue to use similar forms. Therefore, what is identified are clear tendencies in the corpus of films analysed here. Some can be seen as representatives of contemporary Hindi cinema, others show significant differences.

In the analysis I will put an emphasis on song and dance sequences for various reasons. Firstly, song and dance is a primary marker of Hindi cinema and even more so due to the recent globalization processes, as it serves to demarcate Hindi cinema from other cinematic forms (Gopal/Moorti 2008: 1f). Since contemporary films mostly adapt the realist mode in the narrative space, song and dance offers a greater variety of modes of representation. Secondly, it is a space displaying a high density of hybridization as different music styles, dances as well as imageries are used. Thirdly, song and dance also play a crucial role in the representation of love and the erotic, which is of major interest in this context as the study puts an emphasis on the negotiation of gender conceptions. Fourthly, in recent years song and dance sequences have also increasingly been integrated into the narrative of Hindi films (Vasudevan 2000a: 10). This phenomenon is tightly connected to the adaptation of the realist mode and other characteristics of globalized Hindi cinema. Thus, the focus also lies on the relationship between song and dance and the narrative space. Generally, we can say song and dance is of particular relevance to the objective of tracing the mixing and negotiation of filmic codes in contemporary Hindi films.

Let us now turn to the second level of investigation, which is more specifically connected to the major object of research: the gaze. The main focus of my approach lies on how gender conceptions and relations are negotiated. In this context representations of visual interactions as well as their corresponding spectator constellations are relevant. As the title of the book suggests, the aim here is to approach the gaze from an intercultural perspective. Therefore, two concepts and their theoretical background shall be brought together, negotiated and deconstructed by their interplay. On the one hand, feminist psychoanalytic theory has conceptualized the erotic gaze, which is built into filmic texts as fundamentally male and objectifying. Laura Mulvey's seminal work in this context has been widely discussed in Western and Indian film studies. Her main argument is that the female body is displayed as object of desire and erotic spectacle, while the male figure has agency and pushes the narrative forward (Mulvey 2009 [1975]: 15). On the other hand *darshan* is a concept of the gaze originating in Hindu religious worship. It refers to the act of the devotee looking at the deity's image, which in turn gazes back. Consequently, seeing and being seen lead to a union of the two which gives blessing to devotees (Eck 1985: 6). In Indian film studies, representations of this gaze and its influence on scopic regimes in film texts as well as on star images, have been identified (Vasudevan 2000b, c; Prasad 1998: 72ff; Taylor 2003). As the two approaches both refer to core elements of Western and Indian philosophical concepts, their application and negotiation leads to more general questions of intercultural relations. Thus, the study on the one hand uses the approaches as epistemological lenses, but on the other hand also touches upon a deconstruction of basic paradigms of thought in Western and Indian contexts.

It might be surprising to some readers that a religious concept such as *darshan* is applied in the context of gender and love relationships, especially focusing on the erotic and sexuality. Yet it should be remembered that the dichotomy between the erotic and the religious that might lead to such a reaction is deeply rooted in specific traditions of Christianity. Religions like Hinduism and many others worldwide have always involved erotic elements. The best example in Hindu belief is the relationship between the deities Krishna and Radha, whose mutual love is mostly described as essentially passionate and sexualized. In some religious movements in India this relationship is also seen as a model of love between the deity and the devotee, such as *bhakti* (King/Brockington 2005: 3). Furthermore, the presence of deities and the sacral is much more common in Hindi films than in Western cinema. Rachel Dwyer states that films as such have a religious significance, too (2006b: 4). Thus, it is not surprising that *darshan* plays a role in the filmic context.

Both theoretical approaches to the gaze shall be scrutinized for correlating, overlapping and contradicting conceptions of self and Other, or subject/object relations. Corresponding to the gender focus, woman's confinement to the object position as a "bearer, not maker, of meaning" (Mulvey 2009 [1975]: 15) is of particular interest in this context. In contrast, the underlying principle of *darshan* states that the object of the gaze holds power, because only if it gazes back can the union be achieved. Ultimately, these two assumptions in the context of the film analysis lead to the questions of how desire is represented and how desiring positions are determined. A special focus lies on the representations of female desire and sexual identity, precisely because feminists have argued that in the patriarchal discourse this is near to impossible. Luce Irigaray speaks of a "hommosexuality" as she argues that in predominating systems of representation only male identity is sexed. The seeing male I/eye constructs sexuality as always the same, namely a masculine thing (Robbins 2000: 153). For the analysis of the film corpus this means that various notions of femininity and masculinity have to be taken into account. Moreover, their negotiation in the context of differing concepts of love, the body and the erotic is at the centre of the analysis. It shall be investigated whether forms of representations in the film corpus adhere to what Mulvey calls "a new language of desire" (2009 [1975]: 16).

Thirdly, the following film analysis touches on different aspects which can all be seen in the context of the contestation of dualism: modes of representation, spectatorship and star image. Let us first focus on the modes of representation and related research questions. In terms of the realist mode the main focus lies on the ways it is renegotiated in the space of song and dance. As the narrative space is dominated by it, song and dance sequences offer alternative scopic relations. Various devices are used, transformed or opposed in different stages of the filmmaking process. For example, the mise-en-scène in a song and dance sequence can reflect the adaptation of the realist mode in the film, generally by inserting the lover's enchanted dance into New York City's everyday bustle. The most prominent characteristic of the realist mode, continuity editing, is also exploited in various ways to achieve new forms of representation and alternate the scopic relations. On the one hand, there are specific devices which have been established to represent darshanic gazing. For example, dialogues between devotees and (often mute) *murtis* of deities (the image or form the deity takes as object of worship) are common in films and often represented by shot and counter shot. Moreover, interactions in the religious context such as the ritual of *puja* frequently appear in similar forms of representation. On the other hand, continuity editing can also be negotiated and played on in the context of *darshan*. A short delay or missing establishing shot can suspend the expectations built up by conventional shot/counter shot series. Thus, desire and power positions signified by the gaze between two characters can shift easily, opening up alternative perspectives on gender relations, too.

The other mode of representation relevant in this context is the iconic mode. Generally, iconicity in films can be characterized as static and emblematic. In Indian film studies the definition by Radhyaksha and Kapur is most common, so Vasudevan refers to it by describing the iconic image not only as static but also as binding condensed, multilayered meaning (2000c: 388). This is interesting in so far as Mulvey, in contrast, sees iconized representations as 'flat'. She refers to fragmented, mostly close-up shots of the female body and argues that "[i]n contrast to woman as icon, the active male figure (the ego ideal of the identification process) demands a three-dimensional space" (2009 [1975]: 21). However, in the context of *darshan* iconized images of the female figure can have very different effects. Representations of the male figure in song and dance sequences are also frequently marked by iconicity. When notions of *darshan* in the filmic context are evoked, the analogy of iconized images and *murtis* evolves. This can also be found in representations of the couple as discussed by Gayatri Chatterjee. She argues that, similarly to religious icons, especially of Krishna and Radha, the couple can appear as dual figure (2005: 94f). Consequently, Mulvey's concept has to be reconsidered in this context.

Generally, the iconic mode is deeply connected to filmic representations drawing on *darshan* and therefore has effects on spectatorship. While the realist mode creates the illusion that the spectator is peeping into a private world, darshanic notions of gazing invite the spectator to look at the object and receive the blessings if the object gazes back. This raises various issues with regard to spectatorship and cinematic pleasure when examined from the intercultural perspective my study takes on. In her concept of scopophilia Mulvey draws on Freud, putting voyeurism at the core of the pleasures in looking. Similarly to the private and forbidden (body parts) that arouse the objectifying, erotic gaze, the hermetically sealed world of the cinema screen endorses the voyeuristic desire of the spectator (Mulvey 2009 [1975]: 17). This form of voyeurist spectatorship, however, produces a feeling of guilt, as Mulvey argues (Ibid.: 22), or shame, as Katja Silverman states (1994: 277). In opposition, *darshan* is marked by exhibitionism as it invites the gaze, but with a crucial difference: the object to be looked at holds power. In terms of spectatorship, this can mean that the darshanic gaze engages a form of spectatorship relying on public viewing based on communal relations, according to Madhava Prasad (1994: 103).

In this context the modes of address employed in the films are of essential significance. The main focus in my analysis lies on the frontal, direct address. Vasudevan defines this mode of address as shots which are characterized by frontal staging, the direct look into the camera and stylised performance (2008: 138). It will become clear that in the film corpus the frontal, direct address is often used in moments of intensive gazing in the song and dance sequences. Taylor and Sanzaro also point at the predominance of close-up shots of the lovers' faces looking directly into the camera in the context of *darshan* (Sanzaro 2007: 19; Taylor 2003: 307). Generally, the term frontality is applied here to refer to shots that are marked by frontal positioning and by different ways that enable alternative forms of spectatorship.

However, in terms of spectatorship it is important to point out that my approach is not based on the assumption of an inscribed spectator. The criticism of psychoanalytic film theory and its deterministic perspective on media recepients is taken into account here. Especially representatives of Cultural Studies such as Stuart Hall have pointed out the complex processes of meaning-making in the reception process (cf. Hall 2005 [1973]). Thus, it might be most useful to differentiate between inscribed and actual spectator, as Rajadhyaksha suggests (2000: 290). This approach bestows agency on the spectator, and the analysis can regard the inscribed spectator in terms of non-deterministic viewing positions. This discussion offers great insights into more general issues connected to spectatorship and related dualistic concepts. For example, the dichotomy between private and public is of major interest: which conventions are used to represent specific forms of eroticism and how are they renegotiated in the film corpus? Moreover, identification emerges as a concept highly contested in the intercultural approach as it is intrinsically connected to constructions of the relation between self and other. The concept of union in *darshan* of the deity and the devotee withstands Eurocentric notions of symbiosis. Rather it holds a concept of identification which overcomes the dichotomy of self and other so prominent in Western discourses. What does this mean for filmic representations of darshanic gazing and spectatorship in this context? In the analysis special attention is paid to the effects this underlying concept of identification can have on inscribed spectator positions.

The last of the three principal aspects of the analysis is the star image. Due to clear tendencies in the film corpus this part of the study is mainly concerned with the male lead actor in all samples: Shah Rukh Khan. Although other films have strongly influenced the on-screen image of this actor, Karan Johar's staging of Shah Rukh Khan has contributed significantly in shaping it. Certain techniques and devices predominant in Johar's style are intrinsically connected to Khan's star image. Some of them present representations of *darshan* and other forms of the gaze. In general, the star image shall be regarded here in the context of spectacle. Mulvey describes how the display of woman as sexual object is a source of pleasure in film. The objectified female body thus serves as erotic spectacle (Mulvey 2009 [1975]: 19). For the analysis of the spectacle of the female and male stars in the film corpus, however, this approach is too limited. Indeed, taking darshanic notions of the gaze into account breaks up Mulvey's fixed position of exhibitionist as female and passive. Moreover, in Johar's particular staging of Shah Rukh Khan's male emotionality, desire and even the act of gazing itself are moved to the centre of the spectacle. At the same time the female lead actress is hardly ever found on display as erotic spectacle. While this might grant even more attention to Shah Rukh Khan, it also serves a seemingly crucial purpose in all films: to establish female subject positions and represent female desire. I would argue that this element of Karan Johar's films has also become part of Shah Rukh Khan's star image.

Due to the intercultural perspective of the research, special attention shall be paid to conventions established in film studies that ascribe certain effects to devices. These shall be scrutinized and reflected upon, taking into account the hybridization processes. The focus clearly lies on mise-en-scène, camera and editing techniques in the context of the outlined theoretical concepts. Naturally, my own position as a spectator socialized within Hollywood cinematic culture as well as a researcher socialized in Western media studies is part of this reflection process. The challenge of overcoming internalized viewing habits in the face of global cinema has been part of this research project. It is evident that my personal reception context connected to German speaking audiences in the midst of Europe plays a role in the approach to and indeed in the choice of the research object as such. After all, the collaborations of Karan Johar and Shah Rukh Khan which form the film corpus have been milestones in the opening up of new audiences to Hindi cinema, especially in Europe.

The book is structured into three main parts, starting with a general introduction to Hindi film and its aesthetics in order to contextualize the object of research in a wider context (Chapter 1). It is important to point out the conventions and filmic traditions which the films discussed here refer to or which, in some cases, they dismiss. In the second part (Chapter 2) the theoretical framework is described in detail and the fundamental differences between the concepts of the gaze as well as convergences of it will be pointed out. Furthermore, the implications for the methodological shall be considered. The last part (Chapter 3) is the analysis of the samples focusing on various different types of song and dance sequences, followed by a general conclusion.

State of Research

The field of film studies offers a variety of approaches towards the gaze. My research focus is localized by the seminal works primarily used here. Laura Mulvey's article "Visual Pleasure and Narrative Cinema", originally published in 1975, is the basis for the conception of the erotic gaze taken as a starting point from psychoanalytical film theory. This approach has been discussed in the context of Hindi cinema as well and I refer to Asha Kasbekar, who applied Mulvey's concept to the analysis of Hindi films. In the case of *darshan* Ravi Vasudevan's written work and applied analysis mainly directed my research interest. Furthermore, the approaches to *darshan* by Francis Sanzaro and Uttara Coorlawala play an important role in the development of arguments that are central to this study. It is along these lines that the state of research has been compiled. As we will see, the literature on darshanic gazing in Hindi cinema is dense, but limited to a number of seminal texts, which will be introduced below. In contrast, the psychoanalytical approaches require a more rigorous selection, as reactions on Mulvey's as well as other concepts of the gaze in cinema are abundant.

For the general approach to Hindi cinema concerning historical and social background, as well as its aesthetics and characteristics, four reference works were of major importance to this study. Rachel Dwyer's "All You Want is Money, All You Need is Love: Sexuality and Romance in Modern India" (2000) as well as her collaboration with Divia Patel "Cinema India: The Visual Culture of Hindi Film" (2002) are seminal works of Indian film studies. Not only do both works offer detailed introductions to the film culture and its social backgrounds, but the former also has a special focus on notions of love, desire and intimacy, which are highly relevant to this study. Recent trends and characteristics of the Bollywood industry are outlined by Rajinder Dudrah in "Bollywood: Sociology goes to the Movies" (2006). Although his work is more concerned much with various reception contexts as well as other cultural forms associated with films, it is relevant for an understanding of the samples which adhere to the Bollywood cultural industry. In German-speaking film studies Claus Tieber has published a basic reference work titled "Passages to Bollywood" (2007), which offers an excellent overview of Hindi cinema. Apart from these seminal works, there is an anthology edited by Jigna Desai and Rajinder Dudrah, "The Bollywood Reader" (2008), which brings together the most influential authors of Hindi film studies such as Ashis Nandy, Madhava Prasad, Ashish Rajadhyaksha, Vijay Mishra and many others. As it covers diverse issues relating to Hindi film I have been using the anthology extensively.

The literature more specifically interested in the gaze will be shortly outlined in two sections. Firstly, let me refer to the works used to extend and revisit the basic concepts presented in Laura Mulvey's essay. Mulvey herself offers some further insight in her edition of collected essays published with the title "Visual and

Other Pleasures" (2009), in which she reflects on her original essay. Other authors concerned with psychoanalytical film theory contribute to a better understanding of the mechanisms behind the filmic representations of the gaze as well as the underlying philosophical concepts. In terms of the phallic gaze Katja Silverman's text "Fassbinder and Lacan: A Reconsideration of Gaze, Lack, and Image" (1994) adds to central issues of this study although concerned with a very different type of film. Furthermore, Anne Friedberg offers insights into the concept of identification in "A Denial of Difference: Theories of Cinematic Identification" (1990). These and other (re-)considerations of the gaze as well as Mulvey's concepts help to develop further the basic framework of the erotic gaze. One particular contribution focusing on the erotic gaze and Hindi film shall be emphasized here: Asha Kasbekar's essay "Hidden Pleasures: Negotiating the Myth of the Female Ideal in Popular Hindi Cinema" (2001), which comprises many aspects of erotic gazing in the context of narrative as well as song and dance.

Further discussions of the gaze in Indian film studies often include references to Mulvey. Scholars such as Rajadhyaksha (2000) have further developed Mulvey's concept and in the case of Prasad also put them into the context of other scopic regimes like *darshan*. The latter refers to this in his seminal work "Ideology of the Hindi Film: A Historical Construction" (1998), which points out the private/public divide in filmic representations, which is highly relevant to this study, too. Apart from the already mentioned work of Vasudevan, Woodman Taylor contributes to a better understanding of darshanic gazing in Hindi film. In the essay "Penetrating Gazes: The Poetics of Sight and Visual Display in Popular Cinema" (2003) the hybrid nature of *darshan* and the interaction with cultural forms such as *nazar* (a concept predominating in Urdu literature) are emphasized. Furthermore, the applied analysis of Gayatri Chatterjee (2005) points out important characteristics of filmic representations of *darshan*. An interesting approach to *darshan* as "mode of perception" is introduced by Francis Sanzaro (2007). In terms of performance tradition and its connection to scopic regimes encompassing *darshan* and psychoanalytic concepts, Uttara Coorlawala served as a major source of inspiration (1996). More generally, an understanding of *darshan* was enabled by the works of Diana Eck (1985), Christopher Fuller (1992) and Lawrence Babb (1981), which all describe the gaze in the context of religious worship.

1. Understanding Hindi Cinema, Understanding Bollywood

Indian cinema is founded on long and diverse traditions of film making. In recent years, the global popularity of the cultural phenomenon Bollywood has led to a misleading identification of it with Indian films in general, especially in Western countries. However, only some of the films that are produced every year in India can be considered a part of the emerging culture industry which is usually referred to by the term Bollywood. Thus, a precise contextualisation of films, including a definition of terms, is indispensable. Moreover, the historical development of Hindi cinema shall be traced in this chapter. Altogether the contextualisation shall enable a better understanding of the modes of representation based on their origins and related conventions. Recent transformations and innovations that are relevant for the following analysis are highlighted.

Generally, the Indian film industry is one of the oldest in the world and the biggest by number as well as distribution. Every year over 800 films are produced in 16 different languages and address audiences in different regions in India and beyond (Tieber 2007: 43). It is important to keep in mind, though, that only 10% of these films are successful; the number of flops at the box office is immense (Ibid.: 56). After the country became independent in 1947 the film industry has become one of the most significant industries there. Regional cinemas have emerged according to the different languages, Hindi being one of them. The Bombay-produced Hindi cinema, on which the focus of this study lies, can also be considered a pan-Indian popular culture due to its widespread distribution (Dwyer/Patel 2002: 9).

Depending on the focus of research, Hindi cinema can be seen as "third cinema" emphasizing the national and postcolonial aspect (cf. Vasudevan 2000a, b), as part of a Bollywood popular culture and culture industry (cf. Dudrah 2006) or even in the context of "Bollyworld", a term hinting at the global and transnational aspects (cf. Kaur/Sinha 2005). This study is exclusively concerned with big-budget commercial Hindi films which are predominantly seen as belonging to the Bollywood culture industry. The analysis is situated in a negotiation between Western and Indian concepts of perception and, more generally, modes of thought.

Taking a Look Back: Historical Development of Hindi Cinema

The history of film in India starts as early as 1896 with the first public screening by the Lumière brothers in Bombay, only some months after the first one in Paris. By 1913 Dhundiraj Govind Phalke had produced RAJA HARISHCHANDRA, which is commonly seen as the first Indian feature film (Dwyer/Patel 2002: 13). The story is taken out of the *Mahabharata* and thus the film established the genre of the mythological film (Ibid.; Tieber 2007: 15). At the time cinema was regarded as a low profession, especially for women, as not even prostitutes would play in films. It was Phalke's daughter who was the first actress, which already foreshadowed the joint family system in the film business (Tieber 2007: 16). Another important event in the early days of cinema was the introduction of censorship in 1918 by the colonial authorities, primarily to ensure positive representations of the West (Ibid.). As we shall see, censorship by colonial and later national institutions had a considerable impact on forms of representation.

With the introduction of the first talkies in 1931 Indian film began to diversify rapidly. Regional studios produced films in those languages that were widespread in a specific part of the country. The most significant up to today have been the Bengali cinema, mostly produced in Calcutta; the Malayam cinema in Kerala; the Telegu and Tamil cinemas in South India (Dwyer/Patel 2002: 8; Tieber 2007: 19). As Dwyer and Patel emphasize, out of the regional cinemas it is the „Bombay-produced, Hindi-language cinema that is not only screened across India but is also dubbed into local languages“ (2002: 9). Language can be seen as a principal reason for its dominance, as Hindi is the designated national language and is understood in most parts of the country.

In the 30s a studio system similar to that in the United States of America developed and enabled the first boom of Indian films. But in contrast to its equivalent in the USA, there was never a homogeneous style nor were standards set up. The most famous studios include *Bombay Talkies*, *New Theatres* in Calcutta and *Prabhat Film Company* at Pune (Tieber 2007: 20). The huge amount of black money infiltrating the film economy after the Second World War caused the downfall of the studio system, as independent producers emerged and stars were paid enormous amounts of money (Ibid.: 22; Dwyer/Patel 2002: 19). The following period is remembered as the golden age of Indian cinema. In the 50s the so-called formula films of Hindi cinema were hugely successful and were predicated on stars, music and dance (Dwyer/Patel 2002: 21). The cinema starred actors such as Raj Kapoor, Dilip Kumar and Nargis, while the most famous directors were Mehboob Khan, Guru Dutt, Raj Kapoor and Bimal Roy. During these years India also saw the rise of the highly influential playback singer Lata Mangeshkar.

In the following years profound changes took place in the film industry. The crisis of the Indian nation state, which reached its peak with the declaration of the State of Emergency in 1975, affected Hindi cinema in various ways. As

Prasad states: „new expectations arising out of the political upheavals of the period produced the conditions for exploration of new forms, narratives and characterological innovations“ (1998: 132). In Bombay a new star emerged who would dominate Hindi cinema for almost the next twenty years: Amitabh Bachchan. The popularity of the "angry young man" character which Bachchan played in many films of the 70s was the answer to the repression, poverty and corruption of those years (Tieber 2007: 96). Furthermore, the character of Vijay that he played in many of his films combined the romantic hero who fights against injustice with the man defending family values (Dwyer 2009: 106ff). Thus, Bachchan represented a new star image, and while a general decline of the cinema began, he attracted large audiences as all but a one-man-show.

In the 80s Hindi cinema suffered a severe crisis, and only with the comeback of the romantic family film in the 90s did another boom take place (Dwyer 2000: 138; Tieber 2007: 122). The focus of this study lies on films of this period as well as later productions that have been strongly influenced by the developments taking place then. Generally, the romantic family films were dominated by issues such as changing gender roles, consumerism, the negotiation between East and West, as well as the relationship with the diaspora (the Non-Residential Indians). The joint family became the primary arena where resulting conflicts were dealt with (Tieber 2007: 122; Dwyer 2000: 96ff). The films that Dwyer calls „big-budget, plushy, romantic films“ (Dwyer 2000: 100) especially targeted the new middle classes as well as the Indian diasporic community, predominantly in North America and Europe. Furthermore, radical economic reforms enabled the liberalization of the country and the local market opened up to Western influences. In 2001, the Indian film industry was granted industry status, which facilitated investments (Desai/Dudrah 2008: 13). The new ways of financing films have had a great influence on the modes of film production and thus on the aesthetics of Indian films (Ibid.; Tieber 2007: 44, 174). Some of the major consequences of this restructuring process have become quite obvious in recent years, such as the growing importance of screenplay and authorship. In contrast, Hindi cinema had previously been characterized by a "fragmented, episodic structure" (Prasad 1998: 43) of the text. Romantic family films have largely informed the conception of Bollywood films as exuberant, often 'kitschy' boy-meets-girl stories with happy endings.

As we have seen in this short historical overview, the romantic family film is, however, only one trend dominating in the 90s and early 2000s. Other genres and film styles have always existed in Hindi cinema. Particularly of note is the Indian art house cinema, which underwent a very different historical development from the 60s onwards. This was primarily due to the government support it enjoyed. While in the golden age cinema tried to unite artistic value and mass popularity, the „New Indian Cinema“ developed a depreciating stance towards commercial cinema (Tieber 2007: 67). Popular films continue to be associated with escapism, melodrama and mere entertainment (Desai/Dudrah 2008: 10) and are seen in opposition to various other forms of cinema, which are mostly demarcated by the use of the realistic mode. Consequently, the melodramatic and the realist mode are significant markers which, depending on the context, can signify difference among traditions not only of Indian film but also of global cinema.

As already mentioned, audiences outside India became highly significant in the 90s. The importance of NRI (Non-Residential Indian) communities influenced modes of production as well as representation in Hindi cinema. When, in 1998 the film Dil Se … (Mani Ratnam) starring Shah Rukh Khan became the first real box-office success in Great Britain, it became clear that a great change in audiences of Indian films was taking place. The same film had failed at the Indian box-office, but with the profit from the overseas market it nevertheless earned a remarkable amount of money (Dudrah 2006: 33ff). This was a key event as the overseas territory of distribution had used to be rather insignificant compared to those into which the Indian country had been divided: Bombay, Uttar Pradesh, East Punjab, Eastern Circuit, Central Province Berar, Central India, Rajasthan, Nizam Mysore, Tamil Nadu and Andhra (Tieber 2007: 52). Consequently, certain directors and actors (such as Karan Johar and Shah Rukh Khan) became associated with the transnational distribution of Hindi films, which will be treated in more detail later on in the context of the Bollywood culture industry. This study particularly focuses on this kind of Hindi film from the perspective of globalization processes.

To understand this development in recent years it is interesting to take a closer look at audiences and viewing practices related to Hindi cinema. In India audiences are extraordinary in many ways. First, the sheer number of moviegoers is remarkable; Pendakur estimates that the „actual theatrical attendance may be around 26 million a day“ (2008: 58). Furthermore traditions such as touring cinemas (Ibid.) or the practice of repeated viewing (Tieber 2007: 64) have influenced the cinema tradition to a great extent. In general, the style of Hindi cinema in particular is very present in Indian everyday life and can be seen as an „all pervasive visual culture“(Dwyer/Patel 2002: 8). Audiences are very diverse and may be differentiated according to genre, historical period or region. On the one hand there are the big budget productions, which nowadays primarily cater to the new middle class and the diaspora (Dwyer 2000: 96ff). On the other hand young, underprivileged men of the working classes constitute the major group in other cinema halls, as Derné shows in his ethnographic work on movie-going in India (2000: 52). This is relevant in so far as it hints at the wide range of audiences the films cater to and seek to attract. However, we have to keep in mind that the commercial cinema involves many different genres which are also shown in different kinds of cinema halls (cf. Dwyer 2000: 99). The popularity of Hindi films with NRI audiences has led to more recognition in Western societies, too. Due to eurocentric perception of the global mediascapes, it has often been ignored that Hindi films have always been distributed in large parts of the world. Raj Kapoor and his films, for example, enjoyed great popularity in the Soviet Union. Although Tieber argues that there has never been a relevant audience outside India and the Indian diaspora (Tieber 2007: 9), I would like to point out the great variety of contemporary global audiences in countries such as Nigeria (see Larkin 2008), Germany and Austria (see Mader/Budka 2009) or even Peru (see Hirzer/Mader 2011). These audiences might not be very large in number, but contribute nonetheless to a globalization of Indian film.

Nevertheless, the major significance of commercial cinema in the 90s lies in the opening up of diasporic markets and the Western ones which go hand in hand with them. The resulting shift in priorities is mostly due to the spending power of the audiences in question. In 2007 Tieber already stated that only 35 percent of the income of the industry was made in India (2007: 52). Consequently, the modes of distribution have changed a great deal in the past 15 years: production companies have their own selling agencies, distribution has become more structured in general and marketing has improved (Ibid.; Pendakur 2008: 62). Increasingly, foreign companies have been investing in the Indian film industry and co-operations are much more common. To give an example: just recently the blockbuster *My Name is Khan* (Karan Johar, 2011) has been released worldwide and distributed by Fox Star Entertainment.

Definition of Terms

The use of the term Bollywood is controversial, as it is associated with an appropriation of Indian cinema by Western discourses (Desai/Dudrah 2008: 2). Its origin is usually traced back to a European denomination of the film industry based in Bengali Tollygunge as "Tollywood", but sometimes is sometimes said to have been coined in a British novel of the 70s (Govil 2008: 203). Before the 90s it was interpreted as a prejorative term signifying negative sides of Hollywood and its mass media production. Moreover, it implied an imitation of the US American culture industry in India (Tieber 2009: 7). Only in the 90s, with the increasing globalization of Hindi cinema, was the term Bollywood re-evaluated. Especially in Western countries it is often used to refer to Hindi films in general, but as Tieber points out, Bollywood today means much more than just films (Ibid.).

In his essay "The 'Bollywoodization' of the Indian cinema" Ashish Rajadhyaksha points out that Bollywood as a culture industry cannot be equated with the national film industry. It is a "diffuse cultural conglomeration involving a range of distribution and consumption activities from websites to music cassettes from cable to radio" (2008: 192). He goes on to state that although Indian cinema can be seen as part of Bollywood, not all films are:

> The difference between the 'Bollywood' movie and the rest of the Hindi and other language films being made would be, say, the difference between Karan Johar and David Dhawan, between Shah Rukh Khan and Govinda, between PHIR BHI DIL HAI HINDUSTANI and ANARI NUMBER 1 (2008: 196).

In conclusion, Rajadhyaksha defines the difference as one "between a low-end local production with little ambition to new global markets, and a glossy internationalized production" (Ibid.). As we can see, director Karan Johar and actor Shah Rukh Khan are mentioned here as markers of a globalized Hindi cinema and the culture industry Bollywood. This has been significant for the selection of films analysed in this study, which exclusively adhere to the Bollywood mode.

Not only has the term Bollywood been re-defined in academic literature, but the object of research has changed as well. While major works in Indian film studies are concerned with Indian popular cinema (Nandy 1998) or the Hindi film (Prasad 1998), various anthologies have been published in recent years supporting the use of the term Bollywood, which they even use in their titles, and justifying this use in similar ways. Dudrah and Desai, for example, introduce "The Bollywood Reader" stating that Bollywood has become "the dominant globally recognized term to refer to Bombay's (Mumbai's) prolific Hindi-Urdu language culture industry and cinema" (2008: 1). The term also signifies the hybrid nature of the Hindi film industry as Kaur and Sinha explain in the introduction of "Bollyworld". In their anthology about Song and Dance "Global Bollywood" Gopal and Moorti stress the global aspect of Bollywood furthermore: "We use the term Bollywood instead of Hindi commercial cinema to capture the global orientation of this formation" (2008: 4).

However, in Western countries Bollywood is still often associated with *kitsch* and triviality or seen in exotistic ways (see also Dudrah 2008: 243). Consequently, I decided to predominantly use the term Hindi film even if most of the films discussed here could also be called Bollywood movies. As I am partly applying psychoanalytical theory to Indian films, I also want to signify by using this term that I am aware of the danger of reading Indian cinema "within Eurocentric hermeneutics" (Desai/Dudrah 2008: 2). Quite the contrary, the aim of this study is to question fundamental paradigms of thought in Western film studies. At the same time I do not wish to dismiss the important issue of globalization and the development of the culture industry, which is implicit in the term Bollywood.

Characterising Contemporary Hindi Film

The contextualisation of the modes of representation central to the analysis demands a closer look into the changes taking place in Hindi film aesthetics and conventions. The modes of production and related social and economic processes shall be partly addressed, too. First and foremost, an analysis of Hindi film should emphasize its hybrid nature and origins. From the very beginning, Indian cinema has drawn on a wide range of cultural forms and traditions. In the 19th century, Indian visual culture was influenced considerably by emerging Western technologies, such as photography or printing, as well as by Western theatre. The colonial cultural forms were partly fused with local and indigenous forms (Dwyer/Patel 2002: 10). Thus, performing traditions like those of the Parsi theatre, which included many features which can be found in contemporary Hindi films, such as song and dance sequences or the series of attractions (Ibid.: 14), were already hybrid. Consequently,

> Much of Indian cinema is thus the product of a new public culture that arose during the nineteenth century, the hybridity of which is inherent to its very nature, as it brings together traditional Indian images with industrial technology (Dwyer/Patel 2002: 13).

The incorporation of different styles and imageries has continued. Even today Indian cinemas, as Desai and Dudrah state, "make reference to and rework the styles, forms, aesthetics and/or semiotics of a wide variety of cultural forms" (2008: 4). This has to be kept in mind when applying both Indian as well as Western theoretical and aesthetic concepts.

Moreover, Hindi cinema should not be seen as representing anything like an 'Indian culture', which would grossly underestimate the cultural diversity of the nation. What can be identified is a dominance of Punjabi culture in Hindi films, especially in recent years. Not only is this reflected in the high number of Punjabi producers, directors and actors in the Bombay film industry, but also in the representation of Indian culture in the media. Dwyer and Patel state that "Punjabi culture [has been inscribed] as the national public culture of India" (Dwyer/Patel 2002: 19). It is important to mention at this point that a considerable number of these Punjabis are members of the Muslim minority, which was even more the case before Partition in 1947. The influence of Indo-muslim culture, for example, in linguistic terms by the use of Urdu language, has been enormous, but is often not acknowledged much due to the political tensions between the religious communities. In this regard the term Hindi film might be misleading as Martin Gaenszle points out, because the Hindi language used in the films leans heavily on Urdu, which is the national language of Pakistan today, but used to be the language of both Punjabi Hindus and Muslims (Gaenszle 2009: 50). Although I will not refer much to this aspect of Hindi film in the study, it should always be kept in mind that what is represented as a homogeneous culture in the films is a construction based on a complex amalgam of ethnic, religious and regional relations that are transferred and, thus, transformed in the imaginative space of the media text.

A Classification According to Genres?

The application of Hollywood genre classifications on Hindi films is problematic, as the latter very often unite elements which we would not find united in a Hollywood film (Thomas 2008: 25; Dwyer 2000: 106). In films from the early days of Indian cinema we can distinguish between the historical, the mythological and the stunt film (Dwyer/Patel 2002: 9). The 50s brought about a new genre which is often called 'the social', aligned with middle class culture (Ibid.). During the golden age of Bombay cinema a form called 'Masala film' was established, which has made genre distinctions even more difficult. It included characteristics of all genres, led to a maximum of spectacle and was based on a successful formula: "In a loosely knit story one can see big city underworld crime, martial arts fights scenes with exaggerated hitting noises – (...), car stunts, sexy cabaret, elaborate dance sequences with dozens of extras, comedy, romance and family melodrama" (Desai/Dudrah 2008: 12). It was not until the 90s, when with the emergence of the romantic family film, the *Masala* film or the "omnibus genre" (Dwyer 2000: 106) was pushed back and a restructuring of Hindi films began (Desai/Dudrah 2008: 12).

Let me now describe the genres of Hindi cinema which are identified in academic literature and provide examples of recent films which can be seen as representatives of, or partly draw on, the genre's conventions. I will primarily refer to Dudrah, who lists the mythological or devotional film first (2006: 175ff). As mentioned before, the first Indian feature films were religious and could be seen as first representatives of this genre. At the time, the religious overtone and the stress on national traditions was also a subversion of the colonial rule (Ibid.; Tieber 2007: 15). Most of the time mythologicals represent or draw on the Hindu epics and legends about the lives of gods and goddesses or religious men and women. However, neither are the films exclusively concerned with Hinduism, nor do audiences only consist of Hindu people; Muslims, Christians and Sikhs are part of the audience, too (Dudrah 2006: 175). It seems that devotional films nowadays have been replaced largely by TV serials based, for example, on the RAMAYANA or MAHABHARATA and are hugely popular (Pauwels 2008: 39). With its special focus on *darshan*, the influence of this genre is of major importance, as forms of representation of the gaze in a religious context originate in mythological films.

The next genre which can be rather clearly distinguished is the historical film. These films are usually based on real persons of Indian history, but also involve the myths surrounding them. Consequently, they have always been used to tell history from an Indian point of view, and thus some of the films were very political during the British colonial rule. A crucial characteristic of this genre is the display of splendour and riches, which was probably used to strengthen national esteem (Dudrah 2006: 176). A very recent example which impressingly depicts a glorious past, as it is set at the Mughal court in the 16th century, is JODHAA AK-

BAR (Ashutosh Gowariker, 2008). The film is about the marriage of the Mughal emperor Akbar to a Hindu princess and stars two of the most popular actors in Bombay, Hrithik Roshan and Aishwarya Rai.

As already mentioned, the social film as a genre emerged after Independence. Primarily, it addressed a middle class audience. These films have generally been more oriented towards Western film traditions in terms of realism. Furthermore, they emphasize the narrative (in contrast to spectacle) and broach contemporary social issues (Dwyer/Patel 2002: 9). Apart from that, Dudrah points out the significance of emotions evoked in the audience and the representation of "the complex interplay of personal identity, love, human relationships, family and the law" (Dudrah 2006: 177) as part of social changes. The emotions of characters are often represented in songs (Ibid.). A subgenre of the social film which could also be seen as another genre is the 'Muslim social film' (Ibid.). Their popularity is mostly due to the abundance of music, Urdu poetry and dance. A very prominent subcategory is the courtesan film, which features a popular female figure described by Dwyer and Patel in the following words: "She is portrayed as a victim of men's lust and as an object of the viewer's pity, but also delights the audience in being the object of the male gaze as she dances for his entertainment" (2002: 69). This is in so far relevant as these films have constituted scopic relations, putting the female body on display and in the position of the object of desire, which has also influenced other genres. One of the most famous courtesan stories is the one of Umrao Jaan, which was adapted once again in film by Jyoti Prakash Dutta in 2006.

The distinction between social, *Masala* and romantic films is quite difficult to delineate at this point. Prasad, for example, describes the films produced between the 50s and the 70s as feudal family romances and ascribes to them a basic formula (Prasad 2008: 46) very similar to the one quoted above for *Masala* films and to the underlying structure of the romantic films of the 90s. The most prominent examples of *Masala* and of formulaic films are Bachchan's 'angry young man' films which followed in the 70s. The origin of the genre was in the 60s' stunt films also referred to as the 'all-action film' (Dudrah 2006: 178). The persistent dominance of action films in Hindi cinema was finally terminated by the rise of the romantic film of the 90s. Although the latter partly followed the formula too, the films were by no means *Masala* films, as the action parts and other elements were increasingly erased. Instead, the family stories guaranteed 'clean' entertainment (Tieber 2007: 125). Films such as HUM AAPKE HAIN KAUN (Sooraj R. Barjatya, 1994) and DILWALE DULHANIA LE JAYENGE (Aditya Chopra, 1995) gave rise to new stars, a new genre and a new ideology in a changing environment for Bombay film making.

More than 'Running through fields, hiding behind trees': Conventions of Hindi Cinema

As it is impossible to give a complete overview here, I will focus in the following on crucial characteristics which are relevant for this analysis, either because the films in question draw on the established forms or because they try to differentiate themselves from them. Therefore, more complex debates concerning conventions and their meaning, in a larger context cannot be taken into account.[1] Dwyer and Patel identify some of the most flamboyant characteristics which are often referred to in discourses on commercial Hindi cinema: "Its films are criticized for their excessive length, their complicated plots within plots, their song and dance sequences, their colourful costumes, and their incongruous locations" (Dwyer/Patel 2002: 7); for their part they conclude that the inconsistencies as such define its style (Ibid.). Moreover, they add the distinctive narrative structure, the lack of realism and the abundance of emotionality as further characteristics (Dwyer/Patel 2002: 9). We can find similar listings in most of the seminal works (Tieber 2007: 65; Thomas 2008: 26; Desai/Dudrah 2008: 1). A frequently mentioned characteristic of Hindi film is the recurrence of the "boy-meets-girl love story" (Dudrah 2006: 33). However, as Tieber describes, love in general is central and can also mean the love between sister and brother, parents and children, friends, or the patriotic love for India (2007: 23). It is very important at this point to question what is meant by love in general. Very often the Western concept of romantic love is imposed on other cultural conceptions. Some of the central concepts as well as their implications for filmic representations will be elaborated further in the course of this analysis. But to show how important the understanding of culture-specific conceptions of love is, let me draw on an example described by Dwyer and Patel: conventionally particular seasons for romance can be identified in Indian films. Love in union, for example, is located in spring, while the rainy season stands for love in separation. This convention goes back to categories of love in Sanskrit theory called *rasa* (Dwyer/Patel 2002: 60). In the films, codes can be found which refer to such concepts of love which might be overlooked by a viewer not familiar with the cultural context. As my analysis focuses on romantic family films, the diverse codes used to represent not only love, but also desire, the body and gender differences according to genre conventions are of central interest. Furthermore, the gaze is often a significant element and signifier in this context.

Another very prominent convention that has its root in censorship is the so-called kissing ban. Although there are so many films depicting love relationships between men and women, kissing was highly uncommon from Hindi film screens until recently. For many Western recipients this is irritating, especially in

1 For a detailed account on the debate see Prasad 1998 or Vasudevan 2000b.

contrast with the otherwise quite erotic and sexually connoted elements of the films. The origin of the kissing ban can be traced back to the British and afterwards to the Indian censorship code, although it never explicitly referred to kissing (Prasad 1998: 88f). Over the years, kissing has come to be identified with Western culture and the kissing ban is still widely regarded as part of the national film tradition (Ibid.). Prasad also discusses the ban in the context of the prohibition of the private and the visibility of the romantic couple, which will be dealt with later on in the analysis. Today many filmmakers use kissing scenes in their films, but the enduring influence of censorship is still apparent. Many codes and symbols which were used to represent sexuality and the erotic are still present in contemporary films. The use or the dismissal of kissing on screen is an important marker, and films like the ones analysed here which adhere to the ban convey certain positions on issues such as tradition, intimacy and so on.

An important source for the conventional motifs which should be emphasized here has been Hindu mythology. The swing, for example, refers to the lovers Krishna and Radha, who represent romantic love as well as sexual attraction (Fuller 1992: 194). In addition, there are many "chronotopes of romance" which are "associated with remote or even fantastic places, accessed in dream sequences or without diegetic explanation" (Dwyer/Patel 2002: 58). The mountainous regions of Kashmir as well as Switzerland are a well known example, but also "earthly paradises of parks and gardens in full bloom" or "waterfalls and rivers marking the eroticism of water" are also very common (Ibid.). These are just some examples of motifs common in Hindi films of the past and present.

Trademark Song & Dance: Spectacle as Central Feature of Hindi Cinema

Desai and Dudrah introduce the terms 'spectacle' and 'melodrama' to describe central features of Hindi cinema (2008: 1), a distinction which is also quite useful for this study. Although spectacle can be located on different levels of the filmic text, the major element is the song and dance sequence. Generally, song and dance strongly demarcates Hindi film from other film traditions, especially from Western ones. As Gopal and Moorti mention, they mark Indian film for in- and outsiders (2008: 2). Song and dance sequences are "dense nodes of signification" and while narrative might be repetitive, they offer innovation as well as originality (Gopal/Moorti 2008: 5). Consequently, they should by no means be seen only as catering to the general demand for spectacle in Hindi films. They can play an extra-diegetic role by referring to and negotiating between cultural forms. But they are also crucial for the narrative as they often further and enhance it (Dudrah 2006: 48; Dwyer/Patel 2002: 37). Thus, "Bollywood musical numbers can operate both at the levels of narrative and spectacle" (Dudrah 2006: 49).

Moreover, song and dance sequences play an important role in the structure of Hindi film. In terms of the narrative, the films are often non-linear, and disjuncture can be seen as a function of song and dance. This non-linearity is one of the major differences to Western aesthetics, and it is located in the context of a postcolonial Indian film industry which gave privilege to attractions and other elements of popular cinema: "In this milieu, a straight-forward linearization of the narrative form, into a pattern of cause and effect on the Hollywood model, did not emerge as a clear-cut agenda" (Vasudevan 2000a: 7). This will be discussed more extensively in the context of the different approaches to the gaze in film studies.

In general, song and dance sequences can be described as "powerful acts of imagination" (Gopal/Sen 2008: 157) which do not adhere to the rule of realist cinema. The continuity of the narrative is broken in time and space as for example with rapid location changes (Dwyer 2000: 37). But as Vasudevan points out, the tendency to integrate song and dance into the narrative has increased (2000a: 10). There are various strategies of incorporation which have resulted in established forms such as the staged performance situating the sequences in the context of a stage show, a courtesan dance or wedding dance. Another common strategy is to present song and dance sequences as the fantasy or dream of a character. However, there are many films which do not employ such strategies, but in which song and dance is still significant to the story. Usually their function is to "allow an expression of feeling that cannot be articulated otherwise" (Dwyer/Patel 2000: 37), such as the feeling and declaration of love. In this context, Gopal argues that the missing kiss has been a major reason for the song sequence to become "the primary device for constituting the romantic couple" (Gopal 2011: 23). Thus, historically generated codes of love and eroticism are engaged. This function of song and dance is particularly relevant to my analysis.

The sequences also aim to establish interiority and subjectivity of characters (Gopal/Sen 2008: 150). Dwyer even speaks of a language of love, which is characterized by an excess of meaning in the sense of Kristeva (Dwyer 2000: 113). Without going into detail here, it is clear that the abundance of metaphorical language and the hyperbole of feelings in love songs sometimes create an ambiguity typical of song and dance. Furthermore, we can find the same ambiguity on the image level, for example when the differentiation between objective and subjective camera is not clear (Schneider in Krauß 2007: 148). Secondly, we can also find "elaborate codes of eroticism" (Dwyer/Patel 2002: 91) in song and dance sequences, which allow, for example, transgressive pleasures. The most prominent one is the wet sari scene, which not only displays the heroine's body, but also establishes associations with the erotic mood of the rainy season (Ibid.). Thus, the display of the female body, as well as the erotic relationship between lovers is one of the main attractions of song and dance.

In general, the music in Hindi film is a mix of different music styles across cultures ranging from Indian classical music to rap music. Their historical roots mainly lie in folk and classical theatre traditions (Dudrah 2006: 49; Dwyer/Patel

2002: 14f). Accordingly, the dancing incorporates very diverse elements, which results in the very hybrid nature of song and dance sequences (Dwyer 2000: 115). As Dwyer and Patel point out, most of the musicians and singers working in the film industry have been trained in classical music (2002: 36). The lyrics of the songs are strongly influenced by Urdu literature and by its poetic forms such as the *ghazal* (Dwyer 2000; 40). Moreover, song and dance sequences play an important role in the commodity and consumer culture established in the 90s, as they display goods such as designer clothes and lifestyle elements such as touristic activities in foreign locations (Gopal/Moorti 2008: 43). The spectacle and abundance of the sequences also reinforces the idolization of stars (Dwyer 2000: 123), who can also be seen as central elements of spectacle as discussed below. Consequently, song and dance is both: commodity and art form.

In recent times, song and dance has been much engaged in globalized culture production, due to its general openness in incorporating and transforming many different musical styles as well as other cultural forms (Sen 2008: 85). This crucial role of song and dance in globalization processes can also be explained by its universal appeal despite serving as a marker of difference to other film traditions such as Western cinema (Gopal/Sen 2008: 156). Thus, the sequences can be seen as a highly hybridized space merging culturally diverse styles, art forms and pop cultures as well as corresponding forms of representation. Although it is subject to decline and transformation, song and dance is still present in all genres of contemporary Hindi film, and thus "is the single most enduring feature of popular Hindi cinema" (Gopal/Moorti 2008: 1).

Spectacle of the Idols: Stars as Attraction in Hindi Cinema

Another major attraction of films is the stars, who not only receive extra-space in the song and dance sequences, but are generally part of the spectacle in various forms. In India, film stars are, as Dwyer states, "national icons of beauty, desire and utopian beings" (2000: 119). They are often perceived and worshipped like gods and goddesses (Tieber 2007: 96; Dwyer 2006b: 164). Sometimes fans even dedicate shrines or temples to stars (Hermann Pfandt 2010; Dwyer 2006b: 164). This star-worship is crucial for an understanding of *darshan* in the filmic context, as we will see in the analysis, as it highly influences scopic relations in films but also conceptions of spectatorship. The iconisation of stars is reinforced by the characters they usually play, who often represent ideals and sometimes even bear names of deities out of the Hindu epics such as Arjun or Rama (Tieber 2007: 27). Of course, the stars also embody idealized versions of masculinity and femininity (Dwyer/Patel 2002: 20)[2], which is particularly relevant for this study.

2 Interestingly, the actress playing the legendary Mother India, signifying Indian womanhood (and thus, Hinduness and good femininity) for decades, was Nargis,

The relationship between the Indian public, fans and film stars is very complex. According to Dwyer, much of the star creation in Bollywood is very similar to its equivalent in Hollywood. Consequently, Dyer's concepts of stardom[3] can be applied in this context (Dwyer/Patel 2002: 32). But if we consider the star as image or sign (Dyer 1998 [1979]: 34), we have to take into account differing elements of India's visual culture. This is a major aspect of the following analysis, in which the star in the context of *darshan* shall be discussed extensively. In Hindi film certain elements contribute to the great importance of stars: within the melodramatic mode the star performance is even more in the foreground (Dwyer/Patel 2002: 32), songs and dialogues are explicitly used to create stars (Dwyer 2009: 103), and close-ups are extensively used (Dwyer 2000: 116). Nevertheless, it makes sense to look at stars in terms of on- and off-screen personas as well as the multiple meanings the star image signifies. In India, film magazines such as *Stardust* are highly influential in the creation of off-screen personas and nurture the voyeuristic fascination of film audiences (Roy 2008: 114). In many ways moral standards are different concerning stars so that, for example, extramarital affairs such as the one between Nargis and Raj Kapoor are more or less accepted (Tieber 2007: 96). On the other hand, female stars are still expected to fulfill moral conventions, which is paradoxical nowadays as "actresses are expected to represent globalized images of a liberated female sexuality, but are still circumscribed by shifting yet narrow definitions of 'Indian' femininity" (Govindan/Dutta 2008: 181). This should be kept in mind when analyzing representations of femininity in Hindi films. Furthermore, the relationship between recipients/fans and stars in India is considered to be more 'personalized' than in the context of Hollywood, a phenomenon which has been parodied in the 2007 film *Om Shanti Om* (Farah Khan). Another situation in which this became very apparent, ocurred in the 80s when Bachchan was severely injured while filming *Coolie* (Manmohan Desai, 1983). Fans not only prayed but also offered to give him their own limbs to save his life (Desai/Dudrah 2008: 9)! Dyer subsumes the on- and off-screen persona in the "concept of a structured polysemy" comprising the "complex totality" of the star image as well as its "chronological dimension" (1998 [1979]: 63).

In some cases, as with Amitabh Bachchan, the star persona is so dominant that the character seems to be diminished in favour of the star. Mishra describes the situation that evolves when the star as parallel text displaces the filmic text itself and "the actor becomes the film" (Mishra 2008: 41). The complex relationship between stars and characters outlined by Dyer (1998 [1997]: 20f) is thus

---

a Muslim. Roy concludes that her religious identity was neither present nor absent (2008: 109), which could also be said about present day male actors such as the four Khans (Salman, Amir, Saif Ali and Shah Rukh).

3 Richard Dyer's „Stars" and „Heavenly Bodies" are the seminal works of star studies in the context of Hollywood.

complicated even further. To a great extent, the 'angry young man' films of the 70s turned Amitabh Bachchan into the rebellious hero he represented on screen (Dwyer 2009: 102). As Dwyer notes, the overlap of hero and star sometimes reaches such an extent that the star becomes a hero in the narration of the star text (Dwyer 2000: 119). Undoubtedly, Amitabh Bachchan has been the biggest star of Indian cinema and has reached international stardom (Dwyer 2009: 99). In contemporary Hindi cinema and Bollywood, Shah Rukh Khan is one of the most significant male stars. His career is unconventional in many ways: Khan is not of a family film dynasty; he played a psychopathic hero in his first successful films (Creekmur 2005: 365); and he first starred in a TV series before making the switch to film (Dwyer 2000. 119). His off-screen persona offers more than one 'filmi' story such as the romantic story of how he came to marry his wife Gauri, a Hindu (Chopra 2007: 66ff). In recent years he has been a pioneer of the new order in Indian film industry. Khan, more than any of the other actors, has been operating in advertisement, business and marketing, using his star persona (Chopra 2007: 156ff). Besides creating this 'brand SRK' in India, he has also successfully launched new markets in the global economy (Vajdovich 2010). At the moment Shah Rukh Khan is probably the most well known (Indian) actor in the world and can thus be seen as a global sign and signifier.

Spectacle of Feelings: Melodrama as Central Feature of Hindi Cinema

Apart from spectacle, the melodramatic mode is the second central and structuring characteristic of Hindi film, which shall be described here. Elements such as the role of coincidence in plots, the importance of a moral message and the centrality of emotions are dominant and redound to the non-linear structure of the films (Tieber 2007: 57f). In melodrama, the display of emotions opens up another space where extensive gazing takes place and, although it is most present in the narrative space, while my focus lies on song and dance, it is of interest to this study, too. A central characteristic of this mode is generalization, which we shall look at in more detail by focusing on how characters are depicted. Characters in Hindi films tend to be somewhat standardized, complying with ideals associated with North Indian culture. Thus, heroes and heroines are usually urban, upper-caste, North Indian Hindus. Most of the male stars conform to the corresponding beauty ideal, which is partly rooted in colonial stereotypes of the tall, fair-skinned Punjabi warrior (Dwyer/Patel 2002: 20). The depiction of other regional or religious groups is very often humorous or exotic (Ibid.). Thus, for example, the Guajarati family in the film *Kal Ho Naa Ho* is set against the Punjabi one and ridiculed. Interestingly enough, many Hindu characters, and in recent years the male protagonists especially, have been played by Muslim actors such as Shah Rukh Khan, Salman Khan or Amir Khan. Furthermore, there are established codes on different levels of meaning. Garments such as the *sari* can be heavily loaded with meaning, referring to social status as well as national and cultural identity (Tieber 2007: 38). Names such as Rama imply the values and principles a characters represents (Tieber 2007: 27) in the framework of the melodrama "with its drive to constantly externalize meaning in a bipolar, non-psychological delineation of character" (Vasudevan 2000a: 13). The embodiments of good and evil, traditional and modern or Indian and Western often determine the characters. The result is similar to what Dyer describes as a stereotype which is absolute and denies limitations, relativity, changeability, historicity and power relations (2009: 207). However, it should also be understood in the context as an important feature of Hindi film aesthetics: "'Generalization – of character, of event, of response – is thus the key to understanding the continuing Indian aesthetic" (Dwyer 2000: 30). Consequently, until the 90s we find dense symbolic meanings in character constellations such as the family, which represents India with different members standing for different ethnicities or religious groups of the country (Tieber 2007: 27).

Both Vasudevan and Prasad give a more detailed account of how the melodramatic mode contributes to distinct character formations (Vasudevan 2000a: 13; Prasad 1998: 70f). Prasad argues that it does not adhere to realist assumptions, because "the characters are objects of emulation or disapproval rather than identification" (Prasad 1998: 70). Thus, plots and characters are also often pre-determined, as has already been mentioned in the context of names referring to the Hindu epics. Mishra calls this performance tradition a "perpetual metonymy" and a strong desire to repeat, which could be seen as a basic characteristic of Hindi cinema, too (Mishra 2008: 33). However, there have been various ruptures in the predominant method of characterisation. Amitabh Bachchan, for example, depicted a very active hero in his 'angry young man' roles. Thus he seems to resemble the bourgeois individual we know from Western cinema, who has agency and whose life is not determined by destiny. However, Bachchan's hero is neither a bourgeois character nor is he able to master his fate in the end (Tieber 2009: 89). A considerable disruption took place in the 90s, which was rooted in the rise of a new middle class culture and corresponding ideas of selfhood. A new understanding of subjectivity was introduced, for example, by films such as *Baazigar* (Abbas Mustan, 1993) and *Darr* (Yash Chopra, 1993), where the psychology of the schizophrenic protagonist played by Shah Rukh Khan comes to the fore (Mazumdar in Vasduvan 2000a: 22f). In recent years psychological delineation of character, along with the realist mode and screenplay cohesion, has increased. These tendencies are apparent in the films which are object of this study.

The excessive display of emotion as well as stereotypical and repetitive representations can also be seen in the context of the *rasa* theory, which is concerned with the study of emotions. As the *rasa* theory is crucial to an understanding of Indian performance traditions, a short excursion shall give some insights. *Rasa* literally means liquid and in drama theory refers to pleasure or fulfilment of all of the desires of the spectator. In this concept of stage communication the *rasas* are generalized emotions and the *bhavas* are corresponding mental states. Through identification with the performed, which is achieved through the *bhavas* as aesthetic devices, the spectator experiences *rasa* or simply pleasure. There are many different categories of *bhavas*, often divided into bodily and mental states. Dwyer concludes that *rasa* depends on generalization: "The rasa engenders emotion in a pure, generalized state, without a personal response" (2000: 30). Moreover, this then is an idealized form of the emotion in question, which in its performance shall have the desired effect on the audience of any kind of performance art. The influence of *rasa* dramaturgy on Hindi film is noticeable, as the generalization of emotions as a principle is perpetuated. Vasudevan also points out the connection between characterisation and *rasa* theory: the reproduction of the 'traditional' aesthetic rooted in folk and urban theatrical forms "is often accompanied by an indifference to coherent character development, as if the objective of the entertainment is the display of a (structured) variety of attributes rather than the outlining of a plausible personality" (Vasudevan 2000a: 9). However, he emphasizes that the 'traditional' is by no means static here, so *rasa* theory interacts in various ways with other elements of the medium.

As this study aims to negotiate between Western and Indian conceptual frameworks, the rasa theory will occasionally be addressed in the analysis of emotions in the melodrama. However, it should be noted that its application in film studies has been criticized, mostly because the hybrid character of Hindi films tends to be overlooked by such approaches (cf. Ibid.; Dwyer/Patel 2002: 28). Accordingly, Dwyer and Patel hint at Western influence on the melodramatic mode in Hindi film (2002: 28). Similarly, Vasudevan presents this as a 'transitional' moment in time, when Western elements are incorporated, which results in a dramaturgy characterized by what he calls "manichaeism" and "bipolarity" (Vasudevan 2000b: 131). He emphasizes that the system of narration includes codes of continuity from Hollywood cinema as well as elements associated with the cinema of attractions. The terms "cinema of attractions", referring to the earliest days of cinema, was coined by Tom Gunning and is sometimes known as 'exhibitionist cinema'. These concepts enable us to describe central characteristics of Hindi films, such as frontality, the direct look into the camera, as well as the spectacle (Tieber 2007: 59). Essential elements of the films such as the song and dance sequences, stars, comedy and special effects can thus be seen as attractions (Dwyer/Patel 2002: 30). But, as Tieber again points out, although frontality, for example, may break the realist illusion of film, it is still integrated into the narrative (2007: 59). Gunning's approach and related issues shall be discussed in more detail in the context of film studies in the next chapter. In conclusion, we may sum up the use of emotions and spectacle, especially in films with familiar and predictable plots, in Thomas' words: it is more important "how things will happen rather than what will happen next" (Thomas 2008: 29).

Recent Developments: From the 90s Romantic Family Film to 'New Bollywood'

The dominant and most successful genre of the 90s is what is often called the 'romantic family film'. After the crisis in the 80s Hindi cinema saw what Kaur sums up as "the rise of technically competent films with their slick production and editing, and their new story lines centring on the gentrified middle classes, trendy youth and rampant consumerism" (Kaur 2005: 310). This development should be seen in the context of economic and political changes in India. The liberalisation of the domestic market in 1991 and the following economic boom had profound social consequences, although the situation of lower classes hardly improved (Majumder 2009: 148f). The changes caused a crisis in national identity as Western values and lifestyles got more and more integrated into large parts of society (Sharpe 2005: 63). Consequently, Hindu nationalism gained support in various segments of society, which resulted in the success of the Bharatiya Janata Party in the 90s (Ibid.: 149). On the other hand, global consumer culture was negotiated in a local context and conventional, rigid frameworks were partly broken up. The most popular representatives of the 90s films deal with these contradictions and the shifting meanings of morality, honour and patriotism in an increasingly globalized India.

In her groundbreaking publication "All You Want is Money, All You Need is Love: Sex and Romance in Modern India" Rachel Dwyer describes the rise of the romantic family film in the context of a conflict involving the culture of the lower classes and the new and old middle classes. The values represented in the "big-budget, plushy, romantic films" (Dwyer 2000: 100) she argues, are those of the new middle classes, which are characterised by an orientation towards Western lifestyles with regard to education, jobs, clothing and leisure activities – thus the younger generations form a metropolitan elite. At the same time the acceptance of a rather conservative lifestyle that includes living with the parents, accepting arranged marriages and in many ways adhering to "non-modern values" prevails (Ibid.: 92).[4] In terms of the film content, the form of the feudal family romance has thus been revived in a setting characterised by the new consumerism, Hindu culture and patriarchal structures (Ibid.: 96ff). Clearly hitting a nerve in Indian society, these films made audiences come back to the cinemas at a time when the industry was threatened by the introduction of cable TV and video. The rise of multiplex cinemas at that time should be viewed in this context, but also situated in terms of global trends and consumerism (Dwyer/Patel 2002: 22).

---

4 The term modernity is highly contested one as mentioned before. Here, Dwyer points out the differences between Western, old Indian middle classes and the new ones. She mentions that rationality and secularism are not part of this new middle class ideology; the caste system as well as feudal values of honour and status are dominant characteristics, which she classifies as „non-modern“ (Dwyer 2000: 92).

Another emerging audience which proved to be crucial in the course of the 90s consisted of the NRI communities, especially in Great Britain and the USA. As mentioned before, the two nations have emerged as key markets for the Hindi film industry. Consequently, issues concerning those viewers, such as the renegotiation of Western influences in their lives, as well as the relationship between diaspora and the homeland, were central in the 90s films (Dwyer/Patel 2002: 60). The most popular ones include DILWALE DULHANIA LE JAYENGE (Aditya Chopra, 1995), PARDES (Subhash Ghai, 1997) or SWADES (Ashutosh Gowariker, 2004). A new image of the NRI emerged: whereas before he/she was identified mostly with the negative sides of Western culture (in roles such as the villain or the vamp), "Bollywood of the nineties took note of the non-resident Indians (NRIs) as cosmopolitan in mind, speaking in English or American accents, but with their hearts and souls in the right place, i.e., respecting all things Indian" (Dudrah 2006: 68). All the films chosen for my analysis are set in a diaspora context and negotiate these issues. However, as the focus of interest lies elsewhere, they are only touched upon occasionally.

While the films of the 60s to the 80s were mostly male-oriented (Chakravarty 2008: 88), the 90s not only brought back female audiences to cinema halls (Tieber 2009: 154), but also reintroduced gender issues to Hindi films. This resulted in an emphasis on and negotiations of feminity, notions of the female body, sexuality etc. In relation to the outlined socio-cultural conflicts, this very often led to the propagation of cultural purity and the projection of nationality on the female body. Thus, the "preservation of nationness" was conflated "with the protection of women" (Fernandes in Sharpe 2005: 62), evoking the female ideal of Sita as a symbol of purity. Sharpe concludes: "Bollywood heroines commonly serve an iconic function in representing family values that Western decadence and materialism have undermined" (Sharpe 2005: 62). Nevertheless, many of the films do speak for women's rights in terms of the fulfilment of their love – a love which is marked by mutual respect. Dudrah describes some of these characteristics in the film PARDES, which portrays the female protagonist as a symbol of cultural purity and the nation, even calling her 'Ganga' in reference to the river Ganges, but which also criticizes sexist oppression (Dudrah 2006: 80f). The representation of feminity and the female body are central aspects of my analysis and should always be read within the discourses of Indian national and cultural identities, even if they are not referred to explicitely.

The Best of Both Worlds: The Ideal of the Arranged Love Marriage

The negotiation between modernity and tradition culminates in the representation of 'arranged love marriage' as ideal (Uberoi 2008: 181), placing the female body in between patriarchal possession and individual desires. The almost obligatory happy ending, thus, is the reconciliation between two competing value systems. As Uberoi explains, the idealistic concept of the arranged love marriage is based on a universal story reflected in many romantic narratives of South Asian cinema, as the conflict between dharma and desire, freedom and destiny (Ibid.). Furthermore, Orsini points out the various cultural repertoires they are rooted in, for example Persian poetry, where very often "love is the prism through which ethical and moral questions are examined" (Orsini 2006: 20). However, the issue of arranged marriages should be seen in political terms, too, as it is one of the main factors in the reproduction of inequalities and particularly the caste system in India (Uberoi 2008: 182; Fuller 1992: 14). The concept of arranged love marriage is also relevant to this study, as the samples negotiate notions of love and marital bliss.

Let us now look at the two key constituents of the arranged love marriage in the 90s films: family values and individual desires. The latter are usually represented by the romantic love of the hero or the heroine, which threatens to be sacrificed for the sake of family. Although models of romantic love exist in Indian culture, such as the story of Radha and Krishna in mythology (Orsini 2006: 23f), the concept of romantic love dominating here is a Western, by now globalized one located to a large extent in consumer culture. Dwyer and Patel describe how sites of romance are very often sites of consumption, such as tourist overseas locations or extravagant styles of fashion and interior design (2002: 52f). To explain this phenomenon, Dwyer draws on the work of Eva Illouz, who outlines how romance is shaped by capitalism: love is often seen as self-realization and an individualistic act; this is on the one hand connected to ideas of equality and mutual understanding in relationships, and on the other hand to the desire for economic wealth and consumerist activities (Dwyer 2000: 14). In the films this results in the display of consumption and commodities, which have become part of the spectacle and attractions in Hindi cinema. However, the concepts of love represented in the films are not exclusive but manifold. What we should also keep in mind is that a whole range of individualistic desires shaped by contemporary socio-cultural conditions interact with what we usually associate with the feeling of love.

The second constituent is as complex, because many things are inscribed into the 'family' microcosm. Firstly, in the 90s the joint family became a marker of 'Indianness' and tradition (Uberoi 2008: 182). The West became identified with individual freedom and was viewed in opposition to the 'Indian' tradition (Tieber 2007: 146). Secondly, the joint family as such evolved as a space marked by unity, religious devotion and happiness, where poverty and political issues were obliterated (Ibid.: 124). In contrast, the traditional Hindu family is marked by rigid hierarchies and patriarchal structures. While in Indian society this social form is being more and more displaced by the modern bourgeois family, the representation of the extended family in films is highly romanticized (Dwyer 2000: 49f), also nurturing the nostalgia of the diasporic audiences. The films that will be analysed in this analysis offer an interesting critique of the family by showing repressive aspects of it, but they also reinforce associated values and contribute to idealization. Furthermore, the concept of family drew a lot on the discourse around female purity, which is supposed to ensure the continuation of the social status of a family as well as the caste system in a wider sense (Fuller 1992: 21). The female ideal promoted by the films, consequently, was marked by chastity and total devotion to patriarchal authority, referring to role models such as the goddess Sita (cf. Pauwels 2008).[5] Sexuality, in general, was suppressed since it is in the family where "we find the de-eroticization of love as it collides with institutions such as those of maternity and patriarchy" (Dwyer 2000: 49). In many of the films, however, this form, which resembles what Prasad calls the "feudal family romance" of the 50s and 60s (Prasad 1998: 55; Chakravarty 2008: 90), is put into question and thus the idea of the joint family is challenged. This happens mostly through the depiction of the private and intimate space of the couple beyond patriarchal control, which has also been outlined in detail by Prasad (1998: 94ff). In connection to the gaze, erotiticism and representations of desire are essential; consequently, the private/public division of space will be discussed more extensively later.

Another important characteristic of the 90s family film consists in the changes in character depictions. In contrast to the 70s films, in which character depictions were very often based on a childhood trauma of the hero, the new heroes "generally exist in and are only defined by their present circumstances" (Creekmur 2005: 369). Moreover, the young protagonists do not rebel against their parents or family. As it is reconciliation the films are aiming for, patriarchal authority is never really put in question (Tieber 2007: 31). Furthermore, physicalness became more essential in films, following a general trend of the 'cult of the body' in the context of the global consumer culture. Whether by fashionable clothes or the displaying half naked bodies, female as well as male bodies became more and more central in the films (Tieber 2007: 132; Dwyer 2000: 50).

At last, one filmmaker who had an enormous influence on the romantic family film should be mentioned: Yash Chopra. His films were instrumental in the development of the styles emerging in the 90s. Dwyer states that not only his "visual vocabulary of romance" (2000: 141) was adopted, but also the form of melodrama he uses became predominant in the course of the decade. Chopra himself calls it "glamorous realism" (Ibid.: 150), which employs both in equal measure: a

5 Sita is generally regarded as the ideal of the virtuous wife. She is the wife of Rama and an incarnation of Lakshmi. When her husband is exiled she follows him to the forest. The demon Ravana abducts her, but Hanuman, the loyal monkey god, rescues her. She has to prove her purity in a trial of fire, which she passes. Nevertheless, rumours persist in the kingdom and Rama sends her away pregnant. After giving birth to twin sons she returns to the earth, with which she is associated with as a goddess (Dwyer 2000: 23).

"driving logic" and "emotional richness" (Ibid.: 141). Moreover, films such as DIL TO PAGAL HAI (1997), as Dwyer and Patel emphasize, have introduced a new urban and fancy style into Hindi cinema (Dwyer/Patel 2002: 50). Consequently, many of the prominent features of Hindi films known in Western countries are part of the Chopra style. For example, the lavish and sumptuous weddings with the bride in full red and the groom wearing a turban with lots of flowers, jewellery and colours are also called "Yash Chopra wedding" (Dwyer/Patel 2002: 95).

New Bollywood and Karan Johar

In recent years the dominance of the romantic family film in Hindi cinema has declined and other genres such as the action film are more frequent blockbusters now. While some actors such as Salman Khan have starred in action films for a considerable time, others have turned increasingly to this genre in recent years. Films such as KRRISH (Rakesh Roshan), DHOOM 1 + 2 (Sanjay Gadhvi) or DON 1 + 2 (Farhan Akhtar), were highly successful at the box office. According to Gopal, this diversificiation of genre can be seen as a characteristic of the Bollywood film industry from the 1990s (2011: 3). In all genres, however, the changes in the film industry have become visible. The significance of the screenplay has enormously increased, the internal coherence of films has been reinforced and there has been an approximation to the realistic mode common in Western cinema (Tieber 2007: 174). In the films this is also reflected in the way characters are more psychologically motivated and coherent, but also in the alienation from the normative rules of the filmic tradition. The latter is described by Mishra in terms of how the beginning and end of films have always been fixed, as the plots draw on mythology and other grand narratives (Mishra 2008: 32f). With the departure from normative rules he fears a collapse of the Hindi film genre (Ibid.: 43). In opposition, I would argue that this alienation from normative rules also allows film makers to explore new forms of representation and intertextual references. Consequently, controversial issues such as, for example, adultery and illegitimate children have been treated very differently from before in films such as KABHI ALVIDA NAA KEHNA (Karan Johar, 2006) or KAL HO NAA HO (Karan Johar, 2003). Despite the many changes taking place in Hindi cinema and the deep anxieties about a the westernization of Hindi films, the continuity of filmic traditions and the mixing of codes in what we could call the 'New Bollywood Film' is remarkable.

One director and screenwriter representing this New Bollywood Film is Karan Johar. In my opinion, his films such as KUCH KUCH HOTA HAI (1998), KABHI KHUSHI KABHI GHAM (2001), KABHI ALVIDA NAA KEHNA (2006) and MY NAME IS KHAN (2010) are important milestones in the development of the contemporary style in Hindi cinema. This is a major reason why my samples are all films he has directed or contributed to. Johar has been working with very influential and innovative people in a variety of areas of the film industry, be it costume designers, art directors or actors. In the following, I would like to mention three aspects which characterize his films as well as many of the New Bollywood films in general: the globalization of Indianness in films, the emergence of controversial issues and breaches of taboos as well as star images connected to these characteristics.

In a discussion at the international conference "Indian Cinema Circuits: Diasporas, Peripheries and Beyond" (June 2009, London) the panel and the audience agreed when watching the fighting scene at the end of DILWALE DULHANIA LE JAYENGE that this was Shah Rukh Khans last tribute to the 'old' Hindi film. It was concluded: "This is where Shah Rukh goes global". Leading Hindi film scholars in the audience agreed that the film is located at the intersection where the contemporary globalization process of Hindi cinema started out. Written by Aditya Chopra and produced by his father Yash Chopra, the film was very much based on the already mentioned Chopra style. One of the supporting actors also worked as assistant director on the set for the first time ever: Karan Johar. The next hit starring Shah Rukh Khan and Kajol (the leading actress of DDLJ) again was his first film, *Kuch Kuch Hota Hai*. Not only has he continued to work a great deal with these actors, but he has also collaborated over and over with art director Sharmishta Roy, who according to Dwyer and Patel "changed the look of Hindi films" (2002: 78) with her work. Especially in the depiction of the diaspora very positive images of a hybrid and globalized Indian identity have gradually emerged. Fuchs describes, for example, how costumes lose their ideological function and how the interchangeability of East and West are emphasized in Johar's films (Fuchs 2009: 44). Moreover, song and dance sequences move away from established dichotomies such as urban and rural as well as East and West. A significant part of this is the commodification of places and stars in the context of a global consumer culture (Ibid.). However, we can also see a utopian multicultural idyll in the films (Tieber 2007: 129). This can also be seen as an imagining of new possibilities of a social world, as Dudrah suggests using the framework of Arjun Appadurai's globalization theory (Dudrah 2008: 247).

On the one hand, Johar's films are clearly globalized in style as well as content, which is probably why they have reached audiences beyond the diaspora (cf. Gopal/Moorti 2008: 35). On the other hand, he is often accused of propagating very conservative values, portraying upper-caste, rich, Hindu families reinforcing values of the ruling class. Another perspective might be that he uses the conservative framework to negotiate controversial issues and point out social conflicts, which sometimes brings sharp criticism. Kamala Ganesh and Kanchana Mahadevan pointed out in their presentation "SRK, Karan Johar and the creation of 'Bollywood'" at the International Conference "Shah Rukh Khan and Global Bollywood" (Vienna, 2010) that Johar takes up "the holy cows" of Indian society such as adultery, divorce, illegimate children and adoption. It is a fact that he prefers to employ the melodramatic mode in his films, thus, his criticisms of injustice and repression are not articulated in political, rational terms, but conveyed by the feelings of the characters. The continuity of the Chopra style can be identified in his films and Johar invariably pays tribute to him, for example, in the credits of *Kuch Kuch Hota Hai*. Consequently, we find glamorous realism and its moral universe in Johar's films, where romantic love is celebrated while the sanctity of the family is upheld (Ibid.: 150). In her recent work, Gopal points out that Johar's films also indicate a rethinking of the family: it is not the locus of power anymore, but dominated by affective and emotional attachments (2011: 77). The emphasis on the necessity of "interpersonal communication" (Ibid.: 78) sets the films apart. Moreover, Johar also goes a step further than Chopra, whose "heroes and, more unusually, his heroines can fall in love more than once and even have sexual relations with more than one partner" (Dwyer 2000: 153). With KABHI ALVIDA NAA KEHNA the relationship between adulterers finds a happy ending instead of a reunion of the family. In contrast, while Chopra's romanticism includes erotic elements, the family "is the location not for eroticism, but for sex, reproduction and love" (Ibid: 163). Johar, however, presents erotic attraction as an essential part of a happy marriage. As Dudrah mentions, many of the 90s films explore the issue of the discrimination of women in Indian society (Dudrah 2006: 177). In Johar's films this is complemented by accomplished forms of representation of female desire and sexuality, which has been a major reason to focus on his work in this study.

Another relevenat aspect of his work has been the continual negotiation of cinematic codes and styles. In her insightful analysis of Johar's blockbusters that are at the centre of my own investigation, Gopal concludes that he converts Hindi film forms into 'attractions' by exaggerating them and the frequents homages to older figurations as well as features first and foremost a sentimental expression: "the older figuration of the family and conugality in Hindi cinema is aestitically memorialized – throught song and dance, melodrama, and even duration" (2011: 82). Otherwise she notes the predominance of the Hollywood narrative structure in the films (Ibid: 65; 83). While Gopal remarks that "the KJo film invents a new relation to the old" (2011: 90), this is primarily seen in the light of a transition to the Hollywood mode. In contrast, the results presented in the following show how the mixing of filmic codes results in a hybrid cultural product, in-between the old and the new, Hollywood and Bollywood. Thus, the use of for example frontality is not merely seen as a citation or homage to former practices of film-making, but the focus lies on its dynamic renegotiation.

A recent film by Karan Johar that is not part of the analysis here, showed again a strong will to touch on controversial issues, not only in India but in the whole world. MY NAME IS KHAN (2010) is the story of an autistic Muslim in the USA who loses his stepson in a racial assault. When his wife leaves him after the tragedy, he tries to win her back by following the president through the

US in order to tell him: "My name is Khan and I am not a terrorist". In the 90s, films such as BOMBAY (Mani Ratnam, 1995) or DIL SE (Mani Ratnam, 1998) were rare examples of Hindi films treating terrorism and religious riots in explicit ways (Tieber 2007: 158ff). Others such as VEER ZARA (Yash Chopra) or MAIN HOON NA (Farah Khan), both released in 2004, raised the issue of terrorism in connection with the conflict between Pakistan and India, but with a strong focus on love and family stories (Ibid.). MY NAME IS KHAN similarly focuses on individual conflicts, which are then allocated in a global dimension resulting in a plea for humanity, religious tolerance and mutual respect. Due to the style Johar employs, we find numerous stereotypical representations of ethnic and social groups in the film. In my opinion, this is another example of the characteristic ambiguity in Johar's films, which on the one hand is one of their great strengths, but which on the other hand makes them an easy target for criticism.

Another interesting aspect of this film is that a Muslim actor is actually playing a Muslim character: Shah Rukh Khan is the protagonist Rizwan Khan. In most of the film blockbusters Karan Johar directed, Khan is playing the lead role. Apart from a personal preference (which is also obvious with Kajol concerning female roles), Johar seems to use Shah Rukh's star image in certain ways. Not only is he one of the actors most committed to the Bollywood mode (Rajadhyaksha 2008: 196), but he has also established himself as the embodiment of globalized Indianness (Dudrah 2006: 85ff). In his analysis of the film *Main Hoon Na* starring Shah Rukh Khan, Dudrah concludes that the actor performs "ultimate masala goals - resolving melodramatic trials, overcoming personal and physical struggles, executing song and dance sequences excellently, mediating a relationship between long-standing religious texts and globalisation" through "the agile human body as a literal and symbolic referent through which projects of selfhood are projected on screen" (Ibid.: 94). He closes with the words: "[Shah Rukh Khan] is the epitomy of the 'now' of global Bollywood's cinematic assemblage" (Ibid.: 95). In this study one aspect of the star text of Shah Rukh Khan will be emphasized, namely its role in establishing different romantic and erotic relationships in Johar's films by drawing on his image as romantic hero. The collaboration of Johar and Khan has resulted in a number of fascinating films all displaying a self-conscious relationship to hybridity, innovations in terms of devices and techniques, as well as a globalized imagery. Ending the delineation of recent developments in Hindi cinema with MY NAME IS KHAN emphasizes the contemporary globalized face of Hindi cinema, as not only does it treat a 'global issue', but its premiere took place in Abu Dhabi, and it was later released worldwide and distributed by Fox Star Studios[6].

---

6 See: http://www.business-standard.com/india/news/fox-bags-rights-for-my-name-is-khan-in-rs-100-crore-deal/365138/ (last viewed: 15.7.2011)

2. Approaching the Gaze in Film Studies and Beyond

Looking is never innocent or a neutral activity, feminist writer Coward states (2001: 33). She adds that the gaze is based on power and thus it is "one of the ways in which domination and subordination are expressed" (Ibid.: 34). Visual cultures enclose different ways of representing the gaze as well as structuring scopic relations that are all embedded in complex, intersecting power relations. The perspective on the gaze in terms of power relationships has been a major field of research in film studies, especially in psychoanalytic approaches. Due to the prevalence of critical feminist approaches from the 70s onwards, gender issues have been at the centre of theoretical discussions in this context. There are many more power relationships played out through the gaze apart from gender (which does not only include male/female but also lesbian, gay, bisexual and transgender identities). As bell hooks points out, the politics of slavery and racism have always denied Black people the subject position of the beholder of the gaze, resulting in an "oppositional gaze" in film spectatorship (2001: 123). Furthermore, a philosophical exploration dealing with conceptions of the gaze leads to deeper insight into the underlying hierarchies and the concept of power as such. In this context, *darshan*, for example, can be seen as reflecting questions on the nature of perception in general (Sanzaro 2007).

We have to understand that the question of who has the right to gaze at whom in which way – be it on screen or in the cinema hall – is crucial. A close analysis on the representational level can offer insights into how power relationships are inscribed into filmic texts. In this study the focus lies on a variety of filmic devices which shall be highlighted in the following introduction to the two major theoretical approaches to the gaze used here: Mulvey's concept of the erotic gaze and *darshan*. Moreover, the analysis and its methods shall be contextualized in the broader field of film studies in this chapter. Most significantly, the necessity of an intercultural approach shall be discussed.

Filmanalytical Perspectives on the Gaze

For my analysis, I have decided to use two approaches to the gaze and visual interaction in general: the idea of scopophilia as conceptualized in psychoanalytic film theory and, here especially, the concept of the 'erotic gaze' by Mulvey, as well as the concept of *darshan* rooted in Hinduism and occasionally applied in Indian film studies. It is important to note that although there are universal biological drives in human beings, love, romance, desire and the erotic are all concepts embedded in certain socio-cultural contexts and discourse. This means that all human feelings are interpreted according to prevailing ideas of the body, the self, gender and an endless list of social relations. In Western society psychoanalytic theory, and especially Sigmund Freud, have had a huge impact on discourses of love and desire (Dwyer 2000: 8, 11f). Freud's basic assumption of an unconscious and repressed desires continues to be a fundamental paradigm of Western thought. As Mulvey points out, her film analysis is concerned with "narratives of desire" (2009: XVI), of which the filmic representations related to the gaze are an intrinsic part. Generally, the psychoanalytic approach reflects more than any other the binarizaton so characteristic of Western discourses. The underlying dualism of Western philosophical thought, which structures the fundamental dichotomies such as self and other/Other, is deeply connected to the gaze in psychoanalytic theory, especially by Lacan. The concept of the split subject relies on objectification, which, Lacan states, comes into being by a child gazing at and realizing it might be gazed at (cf. Mirzoeff 1999: 164), which shows the profound significance of the gaze in the paradigms of psychoanalytic theory. Of course this approach has not gone uncriticized, and later French Feminists' answer to Lacan in terms of a deconstruction of dichotomies shall be addressed. In film theory Mulvey pointed out the relevance of the approach to the gaze in terms of patriarchal regimes of representation. Her basic assumption is that an active male gaze and the female as object of desire are inscribed in film texts ([1975] 2009: 19).
Darshan, on the other side, is firmly rooted in a religious context and Eck defines it in her seminal work as follows:

> In the Hindu view, not only must the gods keep their eyes open, but so must we, in order to make contact with them, to reap their blessings, and to know their secrets. When Hindus go to the temple, their eyes meet the powerful, eternal gaze of the eyes of God (Eck 1985: 1).

This concept of the gaze clearly refers to an encounter with the other as well, however, it is important to note the fundamental differences to the paradigm mentioned above. The two most striking aspects in this introductory description are the reciprocity and the power of the image that is looked at. To understand *darshan* better, an excursion into the philosophical and spiritual background of

Hinduism is necessary. First of all, let us look at the principle of polytheism underlying Hindu religion. We might describe it as "fluidity", (Fuller1992: 30) as there is one god and all other deities are forms and manifestation of the divine. Moreover, there is no absolute distinction between deities and human beings, as all beings are one: Brahman, the absolute (Ibid.) This is a philosophical concept, which in everyday religious practice and belief is not always present (Ibid.). Furthermore, power relations reflected in *darshan* become apparent when the hierarchical inequality in Hindu religion, as Fuller calls it (1992: 3), is taken into account. For example, gender and caste privileges can influence *darshan*: generally, blessings are given from the superior to the inferior, which means from deity to devotee but can also mean from husband to wife.

However, the concept of *darshan* is not restricted to Hinduism, but is a "structure of spectation" (Dwyer/Patel 2002: 33) which pervades visual culture in general and Hindi cinema in particular (Ibid.; Eck 1985: 2). The central assumption is that the pleasure of seeing is not restricted to gazing at something, but also being gazed back at in return (Chatterjee 2005: 103). The conception of the image is a different one, as on the one hand it has a different kind of power (Dwyer/Patel 2002: 33), but on the other hand it offers the beholder the possibility to understand and become familiar with 'the other' (Chatterjee 2005: 103). Concerning Hindi cinema, the scopic regime associated with *darshan* has been influential, especially in the mythological genre where deities are frequently depicted on screen (cf. Vasudevan 2000a, b, c; Prasad 1999: 78ff; Taylor 2003). As Taylor points out, *darshan* in films has been influenced much by another form of the gaze, namely *nazar*. *Nazar* is a concept derived from Persian literature and poetry especially used in the context of lovers' gazes (Taylor 2003: 302). Thus, various scopic regimes interact in Hindi film, some of them common in Hollywood and Western media as well. An approach which takes into account the hybridity and constant renegotiation of forms of representation is fruitful and can reach beyond binaries of 'Western' and 'Other' cultural forms. Thus, we can gain new insights into the pleasure gained through sight. This analysis shall not only touch upon filmic representations of the gaze, but also on concepts of spectatorship as well as star images. Consequently, topics relevant to these issues shall be emphasized in the following theoretical outline.

Scopophilia: Tracing Freud and Lacan in Film Studies

In the framework of psychoanalytic theory, scopophilia refers to the pleasure received from looking. Looking and the gaze are also intrinsically connected to sexual desires and, consequently, they are often part of the repressed desires and sensual pleasures that structure the unconscious. Thus, the holder of the gaze is mostly unaware of it (cf. Barnard 2001: 80). With Lacan the notion of looking as 'the gaze' became most significant as he argued that identity formation happens in the so called 'mirror stage', when the child looks in the mirror and identifies with the image, which is not the self itself but a substitute or signifier (Robbins 2000:114). This is when the awareness that the gazer is different from what/who is gazed at sets in. Furthermore, the gaze makes the individual aware that it may be looked at, which becomes part of identity as such (Mirzoeff 1999: 164f). The mirror stage is also the moment of the entry into language. Later, Lacan partly disassociated the concept from an actual state in child development and put it on a larger scale developing the concept of passage from Imaginary to Symbolic order. In general, we could say that in this theoretical framework objectification is intrinsic to looking/being looked at and thus to the formation of the subject (Pagel 1989: 30). However, woman as subject in his theory only emerges in order to affirm the male subject. Consequently, Lacan defines woman as constituted by lack – she is always defined by what man is not. This has been severely criticized by French Feminists such as Julia Kristeva, Luce Irigaray or Hélène Cixous. Their main concern is with the representation of woman in language and the constitution of female subjectivity (Robbins 2000: 117). Irigaray more than the others refers to the visual in this context as well. Not only in language is the woman a signifier rather than a signified, but also:

> [H]er entry into a dominant scopic economy signifies, again, her consignment to passivity: she is to be the beautiful object of contemplation. While her body finds itself thus eroticized, and called to a double movment of exhibition and of chaste retreat in order to stimulate the drives of the [male] 'subject', her sexual organ represents *the horror of nothing to see*. A defect in this systematic of representation and desire. A 'hole' in its scoptophilic lens (1985 [1977]:26).[7]

The question of female sexuality and its representation in patriarchal discourses is of major interest to my research. Irigaray criticizes the emphasis on sight and the visual that renders woman inevitably as object. We will return to her argument in the discussion of female desire in particular.

As we have seen, psychoanalysis offers various different approaches to the gaze that can and have been applied to filmic texts. Before we continue, however, it is important to differentiate what we mean by 'psychoanalysis'. From the beginning, both Freud and Lacan were concerned with the analysis of artistic and fictional work, but these approaches primarily have been relevant to the humanities. Thus, a discourse has emerged concerned with textual processes and reader

7 It has been pointed out that, in the light of the massive rise of the sex industry and pornography Irigaray's „horror of nothing to see" is out of place. However, I think this quote has to be read within psychoanalytic theory, especially concerning castration fear. Secondly, as pornography mostly forecloses the representation of female sexual desire as well as subject position and displays serious degradation of the female body and sexuality, I would argue that this actually backs up the argument if it is not read literally.

or spectator positions (Kaplan 1990: 2, 13).[8] In film studies psychoanalytic approaches have been used extensively, especially in the various essays published in the British film journal "Screen". Probably its most influential article was written by Laura Mulvey: "Visual Pleasure and Narrative Cinema", published in 1975. Here she argues from a feminist point of view that Hollywood cinema of the 50s and 60s built the male gaze into spectatorship and displayed the female body as spectacle. As Kaplan emphasizes, although psychoanalytical film studies were mostly referred to as Lacanian, "it is an ironic labelling in that many Freudian concepts were central and only limited aspects of Lacanian thought were involved" (Kaplan 1990: 9).

Let us now look at the concepts of the gaze generally used in this context. Although scopophilia means both the pleasure of looking and being looked at, Freud associated it primarily with the objectification of another person by subjecting him/her to the gaze connoted as voyeuristic. This is referred to as active scopophilia, in which sexual desire evolves from looking at the private/the forbidden. The corresponding 'passive' equivalent would be exhibitionism. As Mulvey points out, the latter is associated with a female subject position, while active scopophilia is ascribed to the male gaze ([1975] 2009: 19). She, among others, also argues that cinema evokes the "illusion of looking in on a private world" and thus plays on the "voyeuristic fantasies" (Ibid.: 17) of the audience. Similarly, Metz concludes that in cinema, the objectification is much stronger than, for example, in theatre, and represents an absolutely "unauthorized voyeurism" (Metz 2001: 423). Consequently, the spectator feels a sense of guilt and shame. Silverman puts more emphasis on the notion of shame. She argues that the shame of the voyeurist bears on his knowledge that he could be seen looking at the object of desire (Silverman 1994: 277). Shame is thus connected to power in terms of an overarching gaze that the voyeur is subjected to. In conclusion, this conception of the cinema apparatus as structured by voyeurism is at the core of Mulvey's and the psychoanalytic approach, in general. However, there is another possible effect of scopophilia in the cinema: the narcissicist identification with the image on the screen. As male figures tend to be active and hold agency, a positive identification with them is possible. In the context of stars and the star system this is an important aspect. Mulvey touches on this issue by equating the image on the screen with a pre-subjective image (before the mirror stage). This kind of narcissism is subsumed in the discussion about self and other as well as about subject and object. But as other conceptions of identification are more relevant, this discussion will only be touched upon briefly.

8 Kaplan also mentions: psychoanalysis as ‚talking cure'; as used to explain literary relationships, actions and motive in a text; as an aesthetic discourse focusing on the structure of narratives such as dreams; as a subject in narrative discourses; as an historical, ideological, and cultural discourse (Kaplan 1990: 13).

In general, the concept of the mirror stage has often been applied in cinema studies, due to the association between mirror and screen on a symbolic level (see Metz 2001; Kaplan 1999: 9; Mulvey [1975] 2009: 18). What is relevant for my analysis in this context is the notion of the 'split subject' in the concept. The entry of the subject into the symbolic order is marked by lack. According to Lacan, the phallus represents this divided and split field of vision (Mirzoeff 1999: 165). Consequently, the gaze signifies the phallocentric symbolic order – it is a signifier for what constitutes the subject as lacking (Silverman 1994: 275). It is possible to identify differences between the gaze of 'looking' and what we could call the phallic gaze: while the former is an expression of desire and is from one perspective, the gaze is not individualized but overarching. Silverman compares the distinction with the connection between penis and phallus: the former can stand in for the latter, but can never approximate it (Ibid.: 277).

A Close Reading of Mulvey's "Visual Pleasure and Narrative Cinema"

Mulvey's approach has to be contextualized in the wider historical context of feminist thought. The object of research is not "the act of looking itself, but the viewing relationship characteristic of a particular set of social circumstances" (Sturken/Cartwright 2001: 76). There exists a longstanding tradition in Western (and other) art of depicting women as objects of the gaze, constituting the patriarchal possessive claim on the female body. Thus, cameras have also been seen "as weapons of phallic power" (Ibid.: 78). Although this cannot be said about all the films produced by mainstream Hollywood and especially not in a contemporary context, it is still worthwhile to analyse the unconscious structures of 'looking' and 'being looked at'. Moreover, Mulvey is located in a specific political context. In the introduction to the second edition of "Visual and Other Pleasures" (2009) she emphasizes that the intellectual paradigms her analysis draws on are all rooted in the political left: feminism, psychoanalytic theory, cinephilia and avant-garde aesthetics (2009: IX). Consequently, her work is highly influenced by her activist stance, which is evident in her reasons for using psychoanalytic theory: "psychoanalytical theory gave me a polemical vocabulary" (Ibid.:XV) and "[p]sychoanalytical theory is thus appropriated here as a political weapon" ([1975] 2009: 14). Furthermore, her agenda also involves pointing out what has to be changed and the need for alternative aesthetics in cinema. We have to bear in mind this context of Mulvey's approach, although here it will be used in a very different way and for different reasons. Furthermore, it should be emphasized at this point that Mulvey refers to the Hollywood cinema of the 60s and 70s. Consequently, in contemporary cinema, we might find many changes in the cinematic codes. Furthermore, in other filmic traditions such as Hindi cinema there are completely different codes, as we have already seen to some extent in its summarizing description and will partly explore in the following analysis.

Let us now look at Mulvey's essay in more detail. In general, what she aims to demonstrate is "the way the unconscious of patriarchal society has structured film form" (Ibid.). The main point of her argument is that woman, through the forms of representations of the "female form" (15) in films, is reduced to a silent image as bearer (not maker) of meaning. Drawing on Freud and Lacan, she argues that woman always ultimately means lack, or more plainly, castration. This is the only meaning she attains in the symbolic order and thus serves as "a signifier for the male other" (15). Other feminists have emphasized this as well. De Lauretis declares that "the representation of woman as image" is so pervasive in contemporary media culture that it is fundamental in any analysis of sexual differences. Furthermore, she emphasizes that it is not about positive or negative images, but the denial of the status of subject to women in general (2001: 102; 108). Similarly, French Feminists have argued that the representation of woman in the Symbolic is the Other. However, the latter also criticized psychoanalytic theory and especially Lacan at the same time. This deconstruction transcends the psychoanalytic approach as ideology. In the course of this study I aim to deconstruct, to a certain extent, the approaches used. While the critique of Mulvey might not be too extensive here at this point, the analysis shall continuously reflect the reassessment of her arguments.

Mulvey explains the pleasure of cinema as a result of the presence of the two drives identified by Freud as motivating humankind: sexual instincts and self-preservation ([1975] 2009: 19). The first is the basis of scopophilia as outlined by Freud. The voyeuristic desire to see the private and forbidden is the basis for the objectifying gaze on another person. Mulvey assumes that in Hollywood cinema, this is reenacted by the illusion of a sealed private world which the spectator voyeuristically observes, and that allows him to project his repressed desires onto the performer. The implication of the second drive, self-preservation, is based on narcissism. Mulvey draws on Lacan in this context, taking into account the mirror stage. The image of the mirror is a significant landmark in the development of the ego and subjectivity, but also emerges as ego ideal, which the subject can never be. Accordingly, she traces two reactions to the screen image: the temporary loss of the ego, due to the remembrance of the pre-subjective moment, as well as the production of ego ideals through stars (18). Furthermore, she points out that although the cinema presents the two contradicting drives, the male spectator will inevitably be confronted with the implications of desire in the symbolic order: when desire is born through linguistic articulation (in the Symbolic), so is the castration complex (19). Thus "the look, pleasurable in form, can be threatening in content, and it is woman as representation/image that crystallises this paradox" (Ibid.). This is relevant to an understanding of argument of woman as object of the gaze.

In this framework the representation of women in films is traditionally exhibitionist in order to please the male gaze, which projects its fantasy onto the female figure. The dominating dichotomy of active/male and passive/female in

Western patriarchal society thus structures the gaze. The display of the female form usually has a strong visual and erotic impact, encouraging the male gaze to settle on it. This results in the representation of woman as sexual object and of the female body as erotic spectacle (19). Mulvey states that "the woman displayed has functioned on two levels: as erotic object for the characters within the screen story, and as erotic object for the spectator within the auditorium, with a shifting tension between the looks on either side of the screen" (20). In special instances, the two looks are united, such as when a woman is performing within the narrative. Further examples Mulvey mentions are the close-ups of legs or a face, which are integrated into the narrative and are often enabled through the use of subjective camera. Nevetheless, these modes of representation of woman can provoke the freezing of the narrative and destroy the illusion built up by cinematic narrative. As Mulvey explains, "it gives flatness, the quality of a cut-out or icon, rather than verisimilitude, to the screen" (20).

While the representation of women is characterized by objectification and iconization, Mulvey argues that the male protagonist pushes the narrative forward as active agent. The underlying cause is that "the male figure cannot bear the burden of sexual objectification" (Ibid.). While female figures are determined by exhibitionism and spectacle, the male ones dominate the narrative. Consequently, they represent power and the spectator identifies with them as acting subjects. Moreover, in terms of the gaze, the male protagonist occupies the active power of the erotic look and, consequently, is the bearer of the look of the spectator, too. Mulvey suggests that this can also be seen as the image in the mirror, because the character appears as "powerful ideal ego" (21) and more perfect than the spectator. In conclusion, the female figure is the erotic object of the gaze and represented in an iconic way, where looking at her corresponds to active scopophilia. The male figure has agency and appears to be in control of events, which makes the male spectator identify with him in a narcissistic way. We will come back later to the highly relevant aspect of iconicity and its effects, as well as the dichotomy of narrative and iconic mode established by Mulvey here.

As mentioned before, desire and as such woman as object of desire can also be threatening, as it recalls castration and woman's lack of a penis. Mulvey argues that castration anxiety in the male unconscious is dealt with in films in two ways. Either the woman is castigated and control over her is reasserted in the narrative, or she is fetishized and so ceases to be threatening. The first possibility is associated with not only voyeurism but also sadism and can only work if embedded in a story. The second one, which she calls "fetishistic scopophilia", can for example be seen in the cult of the female star as produced by Sternberg in connection with Marlene Dietrich. Woman in this instance is not threatening anymore as she is "no longer the bearer of guilt but a perfect product, whose body, stylised and fragmented by close-ups, is the content of the film and the direct recipient of the spectator's look" (23).

In her conclusion Mulvey emphasizes the power of cinema to structure the look of the spectator, since it does not simply give woman an exhibitionist role, but "builds the way she is to be looked at into the spectacle itself" (26). More than any other medium, cinema can shift the emphasis of the look and consequently exploit voyeuristic potential in a specific way:

> Playing on the tensions between film as controlling the dimension of time (editing, narrative) and film as controlling the dimension of space (changes in distance, editing), cinematic codes create a gaze, a world and an object, thereby producing an illusion cut to the measure of desire (Ibid.).

It is these codes, Mulvey suggests, that have to be broken down to change the patriarchal order in cinema. As she points out, its dependency on the narrative diegesis and the illusion of a sealed world is challenged by the iconic and fetishized image of the woman, which is an inert contradiction.The key concepts found in Mulvey's article which I apply analytically shall be examined in more detail in the next chapters. Primarily I focus on the voyeuristic and objectifying elements of the erotic gaze, the exhibitionist display of the (female) body as spectacle, as well as the relationship between these iconic representations and the narrative.

Mulvey Revisited: Criticism and Impulses

Since its publication in 1975, Mulvey's article has often been criticized, not least due to its polemical stance, which the author herself points out in later work. A short summary of the critique on Mulvey helps to understand the shortcomings of her famous essay. On the one hand, the criticism has been voiced inside the circle of psychoanalytic film analysis, but on the other hand, the approach as such has been criticized and other theoretical concepts have been used to reveal the weak points of the argument.

In the Screen reader "The Sexual Subject: A Screen Reader in Sexuality" Buscombe et al. generally criticize the vagueness of concepts and theoretical inaccuracy in essays concerned with psychoanalysis and film in the magazine. Mentioning Mulvey and Metz as examples, they point out the weakness of the conceptualization of perception and identification in the context of the mirror stage defined by Lacan (Buscombe et al.: 1992: 45). Similarly, Sturken and Cartwright emphasize that the critique of the approach has frequently noted that this concept implies a spectator in an infantile state (2001: 75). However, this kind of criticism is appropriate only if the concepts of gaze and the mirror stage in early and later Lacanian theory are not distinguished carefully. As Silverman states, the look and the gaze have to be clearly separated, which she demonstrates when referring to voyeurism: the voyeur is subjected to the gaze in the Lacanian sense too, as it is beyond the individual and determines the subject in the visible, or we could say, in the Symbolic. Consequently, voyeurism is closely connected to shame, as the voyeuristic is threatened by the gaze (1994: 277ff). She criticizes the fact that in feminist film theory (and this of course includes Mulvey) the male voyeur is often equated with the gaze, thus ascribing the transcendental status of the gaze to the individual look (Ibid.). Therefore, the essential element of shame in voyeuristic scopophilia is hardly alluded to by Mulvey. In my analysis, however, this plays a significant role. The relationship between gaze and look shall be treated more in Silverman's terms: the issue is not only the representation of woman as object of desire, but the notion that "the male look both transfers its own lack to the female subject and attempts to pass itself off as the gaze" (Ibid.: 286).

Another problem about Mulvey's approach, which she herself points out in a later essay, is the limitation the strict binary oppositions pose. Although she still considers the binary mode of thought as a useful analytical tool, since the representations of difference dominate Western culture, she revises her model to a certain degree:

> There is a sense in which this argument, important as it is for analysing the existing state of things, hinders the possibility of change and remains caught ultimately within its own dualistic terms. The polarisation only allows an 'either/or'. As the two terms (masculine/feminine, voyeuristic/exhibitionist, active/passive) remain dependent on each other for meaning, their only possible movement is into inversion ([1987] 2009: 169).

This issue is broached by many scholars engaging with Mulvey's original text. De Lauretis argues that the question arises in any "theoretical paradigm of a subject-object dialectic, whether Hegelian or Lacanian" (2001: 320) and traces the primary binary oppositions back to Platonic philosophy. As mentioned before, this is another reason for using this psychoanalytic approach here instead of contemporary, probably more innovative ones in feminism and gender studies. It displays a strong affinity with central paradigms of thought in Western culture. In the context of contemporary global consumer culture it should also be taken into consideration that the cult of the body is connected to a commodification and objectification of female as well as male bodies. The visual impact of this can be seen, for example, in modern advertising. However, as Sturken and Cartwright mention: "Part of the tradition of imagining men as objects of desire has involved particular codes of resisting the power of the gaze upon them" (2001: 88), which is valid for large parts of contemporary global cinema.

The second strand of criticism on Mulvey is more concerned with general questions and conceptions in media studies. It is set in the dispute between two 'Grand Theories': Apparatus theory, or subject-position theory; and Cultural Studies, or culturalism (Bordwell 1996a: 3). First and foremost, the concept of spectatorship in psychoanalytic film theory as well as in any other film theory assuming an 'implicit' or 'ideal' spectator, has often been questioned, especially by representatives of Cultural Studies. The spectator has increasingly been seen as actively involved in the process of meaning-making. Consequently, the critique on Mulvey focuses on spectatorship too. bell hooks, for example, argues that Black female spectators develop an oppositional gaze, thus deconstructing the concept of a monolithic audience structured by the male/female dichotomy (hooks: 2001: 130). Furthermore, Stacey investigates the importance of female desire and the complexity of the relationship of female spectators to the female subject on screen (2001: 110). Her ethnographic approach offers insights into decoding practices of actual female audiences, thus putting into question Mulvey's model (1994: 24–31).

Keeping in mind that the filmic content is a text open to different interpretations that are shaped by decoding practices situated in a specific social and cultural context, I will still have to assume certain spectator positions to analyse the visual interactions in the samples. The concepts taken from Mulvey's approach, along with psychoanalytic approaches in general, shall not be applied unreflected and will be enriched through an intercultural approach to other perspectives on the gaze. Moreover, my analysis is influenced by feminist ideology as well, although this might manifest itself in a very different way. While Mulvey stood for a radical critique of Hollywood and support of avant-garde cinema according to the political context of the time, I want to point out certain tendencies in mainstream Hindi cinema concerning gender issues and open up some new perspectives on filmic representations.

Darshan: *What 'Seeing' Can also Mean*

In the Hindu concept of *darshan*, the devotee seeks the presence of the deity and wants to see as well as be seen by the deity. The image of the deity can be a statue, a place, or an object; there is a great variety of forms of manifestation. As Eck states, the two elements are called *darshan dena* (give *darshan* – which we could call the pleasure of seeing) and *darshan lena* (take *darshan* – which we could call the pleasure of being seen) (Eck 1985: 6). Generally, *darshan* is a fundamental part of Hindu worship. Consequently, the eyes and their iconographic representations play an extremely important role in Hindu religious practice. The unblinking eyes of the deity are regarded as very powerful, due to the ever watchful gaze which sees everything. It is through them that the devotee comes into contact with the deity and receives blessings (Ibid.: 7). This emphasis on the gaze results in a rich visual imagery and a predominance on visuality in religious groups, and also in Indian culture on the whole (Babb 1981: 387, 390). A fundamental aspect of *darshan* is that the act of looking is not seen as something passive, as the image form of the deity is gazing back on the devotee (Fuller 1992: 60). Drawing on Gell, Taylor states: "this mutual looking or ocular exchange between a devotee and deity is a visual activity that is both reciprocal and intersubjective" (Taylor 2003: 302).

This means that the subject-object relation stands in stark contrast to what we discussed in the context of Western paradigms of thought. The image or icon is not passive, but exercises power: "the devotee is *permitted* to behold the image of the deity, and is *privileged* and *benefited* by this *permission*, in contrast to a concept of looking that assigns power to the beholder by reducing the image to an object of the look" (Vasudevan 2000b: 139, emphasis mine). More than in other descriptions Vasudevan points out the hierarchical structure of *darshan*. Furthermore, he also takes non-religious contexts into consideration. This scopic relationship and its inherent hierarchy is also fostered with other authorities such as kings or patriarchal family heads (Ibid.). In terms of gender relations this can mean that the embedded hierarchy can ascribe an inferior subject position to women as, for example, the husband is supposed to be seen as god and worshipped as such (Fuller 1992: 20). However, the benevolent gaze is not male gendered as there are female deities who hold power and can give *darshan*.

Moreover, the perceptive sense of seeing is redefined and extended in this context. Gonda explains that an emphasis on the communicative aspect of visual interaction can be found in key texts of Sanskrit poetry and drama. The glances between two people, for example, can express complex feelings resulting in the idea of a kind of language of the eyes. Secondly, seeing can also be regarded as a kind of touching, as the look means contact. Thus, there is a close connection between the activities of touching and seeing. In Gonda's analysis of seeing we find the conclusion that seeing is "a means also of participating in the essence and nature of the person or object looked at" (Gonda in Eck 1985: 9). Similarly, Pinney emphasizes mutuality and corporeality as important aspects of *darshan*. In contrast to Western conceptions it is a tactile, embodied vision meant to enable an encounter and connection (Pinney in Dwyer 2006b: 19). This enhanced model of seeing has to be taken into account in the following, in which it is regarded a form of touching and knowing.

In a philosophical approach to *darshan*, the aspect of seeing as knowing predominates. What it conveys is a perspective on truth, the seeing of the truth (Eck 1985: 25). Ultimately, this should lead to liberation, which is again deeply rooted in the soteriological idea of Hinduism. Generally, liberation in Hinduism refers to the liberation from rebirth which can be achieved in different ways: so-called *yogas* or *margas* (King/Brockington 2005:2). Babb, for example, describes *darshan* in the context of a religious sect. The visual interaction with the deity lets the devotee participate in the superior way of seeing and knowing: "inner powers of the deity become available to the devotee". This enables a transformation of the self and a new perspective (Babb 1981: 400). Consequently, the transitional experience can be taken as another important aspect of *darshan* when we deal with it as knowledge of the self and the other.

Religious Concepts and Practices Related to Darshan

To understand how this concept is applied in film studies, it is important to have a closer look at *darshan* in the context of Hinduism. It is not only a fundamental part of everyday religious practices, as when Hindu devotees perform the puja (a central ritual of Hinduism) in temples or in their home shrines (Fuller 1992: 57). In Hindu culture, *darshan* is also deeply embedded in the key ideas of the relationship between the divine and human beings. Consequently, we need to take a closer look into the fluidity of Hindu concepts, various religious movements as well as mythological sources which are significant in this context.

First of all, it is important to see what *darshan* is in lived religious practice and in the specific context of puja. Every time a devoted Hindu encounters the eyes of the deity he/she seeks *darshan* – be it with a statue in a temple or shrine, a picture or a statue on display in a public procession (Fuller 1992: 57; Eck 1985: 57). To receive it brings fortune and spiritual merit to the devotee (Fuller 1992: 59). Puja is probably the most common way to worship, to seek *darshan* and to reach the desired unity with the deity. The ritual can be performed in different settings, in the temple or, for example, at the family shrine, and varies much depending on the context. Fuller describes the atmosphere of big pujas where many people are assembled. There is music and lavish decoration with flower garlands, as well as rich fabrics covering the statues which represent the deities; it is hot, incense and camphor lights are lit (1992: 57). Consequently, a puja appeals to all senses: seeing, touching, smelling, tasting and hearing (Ibid.; Eck 1985: 11). After diverse greetings and offerings to the deity, the climax is reached when the lamps are displayed by circling them in front of the images (Babb 1981: 394). As both deity and devotee gaze at the flame it symbolizes the transcendence of the embodied forms of both, and thus unification:

> When a camphor flame is shown at the climax of puja, therefore, the divine and human participants are most fully identified in their common vision of the flame and hence in their mutual vision of each other – the perfect darshana (Fuller 1992: 73).

When this unity is reached devotees cup their hands over the flame and then move the fingertips to the eyes. In this way, the power and protective grace of the deity is transmitted to the worshiper, again through his/her eyes. Before closing the ritual all devotees lift their hands in the namaskara gesture to pay homage to the deity (Ibid.: 57). When visiting the temple or performing puja, a red dot called kumkum is usually applied to the forehead. This aspect of identification is relevant to the concept of *darshan* used here and will be discussed below in more detail.

Before we go further it is indispensable to discuss the nature of the image of a deity, or the concept of divine embodiment, in Hinduism. The image of a deity can be many things: sculptured images, paintings (and here also cheaply produced prints which are widespread in India and commonly used in domestic shrines), but also objects such as pots of water or rocks as well as natural phenomena such as the river Ganga (Fuller 1992: 58f). However, it is by no means seen as the 'actual' deity and object of worship. The image is usually called *murti* and the term refers in general to the form of the deity. Only after a ritual of consecration is the divine power installed in the *murtis*. Apart from the pronounced eyes as a distinctive feature of the images, most bear a mark above their nose that symbolizes the third eye, which is the point where the power emanates[9]. In the context of *darshan* this is important, because "when devotees look at images, they are also standing in the field of the deities' power and absorbing it like light through their own eyes" (Ibid.: 60). The relationship between deity and image becomes even more complicated when we take into consideration that human beings, too, can be an image of a deity: a priest can become the form of Vishnu, for example (Ibid.: 61). Thus, neither can the image be equated with the deity nor is there an absolute distinction between them. Generally, devotees can receive *darshan* from human beings as well. For example, on the day of the wedding the bridal couple is divine and also gives *darshan* to the participants (Ibid.: 30; Babb 1981: 394). Furthermore, holy men such as gurus, sadhus or swamis are considered partly divine, too (Fuller 1992: 31). In this context Babb describes a religious movement[10] where seeing and being seen by a guru is the essential aim (1981: 388).

How can this concept of embodiment be understood? An explanation requires going into more detail with the basic belief system of Hinduism. Commonly, Hinduism is regarded as a polytheistic religion, but depending on the perspective, there is either one god or many. Brahman is the most supreme deity, whom all other deities, human beings and everything else are part of (Fuller 1992: 30). Thus, we first of all have to comprehend what Fuller calls "fluidity" (Ibid.) in Hinduism. This is perpetuated in the different forms gods can take on. Vishnu, for example, is encountered in many different incarnations such as Rama or Krishna. In other words, the principle of Oneness does not exclude multiplicity: "At virtually every level of life and thought India is polycentric and pluralistic" (Eck 1985: 24).

Having touched on fluidity as a core element of Hinduism, we can understand why *darshan* or other practices such as the *namaskara* gesture are widespread in human interaction, too. These examples, however, reveal that rigid hierarchies structure religious practice as well as social life. For example, Fuller describes how the *namaskara* gesture marks social rank, as the inferior bows to the superior; only if both people are equal they both do the *namaskara*. He points

9 Among all Hindu gods and goddesses only Shiva actually has a third eye, but the power which he possesses flows through all of the deities (Fuller 1992: 60).

10 Babb refers to the Radhasoami movement originating in Agra.

out that this does not simply signal inferiority, but expresses devotion and adoration as the part greeted in the superior is the divine (Fuller 1992: 4). Another example is the touching of the feet of and the blessings subsequently given by the superior. The feet, as Babb explains, symbolize the idea of power as touching them means total submission and surrender. The underlying idea is that the more powerful protect the weaker and is an essential principle of Hindu society: "Moreover, the gesture suggests reciprocal obligation; he who has been surrendered to, and who has accepted this surrender, is obliged – on the model of the parent or patron – to provide shelter and protection to the one who has surrendered" (Babb 1981: 195). The deity's feet are thus central to worship.

In terms of gender relationships, a general perception of women as inferior to men is expressed in these practices. Married women often seek the blessings of their husbands in ritual or other contexts by touching his feet. It is often said that the husband should be seen as god by a woman (Fuller 1992: 20). Consequently, the same power relationship as between god and devotee is projected onto marital relationships. Although there is the feminine divine power called 'shakti' which masculine power depends on, we also find this hierarchy in divine couples as already mentioned in the example of Sita as the ideal wife (Ibid.: 24). Nevertheless, let me point out again that there is no indication of a gendered nature of *darshan* as such.

Let us summarize some of the central characteristics of the relationship between human beings and deities which structure *darshan*. Firstly, Brahman is in all living beings, and thus the powerful divine can be found in human beings, too. In *darshan* devotee and deity are united temporarily, which is evoked by the surrender of the former and the blessing by the latter, which is the basis of darshanic identification. An important aspect that Babb emphasizes is that seeing and being seen here is a "medium of intimacy between deity and worshipper" (1981: 396), which makes it possible to take in something of the deity: "the beneficiary mingles a superior, apparently fluid-like 'seeing' with his own, thereby appropriating its powers" (Ibid.). Hence, we could say *darshan* is the ultimate encounter of self and other as well as their dissolution. Still, the relationship is marked by a hierarchy similar to that of power relations in society, as Fuller states: "the worshiper is as much a deity's wifely servant as its royal subject" (1992: 81). The ritual can be as much homage and devotion as negotiation of power (Ibid.).

As mentioned before there are different ways which lead to liberation in Hinduism. One of them is devotion, which has emerged as a central principle in contemporary religious practice. This development has taken place in the context of a certain religious movement called *bhakti*[11.] It shall be described briefly here, as it can also offer insights into *darshan* and identification and will become

11 Apparently the word bhakti originally meant ‚to share' and referred to loyality to a master and his obligations to the servant (King/Brockington 2005: 6). Thus it more

more important in the analysis later on. *Bhakti* refers to devotionalist movements which put the personal emotion and relationship between devotee and deity at the centre of worship. In this direct address of the deity the devotee feels great intimacy and at the same time is aware of his/her otherness, as King and Brockington state: "God is the intimate other" (2005: 4). The individualization of worship results in the independence from Brahmanic priests, which is suggestive of a certain subversion of power structures (Fuller 1992: 157). Furthermore, as Vasudevan points out, the female devotee who does not have to rely on husband or priest to show her devotion to the divine puts in question another hierarchy. Her voice is thus one of ambiguity (Vasudevan 2000c: 387). King and Brockington conclude that *bhakti* is not subversive per se, but from a differentiated perspective it "can be employed to both legitimate, and also to contest and subvert the social order" (2005: 6).

Among the devotionalist movements the worship of Krishna has been most dominant in many parts of India. The relationship between him and Radha, the cowherdess, serves as a model of intense, mutual love between deity and devotee (Ibid.: 3). Radha's love for Krishna is very passionate and sexualized. Consequently, *bhakti* in this sense is highly eroticized (Fuller 1992: 156). Moreover, Radha offers a female role model characterized by independence, pride and sexual agency, which is greatly in contrast to other goddesses. For example, Krishna worships Radha's feet and he prompts her to put her foot upon his head in one of the key texts, the Gitagovinda. Fuller states: "Thus Krishan is Radha's lord, but she is also his, and their love denies the inequality of marriage, conventionally symbolized by Lakshmi faithfully worshiping at the feet of her husband Vishnu" (1992: 157). In general, their love is very transgressive as it is cross-caste, adulterous (Radha is married), romantic and sexual without being legitimated by marriage (Ibid.). This is of importance for my study in so far that it shows a concept of love constituted by romantic transgressions, erotic attraction and mutual (and thus significantly female) desire. Furthermore, there are imageries and visual representations associated with it. The very common depiction of the divine couple as entwined and appearing to the eye as inseparable (Eck 1985: 28) already hints at its significance for the concept of the 'intimate other'. Krishna and Radha are "both separate and one" and in the same manner "human beings are separated from the divine" (King/Brockington 2005: 3). It must be mentioned that the relationship of devotee and Krishna in the *bhakti* movements is marked by ecstatic and passionate longing (Ibid.). Interestingly, during worship all devotees identify with the female positions of Radha and her longing for the divine male lover (Coorlawala 1996: 23).

---

or less describes the hierarchical relationship between superior and inferior mentioned before.

However, it is important not to see *darshan* exclusively in the realm of the religious nor its meanings rooted in Hindu philosophy and practice. First of all, a clear-cut distinction between religious and mundane forms is unfeasible and mostly motivated by Western paradigms of thought particularly influenced by Catholicism. Moreover, from the beginning other concepts such as the Arabic *nazar*, which is very present in Urdu poetry, have influenced the predominating modes of visuality in public culture (Taylor 2003: 302; Orsini 2006: 15). As Taylor describes, *nazar* alludes to the glances exchanged by lovers, but can also be located in religious worship as in Sufism (2003: 303). As I will use *darshan* in the context of cinema and popular culture it might be best to comprehend it together with the mythology and imagery of Hinduism as "basic cultural vocabulary and a common idiom of discourse" (Eck 1985: 17), which is used along with other codes in filmmaking. A mixing of codes and mutual influence between them is what makes cinema and other popular forms the vibrant and dynamic cultures they are.

Analytical Approaches to Darshan *in Indian Film Studies*

In general, *darshan* has had a huge impact on visual culture in India. As Eck points out, we find elements of darshanic visual interaction in most visual texts and consequently, in films (1985: 2). Possibilities have been explored to mediate *darshan* in a filmic context, primarily in mythological or devotional films. As mythologicals are not as common as they used to be, this finds continuity in the already mentioned, very popular mythological TV series, some of which offer a true "feast of darsana" (Pauwels 2008: 173). Furthermore, references to *darshan* as well as renegotiations of the concept can be found in non-religious films in many different ways. In Hindi film studies, modes of representation and address have been identified which are used in the context of *darshan* as scopic regime. The two most significant ones that I will focus on are the iconic mode and the frontal, direct address, which are intrinsically connected in Hindi film aesthetics related to the gaze. In the following we will investigate what iconicity and frontality in this context mean, drawing on the seminal texts in Indian film studies concerned with *darshan*.

Iconic signs are usually understood in contrast to symbolic signs which arbitrarily refer to a signified (Prince 1993: 23). In the context of Indian visual cultures, however, iconicity is mostly defined in terms of the representation of the mythic in Indian art as described by Rajadhyaksha and Kapur (Vasudevan 2000b: 137; Dwyer/Patel 2002: 44). The iconic mode is used to "identify a meaningful condensation of image" (Vasudevan 2008: 138) and is found in "cultural work which seeks to bind a multilayered dynamic into a unitary image" (Vasudevan 2000c: 388). In result, the iconic image encompasses condensed symbolic meanings and is characterized by stasis (Kapur in Ibid.). In mythological films we find the iconic mode, for example, in the depiction of deities (in form of the statues and images) or saints. The most famous examples are Phalke's films such as SANT TUKARAM (1936) or SHRI KRISHNA JANMA (1918) (Taylor 2003: 307; Chatterjee 2005: 105). The iconic images strongly recalled the images displayed in temples (*murti*) and consequently actuated visual interactions consistent with *darshan* – between the devotee as character in the film, but also with the audience (Taylor 2003: 307). Furthermore, the long shots foreclosed any narrative action and in some cases were "purely scopic" (Chatterjee 2005: 105), which further patterned the aspect of worship in these scenes (Ibid.). Mainly, the iconic image in Hindi films is characterized by its distribution over the entire surface of the screen and by its function of signifying an already known narrative or discourse. Stasis is another characteristic; however, it should not be understood in a narrow way, as in the filmic context an image can be both iconic and moving (Ibid.: 91). The question now is how exactly this iconic effect is achieved, which leads us to the mode of address.

Generally, frontality and direct address in film studies have been discussed in the context of a cinema of attractions with which early Hollywood films are associated. Contrary to prevailing notions of early cinema as 'primitive' and lacking, Gunning provides the most useful definition of frontality as a model of framing which puts forward the act of display itself and is used to attract as well as control the gaze of the spectator (1989: 9). Moreover, the spectator was directly addressed by acts of exteriority as, for example, the direct look at the camera or gestures of the actor directed at the audience. The cinema of attractions is, thus, marked by exhibitionism and self-awareness (Ibid.). Although some characteristics of Hindi cinema resemble the cinema of attractions, they should not be conflated.[12] One aspect relevant to my approach is the self-reflectivity of Hindi cinema which is similar to early American film (Tieber 2007: 60).

Frontality as well as direct address are negotiated in relation to other codes and modes of representation in Hindi film. As Vasudevan points out:

> At one level frontality would mean placing the camera at a 180' plane to the figures and objects constitutive of filmic space. These may display attributes of direct address, as in the look of characters into the camera, but a frontal, direct addres is relayed in other ways, as in the way the knowledge of the spectator is drawn upon in constructing the scene, through the stylised performance, ritual motifs, and auditory address that arise from a host of Indian aesthetic and performance traditions (2008: 138).

12 Mishra relates frontality as framing device to the theatrical performance tradition of colonial and Parsi theatre marked by the proscenium arch. He emphasizes that transgressions breaking the laws of theatrical frontality took place (Mishra 2002: 9f).

He goes on to describe the relation between iconicity and frontality in tableau in melodrama and in song and dance sequences. Let us first look at the tableau. Dwyer and Patel point out that in the melodramatic mode, frontality is used to make the representations of emotional and moral states more effective (Dwyer/Patel 2002: 45). Vasudevan as well as Dwyer and Patel argue that the static frontal planes of tableau are frequently used for this purpose in Hindi films (Vasudevan 2000b: 138). Interestingly, Dwyer points out that *darshan* is invited by tableau and iconicity is thus reinforced (2006b: 19). Furthermore, Chatterjee mentions various types of iconic imageries and ways that the direct, frontal address is deployed. For example, direct address cannot only be used when characters are actually looking at each other, but also to establish a connection between them or signify a relationship-to-be. Another iconic image is created by the technique of two-shot compositions, which contain two faces of two characters, thus recalling religious icons of dual nature such as Radha and Krishna. In this case "[t]hese gods might both look out towards us or they might look at each other" (2005: 95). Moreover, Chatterjee points out that there are various other camera angles which can produce the iconic effect. Apart from the frontal address, profiles of actors can be iconic images, too (2005: 91). Moreover, if the devotee exchanging gazes with the deity in religious films is positioned not frontally but in an angular position, space is opened up for the audience, establishing a triangular relationship between devotee, god and the audience (107). These examples show a variety of ways in which iconicity and frontality can be connected, but also demonstrate that they do not have to go hand in hand.

In song and dance sequences the frontal address described by Vasudevan is frequently used, including key elements, most of all the auditory relay: "[t]he film song displays this function of 'frontal' address across genres, reaching over and beyond the space of the scene, locking the spectator into a direct auditory relay" (Ibid.). Generally, it could be said that song and dance sequences present a whole "poetics of sight" (Taylor 2003: 301). It is very common that *darshan* is transferred from a religious context to the context of a love story, where it is used to frame desire mostly in song and dance sequences (Ibid.). However, it is important that *darshan* here interacts with and reinforces other visual codes, primarily those of the romantic genre. Close-ups and frontal shots highlight the lover's gaze representing desire and the erotic, but also activate the notion of *darshan* as they resemble the iconic images of the deity inviting the darshanic gaze as portrayed in mythologicals (Ibid.: 311, 313). Moreover, the close-ups of the lovers' gazes indicate the reciprocal visual interaction and are often accompanied by frontal, direct address (Sanzaro 2007: 19f; Taylor 2003: 307ff). The concept of *darshan* gets more complex the more devices such as editing techniques are exploited in its filmic representation, enabling new constellations of visual interaction.

A crucial issue in the analysis of *darshan* in a filmic context is the way hierarchies inert in *darshan* are negotiated and new ones are inscribed into it. This is of great significance for the following analysis, especially in terms of gender relations. In general, *darshan* evokes the following effect:

> [H]ierarchies of power may develop around the image of a character. This character image becomes the authoritative focal point of a scene, occupying a certain privileged position which structures space as a force field of power. In contrast to formulations about looking which have become commonplace in the analysis of Hollywood cinema, the figure looked at is not necessarily the subject to control but may in fact be the repository of authority (Vasudevan 2000c: 390).

In family films the patriarchal authority can thus be marked by darshanic elements, resulting in an omnipresent controlling gaze. Prasad argues that *darshan* in the feudal family romance of the 50s and 60s is part of a scopic regime which displays the splendour of the ruling class in a "hierarchical despotic public spectacle" (Prasad 1998: 78) to legitimize power relationships. Consequently, the representation of the private, such as intimate and romantic relationships of young lovers, challenge this patriarchal gaze (Ibid.: 78f). As Vasudevan points out, we can find challenges and reprehensions of darshanic authority (Vasudevan 2000b: 150). But very often the family narrative evolves around the transaction of this authority and the darshanic position to the son (Vasudevan 2000c: 390). In conclusion, *darshan* as patriarchal gaze is primarily marked by public display and spectacle, which is deeply connected to the exhibitionist character of Hindi cinema in general (Vasudevan 2000b: 151f).

Vasudevan points out various examples of how *darshan* is used in terms of a deification of the male character. Male authority and power can be asserted by a female devotional gaze upon the male character/image (Vasudevan 2000c: 390). We can find iconic images of the male object of the desire, which are deified by the darshanic gaze of the female character as devotee. In terms of camera and editing techniques the gaze can, for example, be conveyed by the upwards movement wandering from the feet of the beloved to the eyes (Ibid.; Vasudevan 2000b: 140). However, this darshanic mode leads to ambiguity, as the concept of devotion draws a great deal on the *bhakti* tradition. The main focus of attention there is the devotee and his/her excessive love for the deity, not for the object of worship. Thus, a feminine subjectivity as well as female desire are represented (Ibid.: 147f). The ambiguity loses significance due to "the framework of masculine authority within which female desire is finally held" (Vasudevan 2000c: 391).

Interestingly, the references to the *bhakti* tradition and to *darshan* in films have effects on the concept of spectatorship, too. Firstly, the iconic images circumvent the identification process and quite frequently the close-up shots do not represent the subjective viewing positions of the actors (Chatterjee 2005: 111). Secondly, the frontal, direct address evokes a direct link to the spectator. As Gunning points out, in the context of early American cinema it is a means of establishing contact with the audience (1990: 64). Furthermore, it can create a distance to the narrative events and characters. What is conveyed then is a symbolized and essentialised message (Vasudevan 2000b: 148; Prasad 1998: 20). Thirdly, the *bhakti* movement has established a female (Radha's) identificatory position full of passionate desire for a male god. In performance tradition associated with *bhakti*, the "locus of the power to construct the love object" (Coorlawala 1996: 23) can shift easily, thus creating ambiguity. In the analysis it shall be further investigated whether and how the shift of the power locus is employed in Hindi films, particularly in terms of the representation of female desire.

Altogether, these relations of spectatorship comply with the self awareness of Hindi film and the corresponding audience expectations. To understand the effects of filmic representations of *darshan* as well as the high degree of symbolized and generalized meaning, it is useful to take rasa theory into account, which is important for any analysis of dramaturgy in the Indian context (Dwyer 2000: 20). The *rasa* of love and the erotic (*shringara*) can be experienced in *bhakti* as the love between Krishna and Radha. King and Brockington point out that it is consequently marked by extreme emotions of ecstasy in reunion and longing in separation. In addition, the lovers are also often portrayed as separate and one, likewise the relationship between devotee and deity (2005: 3). Furthermore, the pleasure of aesthetic performances is provided if the performer manages to convey the *rasa*, meaning the emotion in its essential state, by drawing on the familiar stimulants and determinants of the *rasa* (Orsini 2006: 8).[13] This has implications for acting, which is, however, not at the centre of my analysis.

Darshan in the filmic context also has implications for the construction of star images. Referring to the codes derived from certain styles of looking, Dwyer and Patel state: "While these codes may be less striking nowadays than in older films, their endurance may be seen in the use of spectacle, in particular the depiction of the star" (2002: 46). It is hardly difficult to find analogies between the representation of deities and stars in Hindi film: "Hindi film stars are often perceived as gods by their fans, who may dedicate temples to them" (Dwyer 2006b: 164). The display of the star in films as well as off-screen recalls darshanic relationships to deities, but also to kings and other worldly authorities displaying themselves as spectacle and giving *darshan* (Dwyer/Patel 2002: 73). In reference to Shah Rukh Khan, the star most relevant for this study, Dudrah points out the great significance of the intense iconography and the excessive staging of darshanic interaction for his on-screen star image (Dudrah 2010). Moreover, in the final words

---

13 Determinants are the two lovers and stimulants are the symbols such as springtime. Moreover, there are bodily states which constitute the *shringara rasa*: paralysis, perspiration, gooseflesh, stammering, trembling, change in colour, tears and fainting (Orsini 2006: 8), which can often be identified in films, too.

of the three day conference "Shah Rukh Khan and Global Bollywood" (Vienna, 2010) exclusively focusing on the star, Rachel Dwyer raised the question again which had captivated us all: What is the nature of his charisma? And she suggested that drawing on the concept of *darshan* might yield answers. In conclusion, this study aims to contribute to this debate as well.

Although most of the work focusing on *darshan* has been concerned with either the early mythological genre or the family films of the 50s and 60s, *darshan* is highly relevant for the analysis of contemporary films. Generally, it could be said that:

> Hindu iconography and its relationship of the image and the viewer have, perhaps, an even greater affinity with cinema and the conventions of Indian cinema, whether or not the operation of a melodramatic mode or its sequence of ‚attractions' (see Dwyer and Patel 2002) subordinate the spectacular to the other requirements of cinema (Dwyer 2006b: 4).

In my analysis a special focus will lie on how notions of spectacle and melodrama relate to the gaze. It is of fundamental importance to consider interactions of different visual codes in this context. This has become more significant than ever, as Hindi films continually interact with other cinematic styles and aesthetics (Dwyer 2000: 117). Following Vasudevan, the following analysis will also put an emphasis on how hierarchical relationships are represented, asking questions such as: "who authorises a view, locates a figure in narrative space, who speaks, who sees, who listens" (2000b: 148)? I will investigate how Western and Indian cinematic codes interact and how alternative gazes are created. In this context we should keep in mind that they also construct different selfhoods, as Vasudevan argues in the context of the renegotiation of colonial modernity in films of the 50s:

> [T]he forms of filmic representation are mixed, gesturing to different types of subjectivity, and the look of the spectator operates at the interstices of theses forms, initiating a dialogue between various forms of selfhood (2000a: 13).

Darshan Meets Scopophilia: An Intercultural Approach

An analysis of the erotic gaze in Hindi films demands an intercultural approach which takes into account different scopic regimes interacting in the hybrid Hindi cinema. The following chapter is an exploration and negotiation of perspectives the outlined approaches offer. To exclusively apply either of the theoretical approaches would be problematic (cf. Dwyer 2000: 117). Since Hindi film is in itself hybrid, the filmic codes and representational modes are mixed, as Vasudevan emphasises in his central argument (2005b:151). His focus lies on the interplay between forms of representation related to the iconic mode, or frontal, direct address, and "Hollywood codes of continuity" which refer to a system of narration marked by a character's individuated movement and awareness (Ibid.: 131; 2000c: 386, 388). Due to the increasing incorporation of Hollywood's continuity editing in Hindi films, this is of vital significance. As Kasbekar points out, other styles of filmmaking influence Hindi cinema and bring in more mechanisms of the gaze (2001: 288). If this is not considered, significant layers of meaning could otherwise go unnoticed and the overall result of the analysis could thus be distorted (Coorlawala 1996: 26; Vasudevan 2000b: 151). Consequently, *darshan* as treated here in the context of scopic regimes in Hindi film is seen as a hybrid concept, which already draws on various other 'gazes' such as *nazar*. For practical reasons it shall still be referred to as *darshan*. The two main concepts of erotic and darshanic gaze might sometimes appear like clear-cut entities, which they are not.

Many Indian film scholars have also treated the gaze by drawing on two different theories, namely psychoanalysis and *darshan* (Prasad 1998; Rajadhyaksha 2000; Vasudevan 2000a, b). In particular, Mulvey's approach has often been applied, as well as that of Metz, which is more generally concerned with the cinema apparatus. In Hindi film studies it has also become generally acknowledged that *darshan* is not only relevant in a religious context (Sanzaro 2007: 2). Consequently, the implications of both theories for the analysis of the gaze in the context of the representation of desire or gender relations are obvious. Moreover, both offer insights into deeper philosophical questions posed by the topic, such as power relations, conceptions of selfhood and subject-object relationships. Generally, we could also say that the erotic gaze as it is conceptualized in psychoanalysis, as well as the darshanic gaze, represent ways of encountering and interacting with the Other.

Furthermore, it is also important to see the topic in the context of a debate concerning orientalist notions of Western film studies. As Vasudevan and Rajadhyaksha both point out, significant elements of Hindi film aesthetics, as well as of the scopic regime exploited in films, such as the frontal, direct address and exhibitionist spectacle have been devaluated in the colonial discourse as they are associated with early (and thus underdeveloped) cinema (Ibid.; Rajadhyaksha 2000: 269). Referring to direct address and frontality in early American film, I have already pointed at Gunning's argument that this framing model should be seen in the context of an "alternate cinema". Its practices should not be seen as drawing on theatrical conventions due to a lack of expertise, but rather as using alternative ways of consciously constructing illusion (Gunning 1989: 8). In fact, as in later American filmmaking practices, continuity was a central concern, but was aimed for in a different way (Ibid.: 10). What we can learn from this debate and historical perspective is that if early American cinema is theorized "under the hegemony of narrative films" (Gunning 1990: 64), it cannot be understood as a coherent cinematic form. The realist mode characterized by continuity editing which we find in Hollywood cinema has been institutionalized and established as the universal norm in Western film studies (Ibid.) and is consequently used as a criterion for all films. This leads to severe misunderstandings not only concerning early American films but also film cultures, like for example Hindi cinema. Very often universalist claims lie at the core of such arguments, as for instance with Bordwell's argument that the filmic device of shot/reverse shot could be seen as a "cross-cultural universal" to represent face-to-face personal interaction (1996b: 94). In contrast, my analysis aims to situate filmic devices in the cultural and artistic discourses the films are set in. Furthermore, the continuous renegotiation of different aesthetics and styles in Hindi cinema shall be considered.

Spectacle of the Gaze: Discontinuity, Exhibitionism and Identification

The focus of this study lies on song and dance because it offers a wide space for such renegotiations. Furthermore, it lies at the intersection of narrative continuity and spectacle as discontinuity. As Tieber points out, song and dance numbers evoke discontinuities, but continuity codes which we find in Hollywood films are also deployed in Hindi film (Tieber 2007: 60; Vasudevan 2000c: 388). This is even more interesting in the context of an increasing narrative integration of song and dance sequences. In terms of the gaze, Mulvey notes that the spectacle of woman freezes the action and linear narrative of film ([1975] 2009: 19). Similarly, *darshan* can have the effect of a standstill, a phenomenon which we cannot only find in films, but also in other media. As Pauwels describes, the TV versions of the Ramayana show these typical halts of action where the gods provide *darshan*. Furthermore, in the literary texts which these TV serials draw on, the lyrical meters produce the same effect (2008: 173). Interestingly, the melodramatic mode, which the samples mostly adhere to, displays similar characteristics in the representations of feelings. Consequently, we can find discontinuities on different levels in the films, which open up spaces for negotiation of filmic codes. Although the narrative space is not at the centre of this analysis, its relation to song and dance and the narrative space is of major importance.

As we have seen in the outline of the theoretical frameworks, some modes of representation and corresponding filmic devices are highly relevant for the erotic gaze as well as the darshanic gaze. On the one hand, it is thus important to see the similarities of their function in terms of spectacle, narration and melodramatic mode. On the other hand, the differences between the concepts of the gaze should be pointed out, as the modes of representation are embedded in forms specific to Hindi film like, for example, the song and dance sequence. What Mulvey singles out as primary modes of representation, which subject the woman to the objectifying male gaze, partly correlates with significant markers of song and dance sequences in Hindi film. First and foremost the song and dance sequence is an exhibitionist spectacle displaying the stars (male and female) and inviting the gaze (Dwyer 2000: 117). Many scenes displaying the female star correlate with the erotic spectacle of the female body which Mulvey describes. It can be considered one of Hindi cinema's most important attractions, when, for example, the heroines are depicted in wet saris, which makes up for the fact that censorship has foreclosed other representations of the erotic (Kasbekar 2001: 287). A specific form of song and dance sequences where this display of the female culminates is the staged performance; the most notorious one is the courtesan dance, which is very similar to what Mulvey calls "the device of the showgirl" ([1975] 2009: 20). In both cases the 'to be looked-at-ness' is emphasized and solicits a male erotic gaze, which turns the female body into the object of desire. In the case of the courtesan dance, this is reinforced by the possessive claim layed on the female body by the male beholder of the gaze.

Generally, song and dance complies with exhibitionism, which is an integral part of popular Hindi cinema. The exhibitionist spectacle employs filmic devices such as the iconic mode and frontal, direct address. This is not reduced to the female star but also encompasses the male star and body as a site of spectacle. In Mulvey's framework we cannot conceive this representation of masculinity. An interesting approach in Western film studies is offered by Neale, who argues that a feminization of the male character is the consequence of such a display (1992: 285f). In Hindi film studies, Vasudevan identified representations of the male character as object of desire resulting in deification through *darshan* (2000c: 390). Although we can find evidence of both in the samples, deification and feminization of the male character in the samples, they are not enough to comprehend the scopic relations in these scenes. The general assumption in the concept of *darshan*, namely that the object gazes back, which thus bestows agency to the object, offers a new perspective on the exhibitionist spectacle. This is not limited to the male star and body, but is even more intriguing when looking at the representations of femininity, female stars and the female body. Consequently, it will be a central aspect in the analysis of staged performances in song and dance sequences.

The difference between forms of representation related to the realist mode in Western cinema and the exhibitionist character of Hindi film also demands a general renegotiation of central concepts such as voyeurism and identification.

The concept of active scopophilia as introduced by Mulvey relies on the conception of the fourth wall, which means that the filmic world is seen as a secluded, hermetically sealed space which the spectator glimpses into. The resulting distance and separation of object and look bring about the voyeuristic pleasure essential for scopophilia (Mulvey 2009 [1975]: 17). Not only Mulvey points this out, but it can rather be seen as a general assumption of psychoanalytic film theory. Metz also insists on unawareness as the condition for cinematic experience, only occasionally broken by unusual camera angles designed to direct the attention of the spectator (Metz 2001: 418). In opposition, Hindi cinema is more exhibitionist and interactive, which works against voyeurism in this sense (Tieber 2007: 59). *Darshan*, as we have seen, relies on the acknowledged presence of the spectator/devotee constituting a reciprocal and intersubjective gaze. Thus, how can we conceptualize voyeurism in the context of Hindi film?

Prasad suggests that there is a contracted voyeurism at play (1998: 73). He situates this concept in his general argument of the prohibition of the private in Hindi films. Concerning *darshan* and the erotic gaze, he points out that in song and dance sequences the spectacle of the female body adheres to the ideology of the public sphere: "such spectacle occurs in song-and-dance sequences which are conventionally coded as contracted voyeurism rather than an unauthorized view of a private world" (Ibid.: 93). This shows similarities to what Metz calls the theatrical spectacle, which demands the complicity of the object, as the non-realist mode presents itself as being seen after all (Ibid.: 102). It is only the representation of the private then which invites realist voyeurism as described by Mulvey. The couple which seeks autonomy from the scopic authority of patriarchy brings the pleasure and the menaces of active scopophilia with it:

> It is the representation of the private that engenders the 'shame-faced' voyeurism of the cinema and presupposes the reality of the subject's solitude in the act of voyeuristic perception, and the dissolution of the substantive communal relation into the atomistic individualism of capitalist social relations (Ibid.: 103).

Prasad is making a political and ideological point here. For my analysis, the notion of shame as well as solitude/community will be more significant. Furthermore, the objectification implicit in voyeurism shall be investigated in terms of the conception of self and other, and its significance in the context of a contemporary global consumer society shall also be touched upon.

While Prasad's approach is useful in many ways, Kasbekar further adds to an understanding of how voyeurism is negotiated in scopic relations of Hindi cinema. She argues that erotic voyeurism is one of the main attractions of spectacle for a heterogenous male audience, but has to be legitimized in terms of moral and ideological values for other audiences such as women or authorities (2001: 289). This "permission to enjoy" (292) is ensured by two strategies: distancing and disavowal. The former is, for example, achieved by the creation of an idealised moral universe in the narrative, where a female ideal is propagated that culminates in the fetishization of chastity. In the separate space of the song and dance sequences the display of woman as erotic object caters to the voyeuristic gaze (293). The second strategy is disavowal as in staged performances, where the impression is evoked that the performance demands to be looked at. Furthermore, the diegetic spectator mediates the voyeuristic gaze, which absolves the actual spectator. Sometimes diegetic spectators, such as respectable women or male authorities, reinforce this feeling (295f). Kasbekar argues that this allows a sort of untroubled voyeurism despite, for example, the direct look into the camera. What she calls the fourth look, the imagined, shame-inducing gaze upon voyeuristic pleasure, is suspended (296). Consequently, the phallic gaze can be used to legitimise voyeuristic pleasure. Kasbekar adds that despite all the exploitation of woman as object of desire, the potential of the staged performances for the representation of female desires and sexual identities, as well as liberating interpretations by female audiences, should not be underestimated (305).

These approaches to voyeurism in Hindi films work closely with psychoanalytic theory and the concept of the erotic gaze. Prasad points out that voyeurism opposes *darshan*, as the spectator is privileged when the object actively gazes back (1998: 75). Furthermore, we can see that other performance traditions as, for example, classical dancing also feature shifts of subject and object positions, as Coorlawala describes (1996: 23). In this context, distancing serves a very different purpose and can contribute to a reversal of the power structures implicit in voyeurism. Coorlawala argues that iconized and stylized performances empower the performer if viewed in the context of *darshan*. While the voyeurist spectator has to rely on anonymity, the spectator as devotee seeks identification in *darshan*, which in this case means "a mutually complicit merging of subject-object positions" (Ibid.: 24). However, this depends heavily on audience expectations. The issue of identification is of great relevance here. As Coorlawala points out, a male gaze claiming possession would not be able reach the state in question. What she suggests is that rasa plays a crucial role in such performance traditions (Ibid.). The general aim of making the spectator experience a generalized state of emotion constitutes a concept identification which opposes the psychoanalytic notion.

Let us discuss in more detail the conceptions of identification in the context of the gaze. *Darshan* as unification transcends all embodied forms, and thus devotee and deity become one, adhering to the idea of the divine or Brahman in all beings (Fuller 1992: 73). In contrast, Mulvey argues that identification is based on narcissist scopophilia. The spectator, similarly to the child in front of the mirror described by Lacan, sees an image, which creates a feeling of recognition. At the same time this image shows an ego ideal unachievable to him/her in the form of the star (Mulvey 2009 [1975]: 118), resulting in a general feeling of lack. In darshanic positions, on the other hand, desire does not relate to wanting something, nor does identification relate to wanting to be like something (Desai 2008: 239). Thus the star cannot be compared to an ego ideal. Another aspect of *darshan* is the transformative moment (Coorlawala 1996: 24; Babb 1981: 400). In opposition to this, identification in psychoanalytic theory represents a confirmation of the status quo, because the phallocentric gaze demands the object to reproduce the dominant order (hooks 2001: 126). A different kind of spectatorship can be enabled by *darshan* as Coorlawala states:

> If psychoanalytic feminist theories have generated a 'male' gaze predicated on the power structures implicit in looking, then darshan combined with the rasa theory of aesthetics offers a 'female' model of a reciprocal activity involving mutual recognition. This darshan-rasa model has less hegemonic implications for both viewer and performer (1996: 26).

However, we should not forget that *darshan* is often used to reproduce patriarchal authority. Still, it offers alternatives and means of transformation concerning modes of representation in Hindi films. For gendered modes of representations, such as, for example, the female body as erotic spectacle, this has various implications which will become clear in this analysis.

The Gaze as Signifier of Love and Desire

Because darshanic notions of the gaze appear here particularly in the context of love relationships, *darshan*'s interaction with the erotic gaze as a signifier of erotic desire is extensive. As mentioned before, Hindi films are polyscopic by nature, also drawing on *nazar* which heavily influences *darshan* as lovers' gazes (Taylor 2003: 311). A study focusing on these hybrid forms in Hindi film would have to take into considerations the conceptions of the erotic and love related to the gazes. Unfortunately, this cannot be provided here due to limitations and the major focus of the book on the analysis of the samples. However, let me refer the reader to Rachel Dwyer's work, which examines a great variety of discourses of love, desire and the erotic all relevant in this context (Dwyer 2000). The implications of darshanic gazing in the context of love relationships are treated here on a rather general level. *Darshan* signifies the desire to look and be looked at by the other. Deity and devotee are supposed to attract the glances of each other (Babb 1981: 394). This is the point where darshanic and erotic gaze concur and renegotiations are located. Furthermore, the scopophilic pleasure could then be seen as the blessings the devotee receives if the deity is gazing back. In this new meaning, for example, the role of voyeurism at the centre of scopophilia could be renegotiated. The analysis shall focus on representational modes of the song and dance sequence which could express such renegotiations.

Moreover, it is important to investigate what exactly the blessing can mean in this context. Let us go back to the religious context of *darshan*. There is a model of interaction between lovers based on eroticism and the intimate, which I have already addressed: the divine couple of Radha and Krishna. In *bhakti* worship of Krishna we find a personal and intimate relationship of deity and devotee. As mentioned before, the devotee identifies with the female subject position and maleness can rather be an obstacle to reach god as well as the blessing (cf. Dwyer 2000: 36). Although emotions felt towards the deity are not necessarily eroticized, Radha's "sexual love for Krishna is the perfect expression of devotion" (Fuller 1992: 156). Consequently, we can also understand the display of desire and erotic love in song and dance sequences connected to *darshan* by examining this relationship between deity and devotee. However, it does not mean that, while Sita is the female model used for the fetishization of chastity in the narrative (Kasbekar 2001: 291), Radha is the female figure used to stage the erotic spectacle of the female body. Rather, the reconceptualization of *darshan* in love relationships can be used to propose a counter discourse on femininity beyond these binary oppositions. While the role model Sita as muse rather than erotic object has been reinforced in the context of the nationalist project in postcolonial India (Ibid.), Radha offers a notion of romantic love without simply adapting to Western conceptions.

Similarly, *darshan* can be used to signify lover's union in the filmic context neither adhering to Western representation of the intimate nor the public sphere mostly represented in Hindi film as described by Prasad (1998: 97). Thus, an alternative space of the couple which is both autonomous and intimate can be established. The disempowerment of scopic authorities such as the phallic gaze, the patriarch's or the public gaze can result in the establishment of a female subjectivity and an erotic display of the female body that does not necessarily correspond to the objectification of the erotic gaze. However, the question remains in how far the intrinsic hierarchy between deity and devotee influences the darshanic gaze in the context of love relationships. Also, the model of Radha and Krishna shows the difference between the divine god and his beloved. In what way are modes of representations related to *darshan* structured by hierarchical gender relations? In the analysis of the samples this question will be of major importance. The identification of female and male with deity and devotee give some indication. Interestingly, the samples display strong ambiguities in terms of these subject positions, which results in complex renegotiations of erotic and darshanic gazing.

Let us go back to what comprises the blessing received in *darshan*. It is crucial that the union of deity and devotee transcends the borders of self and other. In this process a transformation is taking place with the devotee as he/she gains a new perspective or truth (Babb 1981: 400; Sanzaro 2007: 6). We could also call it self-recognition as the new perspective is the perspective on the devotee him/herself as part or manifestation of Brahman (the divine which is in everything).

However, it is also the perspective of the other, which might be interesting to investigate using psychoanalytical assumptions. Generally, seeing and gazing in *darshan* is taking in something of the other (Babb 1981: 397). Consequently, on a conceptual level the dissolution of the subject-object relationship takes place and the moment of blessing is characterized by a complete lack of duality. The subject is subsumed into the object and the other way round, which is the liberation that the devotee seeks in *darshan* (Eck 1985: 25; Sanzaro 2007: 6). To sum it up, liberation is found in self-recognition which is beyond the divide of self and other: "Egoism can never survive the union with Brahman. When liberation is achieved, there can be no discourse of meaning for we are outside the spectrum of language. Liberation depends on nothing other than itself for meaning" (Sanzaro 2007: 6). Therefore, *darshan* will also be employed in the study as a critique of perception, as suggested by Sanzaro (2007). General insights into the subject-object relationships in terms of gender relations are highly relevant for an understanding of the gaze on a representational level.

Philosophical Underpinnings: Reflections on the Gaze and Spectatorship

As Sanzaro clearly points out, the concept of *darshan* in many ways opposes that of the gaze in psychoanalytic theory (2007: 17). Generally, concepts in Hindu religion such as the divine as "intimate other" (King/Brockington 2005: 4) oppose the dichotomy at the heart of Western philosophical tradition. The latter refers to the Cartesian subject, which is the basis of selfhood in Western thought and, consequently, is what Lacan built his theory on (Lacan 2001: 138). The Cartesian subject relies heavily on binary oppositions, which stands in stark contrast to the deconstruction of duality described above. In psychoanalytic theory the constitution of the self happens through the split of the subject by the gaze and the introduction to the Symbolic, where it is always marked by lack. Silverman explains that the male look on a woman as object of desire transfers its own lack to the female subject, who takes on the power of the gaze (Silverman 1994: 296). Consequently, the gaze constitutes the subject, but is also the signifier for what constitutes the subject as lacking (Silverman 1994: 275). Silverman suggests that rather than trying to transfer the power of the gaze to 'the Other' (for example, woman), it is important to realize the "impossibility of anyone ever owning that visual agency, or of him or herself escaping specularity" (Ibid.: 294). Rather the reflection of specularity as such can offer new insights here.

The darshanic concept of the gaze goes beyond the visual and specularity as described by psychoanalytic theory. As already pointed out, it is also connoted as knowing and touching. Interestingly, Irigaray associates female eroticism in contrast to male eroticism with touching: "Woman takes pleasure more from touching than from looking" (1997 [1977]: 364). Female desire is thus not representable in the symbolic order and Irigaray asks for a different language (she calls it *Parler-femme*) connected to the multipilicity of feminine sexuality (Robbins 2000: 155). This is in so far relevant to analytical approaches to the gaze as we are looking for visual representations of female (sexual) desire. Regarding the notion that sexuality has been constituted in Western thought as something masculine: "[Irigaray] argues that all the major representations of Western thought, based as they are on the seeing male I/eye, have constructed a logic of the same which she calls 'hommosexual'" (Ibid: 153). This critique of Western paradigms of thought shall be taken into account and contrasted with *darshan* as a concept of the gaze which includes the notion of touching. However, this should not be interpreted in the East/West dichotomyconstructed in orientalist discourses, which often feminize 'the Other' (in this case philosophical concepts opposing Western ones). We would immediately fall back into the established binary oppositions in Western discourse that we seek to deconstruct. Darshanic union, for example, can have various meanings reaching from metaphorical references of sexual union to the representation of love as mutual recognition and self-recognition.

As the concept of *darshan* comprises self-recognition and transformation as well as dissolution of dualities, it can also introduce a mode of perception in the filmic context which transcends ordinary perception (Sanzaro 2007: 17f). While in everyday life we might have to make the distinction between self and other to create an identity, *darshan* offers another vision, which "releases the object from the ego's grip, and teaches that both object and subject are fictional concepts, or, conversely, that each object reflects the all because each object is created in the same process – God, Brahman, self and other included" (Ibid.: 22). Whether hybridized forms of darshanic gazing in cinema could have similar effects is an open question posed by this study.

As the analysis will illustrate, darshanic gazing in the samples also encompasses the spectator/star relationship. In none of the films is the illusion of a hermetically sealed world continual, as devices such as the direct relay as well as the iconic mode are employed. The space which is thus created for the object to gaze back makes the spectator fully aware of their position as well as the act of gazing itself. Consequently, the notion of voyeurism is renegotiated in various ways, which will be central to this analysis. Interestingly, many representational modes and modes of address that serve the male gaze as described by Mulvey (and have the effect of narrative arrest as well as disruption of the diegetic unit/the illusion of realism) can thus enable an interactive spectatorship. Most of all, song and dance sequences, especially staged performances, re-establish the reciprocal relationship, which in the narrative might not be as common as it used to be in Hindi cinema. Furthermore, the concept of looking in *darshan*, which includes a sense of touching as well as involving other senses (Eck 1985: 9), also suggests a different form of spectatorship. As Dudrah states, a notion of the haptic should be included in the analysis of Hindi cinema. The interaction taking place lies beyond mere representation, since cinema 'touches' audiences in various ways, and consequently, it is necessary to conceptualize the notion of bodies in interaction (Dudrah 2010). Similarly, Dwyer suggests taking into account "corpothetics" in Hindi cinema studies, which is a sensory and corporeal aesthetics which Pinney identifies in in the context of popular visual practices (Dwyer 2006b: 19). Furthermore, Coorlawala's approach to *darshan* in the context of rasa theory gives insights into corresponding audience expectations. The experience of rasa is dependent on a certain participation of the audience, mental as well as emotional (Coorlawala 1996: 24). Furthermore, it is not about identification with a single position or evaluation of the performance. For example, in a classical dance performance the experience may be evoked by continual disruptions and constant alternation of opposites: "The same single performer represents empowerment and seduction, religion and sensuality, theatrical artifice and human emotions, male and female, dominant and subordinate positions" (Ibid.).

Situating the Approach within a Methodological Framework

The intercultural approach deployed in this study demands a methodology, which takes into consideration the culturally constituted conceptions of the gaze. This not only has implications for the methods of analysis of visual interactions, but also for concepts of image, screen and spectatorship. Moreover, the positionality of the analysis itself is of great significance in the context of transcultural reception. My reading of the films, highly influenced by my own cultural background as well as socialisation in Western visual culture, is the starting point of the analysis. Consequently, a continuous reflection on methodological aspects and processes is indispensable. These issues can only be touched upon briefly in the following subchapters, which seek to embed the approach of this study in wider discourses of methodology.

The Medium Film in Consideration of the Theoretical Framework

Using a psychoanalytic approach to film usually implies certain preconceptions on the part of the researcher. However, I want to situate my study in a wider field by dealing with the psychoanalytic concepts, not only in order to analyse the filmic texts, but also to view them as part of an ideology which is represented in the text. Psychoanalytic approaches to film have mostly been criticized on the grounds of presupposing an inscribed spectatorship in filmic texts. Especially representatives of cultural studies have pointed out that the actual cinema spectator has agency and interprets films according to the social and cultural context. Bordwell locates this debate in the contention between two Grand Theories, namely subject-position theory and culturalism. Interestingly, he also points out that there are various continuities between them (1996a: 13).

The use of a psychoanalytical approach in this study shall by no means suggest the conceptual presupposition of a determined and fixed meaning in film texts. Contrary to outdated approaches which do not take into account the critique of Mulvey's as well as Lacanian film theory in general, this study contextualizes valuable contributions from Cultural Studies such as the understanding of decoding as meaning-making process (Hall 2005 [1973]). This approach to media deconstructs the presumption that the message encoded by the sender reaches the recipient in a prescribed or intended form (Ibid.). Thus, the recipient is not seen as a passive consumer, and decoding is set in a context, which not only allows for gender- but also culture-specific decoding practices. In contrast, the perspective of psychoanalytical theory is mostly ahistorical, blind to context and cultural differences as well as dismissive of spectator's agency, as Krauß points out in his analysis of masculinity in Hindi films (Krauß 2007: 59). However, by enhancing it with impulses of Cultural Studies approaches, it is of importance not to confound the level of production and reception, of encoding and decoding. Film is seen here as a signifiying practice (Hall 2005 [1973]). Thus, the object of analysis in this study might best be seen as non-deterministic instructions for the spectator on how to read the filmic text (cf. Mikos 2008: 23). Recent research focusing on actual media reception has emphasized the significance of recipient's interpretative practices, context and other factors in the constitution of meaning. Similarly, Rajadhyaksha in a discussion of Mulvey's concepts adds an interesting perspective when he introduces the notion of inscribed and actual spectator. With this distinction he is able to point out the agency of audiences: they "never surrender, or donate, their gaze to an intra-diegetic agency in any unproblematic fashion" (2000: 290). In a reconciliation of text-based analysis and ethnographic approaches (or as we may say of actual and inscribed spectator), media anthropologist Mark Allen Peterson refers to texts as "sites of intersection and struggle between discourses" (2003: 117). Moreover, he points out that media texts offer a variety of spectatorial positions, which are selected by the audience and sometimes experienced simultaneously (Ibid.). Accordingly, my reading and analysis focuses on particular positions of spectatorship that I consider relevant especially in a transcultural context. Consequently, when I address spectatorship in the following analysis, I refer to an inscribed spectator in terms of a viewing position that the filmic text offers, amongst others, but which is never guaranteed to be taken by an actual spectator.

In terms of the gaze, an analytical approach related to *darshan* has to situate it in its larger context of visual culture(s) in India. Eck states that Hinduism generally has a strong "image-making" tradition (1985: 10) and its influence on Indian society results in a visual and highly iconographic culture (Ibid.: 12). Moreover, this visuality cannot be understood without looking at its interdependence with other senses (Ibid.: 11). Although the visual is deeply connected here to the religious, it is important to note that it goes far beyond religious settings as well as the respective religious group. Therefore, it is understood here as a cultural phenomenon encompassing different social spheres and interacting with other visualities. Furthermore, the notion of spectatorship influenced by rasa theory plays an important role. Although the significance of the rasa theory for the film medium is controversial in Indian film studies (Dwyer 2000: 29), this concept of conveying emotions to an audience has to be taken into account, especially in the context of renegotiations concerning the concepts of identification and scopophilia suggested by psychoanalytical film theory. The impact of Western and Indian concepts on signifying practices in popular Hindi cinema shall be considered, always taking into account the generally polyscopic nature of the media texts.

As will become apparent in the analysis of the samples, signifying practices cannot be isolated, as they are deeply intertwined. In fact, the films in question are good examples of how they interact and reinforce each other, especially in a medium which draws on culturally diverse aesthetics and maps of meaning. In Indian film studies Vasudevan most explicitly points out the mutual influence, the merging and subsequent creation of new styles and representational strategies (2000a, b, c). *Darshan* and the erotic gaze as conceptualized by psychoanalytic theory should thus be seen as "part of a multiplicity of visualities which can be deployed both by film producers as well as by viewers" (Taylor 2003: 320). In an excellent, culture-sensitive approach to the gaze, Taylor asks for a contextualisation of the various forms of representation in relation to other systems of visual encoding. These relationships are hybridized in the sense of Bhabha's concept of hybridity (Ibid.). In this study, some of the hybrid forms of the gaze shall be identified. An emphasis lies on the eroticization of *darshan* in representations of love, desire and intimacy.

The hybrid nature of filmic representations and of notions of spectatorship which we find in the samples shall be highlighted by an emphasis on an intercultural approach. The interaction of the two forms of gazing are thus not seen as a simple mixture of two entities; instead a new space of meaning-making is opened in this transcultural field, which could also be seen as a 'third space' referring to one of Bhabha's key concepts (Bhabha 1994: 54f). The fact that I am from a Western cultural background and socialized in the corresponding visual culture designates a specific perspective on the object of analysis. Some layers of meaning might not be regarded at all, and the decoding of others may be heavily influenced by my internalized media practices. For example, identification might be intensified by devices used to evoke rasa as they are read within practices related to the melodramatic mode. Although the process of analysis involves a great deal of reflexion on and abstraction of this perspective, the transcultural reception context abets the visibility of certain elements while it discriminates against others, which might be more prominent in an analysis originating in a different decoding situation. In itself, my gaze as spectator as well as researcher could be seen as located in the third space.

In conclusion, the focus of this analysis lies on hybridized forms of filmic representation which have emerged in recent globalization processes of Hindi film. Secondly, the positionality of the analysis shall be used to deconstruct Western concepts of gazing, but also more generally the patterns of thought predominating in the philosophical context in which psychoanalytical film studies are situated. This might be criticized as a disregard for *darshan*'s and Indian concepts' autonomy as they are put in opposition (defined by negation) to Western counterparts. However, denying my perspective of a Western scholar and media recipient would not contribute to a better understanding, in my opinion. As Hall states: "it is worth remembering that all discourse is 'placed' and the heart has its reasons" (2000: 204).

Methods of Analysis: Approaching the Text

The basic terminology I use for the close analysis of the filmic texts draws on the seminal work of film theory by Bordwell and Thompson (2001). Dwyer and Patel state that although film interpretation along these lines shows shortcomings if applied to Hindi film, basic principles of mise-en-scène, shot and editing outlined by Bordwell and Thompson can still be useful (2002: 42). However, the hybrid character of the samples as well as of Hindi film in general demands great attention to negotiations and transformations of filming techniques. The terminology by Bordwell and Thompson, thus, can only serve as a basic tool. Although the authors state that most often there are no fixed or absolute meanings of framing, for example, they generally ascribe certain effects to devices. Consequently, the methods of analysis have to be continuously related to the theoretical concepts outlined. As Vasudevan states in this context: "Codes such as the Hollywood eyeline match and point of view editing, used to highlight individualized perception, may acquire a different function in a different system of narration" (2000a: 13). The intercultural approach of this study would probably demand a much more complex set of methods. However, in paying special attention to the mixing of codes, the hybridity of the films can hopefully be captured.

Generally, the analysis focuses on camera and editing techniques. The significance of the latter becomes clear if we look back on the quote by Mulvey stating that cinematic codes draw on the dimensions of time and space to create "a gaze, a world and an object" ([1975] 2009: 26). It is editing as well as camera distance she emphasizes as means of controlling these dimensions (Ibid.). Similarly, scholars of Hindi film refer to editing and camera techniques in the context of *darshan* (Vasudevan 2000b: 139ff; Sanzaro 2007: 19f; Taylor 2003: 307ff). Moreover, mise-en-scène plays an important role in terms of the staging of characters. The great significance of frontality as framing device has been discussed above in relation to *darshan* and spectacle in Hindi cinema. This study aims to identify a pool of devices used in filmic representations related to the gaze, which establishes a particular style represented by the selected films.

Despite the fact that western film theory and its terminology as well as methodology are widely used in the analysis, the media texts are not exclusively read within "Eurocentric hermeneutics", as Dudrah and Desai criticize various approaches to Hindi film (2008: 2f). In contrast, the study does not only use theory to analyse the level of representation, but in the intercultural approach takes on *darshan* and the gaze as conceptualized in psychoanalytical theory as epistemological lenses, which constantly interact and open up new perspectives on the other. Thus, the analysis partly entails a deconstruction of basic Western as well as Indian concepts of thoughts and philosophical principles. Therefore, the Eurocentric elements are not left unquestioned.

Furthermore, the concept of spectatorship influences methodology as well. As mentioned before, the study also tries to show that it is not impossible to apply psychoanalytical film theory and the corresponding notions of the gaze, but that one must take the agency of the spectator as well as a differentiated spectatorship into account. On the other hand, performance culture and audience expectations derived from Indian aesthetic theory based on rasa can be incorporated and transformed in the film medium. In the context of the object of analysis we should therefore understand spectatorship in terms of different subjectivities. As Vasudevan states: "the forms of filmic representation are mixed, gesturing to different types of subjectivity, and the look of the spectator operates at the interstices of these forms, initiating a dialogue between various forms of selfhood" (2000a: 13). The film techniques have to be analysed against the background of these presuppositions, which integrate the perspective of the analyst into a hybrid, transcultural context.

Selecting the Films: Karan Johar and Shah Rukh Khan

The films selected for this study are all big Bollywood blockbusters of the 1990s or 2000s. Although the films can all be seen as part of the romantic family film genre, the texts partly renegotiate the established genre conventions as well as the values and norms represented in the films. Apart from DILWALE DULHANIA LE JAYENGE (1995, DDLJ from now on), which was directed and written by Aditya Chopra, the samples share the screenwriter and (all except one) the director: Karan Johar. DDLJ has been considered primarily because it profoundly shaped not just the genre, but specifically Johar's work. Interestingly, Johar appeared in a minor role in the film, and also worked on the set assisting Aditya Chopra. In another film to be analysed, KAL HO NAA HO (2003, KHNH from now on), Karan Johar was only partially involved, as the screenplay is a collaboration between him and Niranjan Iyengar, and the film was directed by Nikhil Advani.

However, some similarities in the forms of representation and style were reason enough to include it in the sample. The other films are KUCH KUCH HOTA HAI (1998, KKHH from now on), KABHI KUSHI KABHIE GHAM (2001, K3G from now on) and KABHI ALVIDA NAA KEHNA (2006, KANK from now on). They were all written and directed by Karan Johar, therefore, they share a set of characteristics, also concerning the gaze. Furthermore, all samples star the same male leading actor Shah Rukh Khan, as well as the same art director Sharmishta Roy. While Shah Rukh Khan's role in the context of this study shall be explained in more detail, concerning the art director it shall only be mentioned briefly here that she highly influenced the style of films from the 90s on. Roy coined the look of a modern Indian lifestyle in films such as DIL TO PAGAL HAI (Yash Chopra, 1997), which restructured essential elements of mise-en-scène (cf. Dwyer/Patel 2002: 78). The films analysed here might not be the most typical examples for the genre, but many of the devices and forms of representation can be found in other Hindi films, too. However, I would argue that they display a resistance towards some trends in contemporary Hindi cinema, such as an increasing objectification of the body (male and female) in song and dance sequences. Instead we find the hybrid codes concerning the gaze that are the central object of this study.

Furthermore, the close analysis of the study is limited to the song and dance sequences of the films. This is due to the dense and frequent occurrence of visual interaction, of the gaze as signifier as well as complex constellations of spectatorship. As Taylor points out, the lover's gazes are never depicted in silence (2003: 311); consequently, song and dance serve as a repertoire which creates "a poetics of sight and visual display that directly affects the meanings films generate for audiences" (Ibid.: 301). Moreover, the creative potential of hybridization processes is nowhere exploited as much as in song and dance sequences. Thus, they could be seen as transcending cultural differences (Gopal/Moorti 2008: 13), which is of great significance to an inter- and transcultural approach to filmic representations of the gaze[14].

However, song and dance shall not be analysed in isolation from the narrative as, although many of the sequences in the samples are set in the extradiegetic space, they have strong implications for the narrative space. All the films follow the recent changes described in the context of globalization processes and, thus, the song and dance sequences are highly integrated into the narrative. Furthermore, the samples tend to adopt Western aesthetics such as Hollywood realism, which may enhance corresponding forms of the gaze in filmic representations. On the other hand, there are frequent references to *darshan* in religious contexts, facilitating the mixing of codes and negotiation of signifying practices in a hybrid space. Karan Johar as the director and screenwriter plays a crucial role in this

---

14 For a list of the song and dance sequences which are analysed in the following chapters, see the appendix.

regard. As a representative of the trend that has been developing the realist mode in Hindi cinema, his screenplays are characterized by internal and logical coherence as well as psychological characterization. At the same time Johar utilizes a dense metatextual framework, religious symbolism and long-established conventions of Hindi film. An example of the latter is the strict adherence to the kissing prohibition in all the films. The fact that his films still extensively exhibit intimacy shows the continuous negotiation between filmic and cultural traditions. While other film makers currently exploit filmic representations which draw on Hollywood conventions and increasingly represent desire in the context of global consumer culture and its commodification of the body (male and female), Johar manages to follow some of these recent trends, but still explores new possibilities rooted in a complex renegotiation between different conventions.

In terms of the gaze it is important to note that the male lead actor Shah Rukh Khan plays a crucial role. His star persona is closely linked to his gaze, for which there is evidence in the research on fan culture in very diverse cultural contexts. Elke Mader points out that in German-speaking communities, fan art of Shah Rukh Khan is distinguished by the clear focus on facial expressions and in particular the look/the eyes (Mader 2008, 2010). In India, the deification of stars is not unusual, but as Adelheid Herrman-Pfandt points out, it is even more the case with Shah Rukh Khan than other contemporary actors, which results in an interesting inter-religious kind of worship. The Muslim actor is sometimes incorporated into Hindu tradition as images of him are displayed in shrines and fans pray to him (Herrman-Pfandt 2010) - receiving *darshan*. Moreover, Shah Rukh Khan himself fosters this star-fan-relationship, for example, with the extraordinary attention he pays to his audience, thereby conveying the feeling of personal interaction, as Nasreen Munni Kabir, who has closely followed the star over several years, points out (2010). Furthermore, it seems that this continues on the level of filmic representation, as we shall see in the following analysis. Shah Rukh Khan is thus an important criterion of the sampling as he consciously seems to activate notions of gazing based on *darshan*. Apart from that Shah Rukh Khan is also a leading representative of the Bollywood cultural industry and certain innovative trends in Hindi cinema. As Rajadhyaksha mentions, the star is committed to the "Bollywood mode" and films such as DDLJ and KKHH can be seen as exemplary (2008: 191). Consequently, he is a symbol of globalization and hybridization, moving in between and negotiating between the dichotomies often imposed on cultural expression: Western/Indian, traditional/modern, sacred/secular, urban/rural, male/female etc.

3. Gazing in Song and Dance Sequences

In the selected films we can find a wide range of song and dance sequences which differ considerably in type, aesthetics, styles and the forms of representation they employ. A general distinction between dream/fantasy sequences and staged performances proves useful, as there are great differences in the according constellations conveying the gaze. As we can see in the third chapter, however, this demarcation can also be dissolved easily, especially in the more recent films. Furthermore, the scope in filmic representations related to *darshan* as well as the erotic gaze is extremely wide. The films offer examples for both with very conventional filmic representations. On the other hand, there are also examples of how the gazes are negotiated and transformed. For example, staged performances which display the female body most explicitly can constitute female desire, and scenes deconstructing the hierarchical structure underlying *darshan* can have a liberating effect in terms of gender relations.

It is important to note that the representations analysed in this study are by no means limited to the samples. We can find similar ones in films by other directors. In his analysis of a crucial scene in VEER-ZAARA (Yash Chopra, 2004), Dudrah points out the significance of the exchange of gazes in the love story which signify *darshan* and *nazar*. Many of the elements he mentions we will encounter in the following: the setting of the temple; the rain as a symbol; the frequent close-up shots showing the gaze; the established connection between gazing and feeling/touching; the iconic images and continuous frontal positioning of Shah Rukh Khan as male protagonist; and the correspondence of the female protagonist's choice of whose eyes to look into, and which man to desire/love.

In my analysis a special focus lies on frontality and iconicity, which has been discussed in the context of theoretical approaches to *darshan*. Frontality in this context is used to describe a series of shots in which frontal positioning predominates. The frequent shot/counter shot series with close-ups of the lover's faces looking directly into the camera is an example of this. Furthermore, I refer to frontal, direct address if these shots display characteristics mentioned by Vasudevan such as frontal staging, the direct look into the camera and stylised performance (2008: 138), whereby the former is mostly emphasized by gestures directed towards the spectator. Iconic images are also identified by attributes that have been discussed before, such as stasis or condensation. However, the analogy to images of deities, which is of great significance here, can also be related to other forms such as camera movement.

These modes of representation and address will be analysed in the context of related filmic devices. As mentioned in the previous chapter, the focus here lies on camera and editing techniques. The arrangement of shots in editing is highly relevant to an understanding of the gaze; for example, shot/counter shots represent the exchange of glances, and point of view cutting indicates the holder of the gaze. Moreover, framing in terms of camera angle or distance are of great importance, too. We will also encounter mobile frames frequently in diverse forms of camera movements. All these devices shall be related to different forms of the gaze and the relation between them, which can offer insights into the multiple negotiations and mixing of codes.

Lovers' Gazes: Darshanic Union in Dream and Fantasy Sequences

The song and dance sequences analysed in this chapter primarily show the union of two lovers as they realize their feelings for each other. I will put an emphasis on the analysis of the songs "Kuch Kuch Hota Hai" (KKHH 1998), "Suraj Hua Madham" (K3G 2001) and "Tumhi Dekko Naa" (KANK 2006). Apart from these, some other examples are referred to in order to support the arguments or facilitate understanding. The three sequences are set in fantasy spaces and give insights into the feelings of both lovers (in one case even three). Consequently, the representation of interiority offers opportunities to investigate the codes of love and eroticism that are central to the gaze. The main focus of the analysis lies on the devices used to evoke notions of *darshan* in the context of the attraction between lovers and their unification.

From the Puja to the Desert: Transferring Darshan *from a Religious Context to the Realm of Love*

The relevance of the darshanic gaze is made clear in the films by frequent references to its religious context. Corresponding camera techniques can be found not only in the scenes displaying *darshan*, but also in the representation of lovers' visual interaction. Especially in KKHH and K3G, the Hindu religion has a strong presence (as do other religions like Islam). Scenes which show the ritual of *puja* and worship in general offer insights into the way *darshan* is implemented on the level of filmic representation. Therefore, let us first have a look at the religious references in the films to enable better understanding of the implications of *darshan* in this context.

The song and dance sequence "Kabhi Khushi Kabhie Gham" shows a puja at Diwali festivities in the house of the rich Raichand family. The ritual is per-

Figure. 1: The puja setting in K3G

formed at the family shrine where the camera first focuses on devotional objects such as the oil lamps, the *kumkum* powder and offerings. Then a medium close-up shot of Nandini Raichand's back follows, in which she pulls the *sari* over her hair. The camera moves to the right and zooms in on the face of the deity's image positioned in direct opposition to Nandini as devotee. This is an establishing shot which gives the basic information of the positions for darshanic visual exchange. The next shot is a medium close-up of Nandini's face, and her frontal positioning indicates that she is looking at the deity's image. As the camera draws a semicircle around her she also looks directly in the camera. At the end of the shot the camera is positioned to our left and it zooms in as she closes her eyes. The darshanic relationship is thus established. In the course of the scene many different shot successions follow, signifying the same. Thus, there are shots starting in a high-angle position and showing the gathering of devotees, after which the camera tilts down to a straight-on perspective on the backs of the deity's images as well as the devotees looking at them. This shot of the family marked by frontality could be seen as a tableau.[15]

The same sequence also establishes the connection between ritual worship and human relationships. Firstly, it serves to introduce all of the family members and show their loving bond. Secondly, when Yash Raichand enters, Nandini turns towards her husband and seeks his blessings by bending to touch his feet. The prayer as well as the gaze she gives to the deities she also gives to her husband before they both turn towards the images again. Thirdly, Nandini's beloved

15 While the form of the tableau is not discussed in detail here, Gopal offers insights into how Karan Johar uses it in his films (cf. 2011: 83ff).

son Rahul arrives, which gives cause for a very interesting exchange of looks that can clearly be classified as darshanic, due to the context it is set in. The moment his feet touch the ground (he has arrived in a helicopter!), his mother senses his arrival and thus turns around to look directly into the camera. What follows is a frontal medium shot of Rahul and then a frontal close-up shot of Nandini's face. Although the spectator is aware of the fact that while she is inside the house unable to see him running towards the building, the editing evokes a shot/counter shot illusion. This results in the building up of tension until their eyes really meet. There are several shots of the mother walking and Rahul running towards the camera. Even when he has entered the house, the series of shot/counter shots continues until a long shot shows them together as he bends down to touch her feet. Significantly, while she is waiting, there is a shot of her back that is very similar to the ones we have seen before of the deities' images. Furthermore, most of the zoom-ins in this part of the scene are directed to her face, drawing the attention and concentration of the viewer onto her. Thus, the mother is staged in a similar way as the deities. However, it is important to note that the darshanic moment between mother and son clearly means a blessing to both of them. This stands in sharp contrast to the gaze of the patriarch, who is distinctly established as the donor of blessings.

Interestingly, parts of this sequence are in a way referred to in the song „Suraj Hua Madham" later in the film. Before we come to know that what we see is Rahul's fantasy of their shared future, a close-up shot of Anjali, his beloved, facing the camera and conducting a puja is cut in without any establishing shot. Until that moment the song and dance was set in a fantasy space surrounded by Egyptian pyramids and desert landscapes. Rahul and Anjali are locked in a passionate embrace, when the scene cuts to the misty close-up of a flame. The camera pans to the left and the close-up I have described before emerges. In this moment it is unclear who her gaze is directed to: who is she gazing at and who gazes back at her? Thus, the erotic love fantasy of Rahul and Anjali finds continuity in a divine setting. The following shot shows Anjali turning around; again she is positioned frontally. But now we can distinguish a deity's image in the background, at which her gaze was previously directed. She then draws the *kumkum* on the foreheads of Rahul's family members. Apart from expressing Rahul's feelings for Anjali as well as his wish to marry her and make her part of his family, this short part of the sequence is also used to bestow a certain divine legitimacy to their love. Moreover, it associates the passionate exchange of glances by the lovers in this song with *darshan* as presented in "Kabhi Khushi Khabi Gham".

Even more frequent are religious references in KKHH; in fact there are far too many to mention all of them here. Let me just turn to two of them that play an important role in the love stories between Rahul and Tina, as well as Rahul and Anjali. The first encounter outside college, followed by the first exchange of intimate glances between Rahul and Tina, takes place in the temple. Later, he

Figure. 2: Gazing back at the beloved: Anjali standing in front of the deity's image (KKHH)

confesses his love for her there (KKHH 1998, 1:17:30). While Anjali is standing in the rain, broken-hearted because she has discovered that he is in love with another girl, Rahul runs to the temple. The following series of shots is strongly marked by frontaltiy. First Tina is shown ringing a bell and looking directly into the camera before lowering her gaze. Then the camera pans to the right and we see Rahul appearing in the entrance behind her. His look is also aimed directly at the camera, looking at Tina and/or the deity. The next two cuts are a shot/counter shot of the two lovers both looking directly into the camera. They walk towards each other and, after making the *namaskara* gesture to the deity, he tells Tina that he loves her. In this scene it is hardly possible to distinguish between the nature of the gaze between the lovers and *darshan*.

Interestingly, the reunion of Anjali and Rahul is also embedded in a religious context, as she is performing a *puja* when he enters the summer camp (KKHH 1998, 2:02:20). While she is circling the lamps and facing the deity, the camera is circling around her. Several cuts show Rahul running towards the building, expecting to find his daughter Anjali there. When he enters calling the little girl's name, both Anjalis turn towards him with a direct look into the camera. What then follows are a number of shot/counter shots with Rahul and Anjali (his beloved), first looking at and then walking towards each other. The series of shot/counter shots starts with a zoom-in on Anjali's face, while she is standing right in front of the deity's image, which we can see in several shots in the background. In this scene Anjali is presented like a deity, as she is the one who is able to give 'blessings' and happiness to Rahul. This idea is not only established by the narrative, but also through camera technique and mise-en-scène. First, the circling camera focuses all attention on Anjali, who is rather static while Rahul is running towards her. Secondly, Anjali is staged frontally and directly in front of the deity's image, which allows an identification of Anjali with the divine.

The two films are not the only ones in which we can find religious references. Interestingly, Islam and Christianity are represented in Karan Johar's films, too. While daughter Anjali in KKHH prays to Allah to help her fulfil the wish of her mother, the female protagonist's family in KHNH is Christian. In the latter, the male protagonist Aman is first introduced to the narrative when Naina's family gathers to pray to god (KHNH 2003, 00:18:00). Jennifer, the mother, explains to her children that in difficult times god sends an angel. When Gia asks when that angel is going to come, there are several shots showing the back of Aman in various angles standing on a boat which is approaching the city. At the same time the background music swells up and the melody of the title song "Kal Ho Naa Ho" resounds. This is repeated several times and a flashback of the first encounter between Naina and Aman, which she disavowed at the time, follows. Jennifer, Naina and the two younger siblings all close their eyes and fold their hands in prayer, which is again a shot marked by frontality. The next cut shows their backs and focuses on the window opposite the road, which is opened when Aman steps outside. Various shot/counter shots follow with Aman in which he is staged frontally, gazing at the family absorbed in prayer. In the course of this scene an analogy between Aman and the angel is established. The iconic representation of his arrival, induced by the rapid cuts of his static, unmoving stature, recalls the representations of deities. Moreover, the series of shot/counter shots with medium close-ups of his face gazing directly into the camera presents him as a potential giver of a benevolent gaze as well as an object to gaze at – or one could say as a deity who might give the blessings the family is praying for. In conclusion, this example shows that *darshan* can also be allocated and negotiated in religious contexts other than Hinduism.

Darshan *as Unification: the Exchange of Glances, the Lovers' Embrace and Dual Figures*

In Indian film studies, two techniques in the analysis of *darshan* in the context of love and erotic desire are mentioned often: firstly, close-up shots of the lovers' gazes indicating the reciprocal visual interaction, which are often accompanied by frontal positioning and direct look in the camera; secondly, the insinuation of the lover's gaze wandering from the feet of the beloved to the eyes, which is evoked either by camera movement or editing style (Vasudevan 2000b: 139ff; Sanzaro 2007: 19f; Taylor 2003: 307ff). In the selection of films we do not find much evidence for the latter, but clearly for "alternating views of lovers gazing into each other's eyes, with prolonged close-up shots of the beloved's intense frontal gaze" (Taylor 2003: 313). As Taylor points out, the erotic connotation has

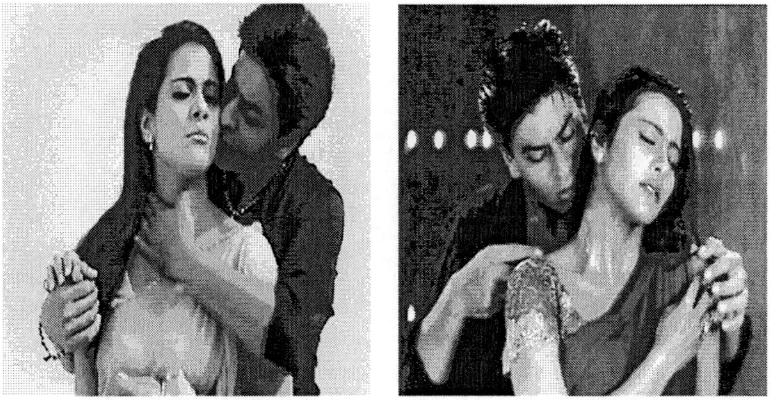

Figure. 3: A recurring image: the Radha & Krishna shot (K3G and KKHH)

been strongly reinforced due to the interaction with the concept of *nazar*, establishing the association with sexual desire and attraction (Ibid.).

In our song and dance sequences that show such intense gazing, we often find physical contact, too. Mostly, they occur in the form of passionate embraces of the lovers, since all sample films exclude kissing. Two forms of embrace are prevalent in "Tumhi Dekho Naa", "Suraj Hua Madham" and "Kuch Kuch Hota Hai": first, there is the common embrace of the couple facing each other and shot from different angles, which is frequently followed by the camera circling around the lovers or by zoom-ins and -outs; secondly, the frontal staging of the couple with the man standing behind the woman embracing her (rarely do we see it the other way round) occurs very often as well. Both types of touching symbolize unification and could be seen as creating a dual figure (cf. Chatterjee 2005: 94). Especially, shots showing two faces in frontal positioning appear like dual figures, which are also common in the depiction of deities, especially the lovers Radha and Krishna: one but separate. Let us, therefore, refer to this as *Radha & Krishna shot*. This impression of a dual figure is reinforced by various shots of one of the lovers appearing behind the other, also marked by frontality. On the other hand, the notion of unification is reinforced in the embrace, starting with a profile shot by the device of the circling camera. As both embraces mostly occur after intense exchanges of glances, the relationship between seeing and touching in the context of *darshan* shall be investigated here further.

The song "Kuch Kuch Hota Hai" demonstrates very clearly that the meeting of the gaze is as essential for a lovers' union as the embraces. In the beginning, we see extreme long shots of Anjali revolving in one spot and Rahul seemingly running towards her. But then a cut shows it is Tina he is running to and they embrace. Various shots of Tina and Rahul embracing as well as exchanging glanc-

Figure. 4: Seeing and touching: amplifying the meaning of the gaze (KANK)

es follow, which visualise the fantasies of the two. In opposition, there is a cut to a shot of Rahul sitting on the ground looking dreamily into the sky. Anjali enters the frame, sits down beside him and, while singing about her desire, looks at him. Her gaze, however, is not returned as Rahul keeps looking straight ahead. Besides other representations of Anjali's lonely position in the triangle, the lack of reciprocal gazes is a key symbol. However, gazing in this song and dance sequence is highly ambiguous, which will become clearer later in the analysis.

In KANK the song "Tumhi Dekho Naa" establishes a very strong connection between gazing and touching or darshanic union and embrace. As the sequence is for the most part not set in a secluded natural paradise but in New York City, the entrance into the realm of the lover's fantasy is marked by the changing of colours. The couple is locked in an intense embrace after eventually giving in to their feelings, when the clothes of the passersby in the background suddenly all turn blue. Interestingly, the colour blue is associated with Krishna and other avatars of Vishnu in Hinduism and thus might be a reference to the divine. The next shot shows Dev looking directly into the camera, which could be seen as frontal, direct address. This is followed by a counter shot of Maya, who is then running down the steps and then falling into his arms. The joint of the two shots in question is achieved not by a cut but a dissolve into a blue screen, which turns out to be her *sari*. This kind of editing is frequent in "Tumhi Dekho Naa" and I will

Figure. 5: Staging the female body: iconic images create distance and enable the object to gaze back (K3G)

come back to it in this chapter. What the first few shots of the sequence show is the close relatedness of embrace and reciprocal gazing. Later on this becomes even more obvious when the song and dance transfers to the scenery of woods in Indian Summer. The first shot in the new setting is a close-up of their faces in profile appearing behind a branch full of orange leaves. The heads move towards each other as if pulled together in an embrace. In the close-up shot they incline their heads slightly from the one side to the other, while their gazes move between the eyes and the lips of the beloved. The next cut offers a long shot staging the couple frontally as they both step out of their embrace, but stay joined side by side. Clearly, the first shot establishes the gaze as emblem of embrace as well as kiss, thus fusing the notion of seeing and touching. The following shot, although not one of the embraces mentioned above, strongly suggests the representation of unification and creates the image of a dual figure.

While "Tumhi Dekho Naa" is basically all about the unification that initiates the song and dance sequence, "Suraj Hua Madham" is characterized more by the tension between Rahul and Anjali preceding unification. Consequently, embraces are not shown so often, but they are nevertheless the climax of the scenes. What we find in this song and dance sequence are various iconic images of the female protagonist marked by a camera movement from bottom to top. However, instead of showing the feet first and moving up her body and simulating the perspective of the devotee, the shots show Anjali standing on a rock from a low angle perspective. She is clad once in a green *sari* and once in a black *sari*, setting her sharply apart from the blue sky and the white rock. Starting from a low angle position, the camera tilts up until the straight-on angle is reached. However, in both cases there is no evidence that it is Rahul's, the beloved/the devotee's, perspective. On the one hand, these shots position Anjali as the focus of attention as well as expose her to the gaze of the spectator. On the other hand, the iconicity creates a certain distance and elevates her to a superior position, recalling of images of deities.

A similar effect is achieved by the embraces accompanied by a circling camera movement. In the same song and dance sequence the couple is united in embrace and this dual figure is reinforced by the camera movement. The scene starts with a long shot of Anjali turning around and running towards the camera. In shot/counter shot technique, the next cut shows Rahul running towards the camera, while a shot positioning Anjali frontally with outstretched arms follows. They embrace and the following medium close-up of their faces shows their passionate unification. The intensity of the embrace is reinforced when the embracing couple is shown in a series of long shots and the camera circles around them. Moreover, they shift from this embrace to a *Radha & Krishna shot* at the end of the shot. The last cut shows a medium close-up of them. Interestingly, this embrace, which clearly symbolizes unity, follows two parts of the sequences in which each of them imagines their shared future life.

In contrast, the embraces preceding this one are mainly *Radha & Krishna shots* that primarily serve to express the mutual attraction Rahul and Anjali feel. The passion is displayed in shots marked by frontality showing him standing behind her and, for example, kissing her neck. The heavily sexual connotation of these *Radha & Krishna shots* will be treated below. Apart from the context, which clearly indicates that their love is not limited to an erotic attraction but that they imagine a shared future, the circling camera has various effects on the staging of this embrace. Firstly, the embrace does not last much longer than others before in the sequence, but with the rapid movement of the camera it seems much longer, thus emphasizing its significance. Secondly, although the couple moves in the embrace, the two stay in one spot, which is the centre for the circle of the camera movement, too. Thus, the focus on the couple is intensified to a great extent. Moreover, this reinforces the notion of unification as well as the dual figure. Thirdly, the predominating long shots combined with the camera movement create an iconic image. In this way, although the spectator takes part in an intimate encounter between the two, a distance is created by the iconicity of the scene. As has been pointed out before, this can be seen as a strategy to resist objectification and to favour a spectatorship based on darshanic identification (cf. Coorlawala 1996: 26).

A very different strategy to represent union in terms of darshanic identification is shown in "Tumhi Dekho Naa". In contrast to the continuity editing which is otherwise frequently used in the film (very much like in most Hollywood films), many of the joints in this song and dance sequence are dissolves. As already mentioned, some of the shots are joined by the dissolve into a coloured

Figure. 6: Dissolves and double exposure as symbols for unification (KANK)

screen that turns out to be a *sari* or the like, which is part of the mise-en-scène of the next scene. The different scenes forming part of the song and dance sequences are marked by the changing of the clothes' colour – of the protagonists as well as the passersby. But this editing technique is also applied within scenes, for example, in a series of shots showing Maya and Dev dancing among yellow New York cabs passing. When they embrace the dissolve editing becomes very obvious as all the shots are medium shots and they overlap heavily. In this scene we also encounter a break with the 180 degree system, which ensures spatial continuity in continuity editing (Bordwell/Thompson: 2001: 231). In the context of the scene this creates the impression of the camera circling around the couple. We could say that this circling, as well as the dissolves, signify unification, as the darshanic moment transcends the boundaries of the realist world, as well as those between self and other. Furthermore, as the shots which dissolve into each other are reversed by breaking the 180 degree rule, the couple appears even more as one, as a dual figure.

The same representation of unity is even more apparent at the end of the song. Various shots of embraces set in different scenes from throughout the sequence are shown again. The double and sometimes triple exposure from one frame to another intensifies the effect described above. In contrast, the problems the lovers have to face in the real world become visible the moment when Dev and

Maya are on their way to meet and Rhea happens to cross their path. The encounter is represented in split screen imagery of the three of them. In conclusion, the song and dance sequence offers a space for the representation of darshanic identification of lovers. Not only do visual exchanges signify this union in *darshan*, but also touching in form of a unifying embrace can be interpreted as darshanic moment.

Visualizing Intimacy: Erotic Codes, Private Space and the Voyeuristic Gaze

As we have seen so far, embraces and symbols of unification have erotic denotations. The specific parts of the fantasy song and dance sequences which emphasize eroticism and employ established codes of the erotic in Hindi cinema shall be analysed here in more detail. The focus is on to what extent the body is presented as erotic spectacle catering for the voyeuristic erotic (male) gaze. Moreover, I will investigate how an intimate and private space of the couple can be established. The issue of intimacy and its connection to voyeurism is touched upon here, but will be addressed again in the context of staged performances in the next chapter. As mentioned before, Prasad's argument is central in this context. He points out that the kissing ban has been connected to the prohibition of the private. It is important to emphasize again at this point that none of the sample films show any kissing, either in the narrative or in song and dance. However, this does not mean that they reject the representation of the private in general. Prasad argues that erotic imagery as for example in the spectacle of the female body, is either marked by a "contracted voyeurism" or by narrative arrest. In contrast, kissing "and by extension the details of a sexual relation between two people, belong to the realm of the private" (Prasad 1996: 93). While Prasad sees *darshan* in this context upholding feudal patriarchal authority and constraining the representation of the private (Ibid.), my analysis shows that it can also operate differently. Especially in the context of darshanic union as outlined before, this is apparent. Therefore, I would agree with Vasudevan, who counters Prasad's argument when he states that: "Even if films exhibit prohibitions around the explicit representation of sexuality, they also display complex strategies to engage the spectator in the aura of the couple" (Vasudevan 2000a: 18).

Let us start with the analysis of such strategies in the samples by first looking at those scenes, which make clear references to established modes of representation of the erotic. The most obvious examples are the scenes which show characters bathing in water or being drenched by rain. As mentioned before, the 'wet sari scene' is a popular device for displaying the female body. Rain is also used as a general metaphor for sex and sexual desire (Sharpe 2005: 67; Tieber 2007: 91). In the samples we can find various examples of this, such as the young Simran in DDLJ dancing in the rain and singing about her still undirected desire in the song and dance sequence „Mere Khawabon Mein Jo Aaye". In KKHH rain also plays an important role in the love story. Interestingly, the first rain shower scene occurs when Rahul confesses his love to Tina (KKHH 1998, 01:19:10). However, this rain starts before that scene, when he and Anjali embrace after he has told her about his love for the other girl. Consequently, another rain scene later in the film establishes a reference to their unfulfilled potential love. In the summer camp they are surprised by a sudden rain shower and Anjali watches Rahul dancing spontaneously in the rain. Subsequently, a highly erotic scene takes place in the pavilion, where the two of them realize their feelings for each other. This scene will be discussed in more detail later. As we can see in KKHH rain is a metaphor for the desire and erotic intimacy of the couple.

These scenes usually encourage the voyeuristic gaze as they serve the erotic display of the female body. Nowhere is this as obvious as in 'wet sari scenes'. In the samples we only find one, which is part of the song and dance sequence „Suraj Hua Madham“ in K3G. The water scene starts with a medium shot of Rahul staged frontally as he emerges from the water with the soaked shirt clinging to his body. Only the third shot shows Anjali, who is lying on the shore with her back to the camera. She throws her head back (so the camera catches her face), while Rahul is leaning over her. The next two shots display the female body more explicitly. First, she is seen falling back into the shallow water, offering a full view of her body in the wet sari, while he rests his head on her belly. Secondly, the next cut offers an even more explicit shot of her body as she rises in the water, throwing up her arm. The frame at first only offers the sight of the body from hips to neck, clearly putting the focus of the gaze on the feminine curves clearly exposed under the wet sari. The camera then zooms out and moves up, while the dynamic movement of the arm reveals even more of the contours of her body. Rahul standing in a lowered position next to her is only revealed in the course of the camera movement, and while she sinks into his arms, her dancing movements focus the attention again on her breasts and belly. The next cut shows a profile close-up of her caressing his neck. As she is positioned on the lower side of the frame, the focus moves from Anjali to Rahul.

The outlined 'wet sari scene' has three aspects which are of great relevance to this study. Number one is the fact that Rahul is shown first and explicitly offers his body as spectacle to the gaze. The direct, frontal address is a crucial device here. As Tieber points out, the display of the male body is increasingly becoming part of Hindi films, too, although he refers mostly to the display of muscles and the cult of the body (Tieber 2007: 91), which is not yet distinct in the case of Shah Rukh Khan in *K3G*. The second important aspect is that the gaze on the female body is not identified with the male protagonist. However, the gaze is ambiguous as it is not clear from the beginning of the explicit body shots who the beholder is. In both of them, Rahul's appearance in the shot is delayed. Nevertheless, the spectator is thus reminded that he/she is a voyeuristic bystander. The general nature of the song and dance sequence as spectacle might classify this as contracted voyeurism. But the third aspect, which is the context of scenes the 'wet sari scene' is embedded in, emphasizes voyeurism and the notion of privacy surrounding the couple. However, it does so only to later reintroduce the spectator into a stylized and distanced space.

Let me explain this further by describing the scenes preceding and following the wet sari scene. Before the scene just analysed, the iconic shot of Anjali in a black dress dancing on a rock is shown. Then a cut shows a close-up of the gravelly surface of a rock. The camera is moving along the stone wall to the left when the couple is revealed around the corner. Rahul is moving towards Anjali and kisses her. She turns around, her back facing him and their bodies pushing towards each other. Some more shots of intense embraces, exchanges of glances and a *Radha&Krishna shot* marked by iconicity from low angle perspective follow until the 'wet sari scene' begins. The fact that the couple is shown only after the camera has moved along the stone wall strongly speaks for a voyeuristic gaze here. Inside the spectacle of song and dance, the intimacy and highly sexualized private space, are thus established. As mentioned before, also the *Radha & Krishna shots* throughout this sequence are also marked by passionate kissing and touching, more so than in others. We could say therefore that the interplay between iconic elements and visualizations of the intimate erotic create an alternative form of representation of the couple. While the voyeuristic gaze is used to mark the intimate and the erotic, it is destabilized by the frequent iconic shots. For example, the 'wet sari scene' is followed by some long and extreme long shots of the couple's embrace, thus creating distance again. Then a highly stylized shot is introduced, showing Rahul and Anjali's profile both looking off-screen left. This arrangement of iconic and erotic shots can be seen as a strategy to engage the spectator in the aura of the couple. Furthermore, it seems that the depiction and visualization of the erotic attraction between Rahul and Anjali was a deliberate intention of the director using conventions and established notions of the erotic gaze. The significance of erotic attraction for the relationship, and also for marital bliss, is emphasized later on in the narrative. When Rahul takes his leave of Anjali in the morning before going to work, he calls her 'sexy' and they draw near for a kiss. Rohan as a kind of voyeuristic bystander interrupts them, which also indicates the limitations of visualizing intimacy in the narrative (2:34:00).

Apart from this deployment of the erotic gaze, there are also other strategies to mix it with darshanic moments. The already described scene at the beginning of "Tumhi Dekho Naa" is an example of how established codes can be renegotiated in this context. After the first shots of Dev with frontal, direct address, the counter shot shows Maya first in a close-up shot positioned frontally and then in a medium long shot running down a flight of stairs. As Dwyer and Patel point out, staircases are frequently used as locations for spectacle, because they offer the chance to display the body in movement (Dwyer/Patel 2002: 72). In this case, the identification of the spectator's gaze with the male protagonist's is established by the shot/counter shot arrangement. Consequently, the erotic gaze on the female body is incorporated here into the darshanic interaction present in the scene. Thus, the erotic is established as component of unification. At the same time, the marker of spectacle signifies *darshan*, which can satisfy the spectator's desire for exhibitionist performance, but is beyond voyeurism.

Figure. 7: Different modes of representation: from the private space inviting voyeurism to exhibitionism marked by iconicity (K3G)

Another interesting scene in the same song and dance number, which displays the female body as spectacle to a certain degree, follows shortly after. A cut introduces a wholly new setting with a New York street in the background and Maya turning towards a mirror. While she is positioned to the left, her mirror image is more at the centre of the frame and she seems to look at herself. In the following, she continues to dance playfully in front of the mirror, thus offering a full view of her body. While her gaze is mostly directed towards the camera during these long shots, a medium close-up follows that shows her profile looking to the left off-screen, from whence Dev enters the frame. Again, this creates an ambiguous situation as there is no establishing shot showing who owns the gaze, and it does not seem that the gaze is the male protagonist's. Furthermore, the play with the mirror on the one hand emphasizes the act of looking at her and at the display of the body. On the other hand, she is looking at herself and the awareness of being looked at is made very explicit. Consequently, voyeurism is made difficult as there is no mediating male gaze of a character and yet the scene displays the female body. Moreover, the desire of being looked at should be seen in the context of female desire and its representation in the film, which will be investigated further in the following chapter.

At last, let me point out another characteristic of "Tumhi Dekho Naa" that is highly relevant to the issues of the gaze, voyeurism and intimacy. The song and dance sequence is partly set in secluded fantasy and natural spaces, and partly in the bustling streets of New York. As a setting for this kind of song and dance the latter is unusual, as we can see in comparison with the rest of the sequences.

Figure. 8: Romance in the midst of New York: the lovers dancing amongst passersby (KANK)

"Kuch Kuch Hota Hai" is entirely set in the ruins of an old castle at the seaside, "Suraj Hua Madham" is mostly set in a rocky and desert like area with Egyptian pyramids and "Tujhe Dekha To Ye Jaana Sanam" from DDLJ is set in the Swiss Alps. Furthermore, Gopal and Sen state that song and dance sequence focusing on individualistic desire make use of vast, empty spaces and also emptied public spaces to privatize the desire of lovers:

> [Empty space] signifies the asocial terrain where the desire of one reciprocates the desire of the other. The evacuation of the social, the emptying out of history occurs because the philosophy of romantic love demands that the self that loves can only come into being in a shared solitude with the other. Love is private, as is well known, but more importantly only the private can love (Gopal/Sen 2008: 152).

In this case, however, the romance happens right in the city of New York and the presence of passersby is emphasized as they, for example, cross the frame in many of the shots depicting intimate physical and visual interaction of the lovers. With the changing of their clothes' colours they even play a significant role in the mise-en-scène. But they never acknowledge the presence of the protagonists. None of them, and that is the crucial point, looks at the couple. Thus, the function of the song and dance to express interiority and subjectivity is fulfilled as much by the scenes set in a fantasy space as by those in a social space. The autonomy of the couple has been established so far that it can also be represented in such a setting. Accordingly, KANK later on shows an unequivocal scene of physical intimacy incorporated into the narrative as well as song and dance, which I will analyse in detail in the last chapter. Moreover, in "Tumhi Dekho Naa" the private can thus be represented in the spectacle, which is intrinsic to the nature of song and dance, due to the fact that the spectator is still enjoying the exhibitionist performance. I argue that this is made possible by the renegotiated form of *darshan* between lovers as described in the previous chapter. However, one essential characteristic of *darshan* that has not been treated in detail so far is crucial in establishing the component of intimacy and the lover's union in the darshanic moment. As mentioned before, *darshan* can also mean self-recognition and transformation, which is expressed in this context as the realization of desire, and particularly female desire. This will be the focus of the next chapter.

The Gaze as Signifier of Desire: Self-Recognition and Female Subjectivity

The song and dance sequences analysed in this chapter all represent interiority and subjectivity of the characters. Consequently, desire plays an important role and its representation has to be investigated in detail. In general, song and dance is used to express what cannot be expressed in the narrative. Thus, transgression usually takes place in such sequences (Gopal/Moorti 2008: 26; Dwyer/Patel 2002: 68). Not only are desires embodied, but also "forms of becoming" (Gopal/Moorti 2008: 26) are represented and concepts of the self created. As the issues of female desire, sexuality and subjectivity are negotiated frequently in contemporary Hindi films, an analysis of song and dance can shed light on what kind of female subjectivities the films in question constitute. An example of this that involves a wide range of desires can be found in "Tujhe Dekha To Yeh Jaana Sanam" when the characters' dreams of what their shared future life would look like are shown. Apart from desires of personal freedom, education and participation in Western consumer society, sexual desire and satisfaction are represented by a scene showing Simran in a dressing gown, romping around with Raj in a hotel room. Although the focus of this chapter mainly lies on erotic desire, it is important to keep in mind that it is always intrinsically linked to other forms of desire.

As some of the central conceptions of *darshan* correspond with the above mentioned functions of song and dance, the darshanic gaze can signify desire in an alternative way. Commonly, the erotic gaze is used to represent desire. However, as mentioned before referring to Mulvey as well as Irigaray, this is primarily male desire. The concept of *darshan* as a transitional experience can enable representations of desire beyond that. The unification and darshanic identification with the other is connected to self-recognition, as in *darshan* the devotee receives a new perspective on him- or herself. This could mean that desire represented by darshanic gazing constitutes new forms of selfhoods, due to the fact that the encounter with the other means to realize one's own wants. Thus, it can also be seen as a liberating transformation of the self, for which indeed, evidence can be found in the films.

Generally, *darshan* in the context of lover's gazes in song and dance clearly signifies desire. As Babb points out, *darshan* is based on attracting glances and glancing at something/someone (1981: 394). Consequently, the darshanic interaction between lovers is predicated on the desire to look at the other and to be looked at as well as to touch and to be touched by the other. Only if both criteria are fulfilled (that is if the other/the object gazes back) do the lovers receive blessing and experience unification. Furthermore, the erotic gaze can serve to constitute the representation of this concept, as it signifies erotic desire. The song and dance sequence "Kuch Kuch Hota Hai", for example, marks the point in the narrative when all three protagonists realize their feelings: Rahul admits his love for Tina, Tina and Anjali feel the same for Rahul. This is expressed by their imagining looking at and being looked at by the beloved. While the girls are first shown alone, each absorbed in their dreams of love, a medium close-up shot shows Tina leaning on a pillar after running down a lane. Rahul emerges from behind her, his gaze fixed on her. Her facial expressions as well as her body language show that she is aware of it. In the imaginative acts related to her, his gaze at her is the primary form of representation of her desire. Similar scenes follow in his and her fantasy, which could be seen as the "visual foreplay": "where a romantic desire is displayed on the screen, before an intense and direct gaze is exchanged between would-be lovers, there is often a play of gazes, a sort of visual foreplay, that takes place between prospective partners" (Taylor 2003: 309). The exhibitionist elements marked by frontality, such as shots of Tina dancing, which clearly serve to draw the erotic gaze on her, can be seen as part of this. In contrast, Anjali's desire is represented by the gaze at Rahul as she is shown sitting next to him while looking at him intensely. It might be concluded that, as her desire does not embrace the notion of being gazed at and fully realizing her own wants (and also her sexual desire), the union symbolized by intense exchanges of gazes cannot take place.

A more explicit example of the darshanic gaze as a liberating, transitional experience can be found in "Suraj Hua Madham". Before the song and dance starts Rahul finally makes clear to Anjali that his interest in her is of a romantic and erotic nature. The scene has already established a highly sexualized atmosphere. While he explains that he desires to have a love relationship with her, he tries to push some *bangles* over her wrist, asking her repeatedly whether it hurts. When he eventually straps them over, he asks again, and when she nods his answer is, "Me, too". Anjali runs away with a smile on her face, and the focus of the camera is on his gaze following her. When the song and dance starts, she is seen from behind, continuing to run. A cut introduces a long shot of Rahul walking towards and looking directly into the camera. The counter shot is a medium close-up of Anjali's, also displaying frontal, direct address, again followed by a long shot of Rahul, who spreads his arms. Here the frontal, direct address is most clearly presented: The gesture serves two purposes - demanding her to come closer as

Figure. 9: Returning the gaze: corresponding shots of Rahul and Anjali (K3G)

well as inviting her and the spectator to gaze at him. The latter is reinforced by the full view of the male body as well as the iconicity of the image. The shots of Anjali are all medium close-ups, which emphasizes the profound significance of gazing in her becoming aware of her own desire.

What follows are various shots showing how they come closer to each other, yet Anjali still does not give in to her feelings and runs off again. An interesting series of shots finally leads to a unifying embrace and intense exchange of glances. First, an iconic image of Anjali appears as she is dancing on a white rock. The shot is shown from low angle perspective. It is followed by another image strongly marked by iconicity of her profile, which is shaded by the sinking sun, which corresponds with some long shots of Rahul's silhouette earlier in the sequence. However, it is not her body which is displayed as in his case, but it marks the moment when she turns to look directly into the camera. This turning point, marked by a close-up shot with a frontal, direct address, is followed by a focus on his gaze on her, emphasizing the erotic nature of the gaze. A shot of Rahul's direct gaze appears to evoke the impression that it could be the counter shot to Anjali's. But then she enters the frame from the right and we see his gaze turning to her, constructing her as the object of the erotic gaze. After this, an embrace of the couple is staged on the same rock, now in a similarly iconic manner. As if to underline the fact that Anjali returns the desire expressed by Rahul's erotic gaze, the embraces are followed by a medium close-up of the two. While only his back is shown, her look into his eyes is at the focus of attention here. Rahul even moves out of the frame. Anjali's gaze with an established eye-match line rests on him, expressing her now acknowledged desire, which not only means the desire to gaze at but to be gazed back at, too. The previously-mentioned scenes that represent the lover's unification succeed this one; these scenes involve elements such as the dreams of a shared future life, the extensive iconic shot of the embraces and the representation of mutual sexual attraction.

My conclusion is that the reciprocal gaze established in the scene described here is of great significance for the following argument. It depicts how Anjali realizes and acknowledges her own feelings and desires. The shot of the typical male erotic gaze on her, which she then gazes back at, emphasizes the erotic nature of the gaze. Male and female body are displayed in the scenes and invite the gaze. However, the images are highly iconic. Moreover. being object of the gaze is tied to the action of gazing back. The reciprocity is, thus, a key element. In general, this song reveals how the exchange of gazes as well as the embraces as darshanic moments bring forth a transformation of the self. This is shown clearly at the end of the song and dance sequence, when a cut changes the image of Anjali running in the desert to her running through the rain in Chandni Chowk. She suddenly stops and sees herself dancing playfully around her father with her younger sister. "Suraj Hua Madham" thus marks her transformation from a child to a woman who has discovered her feelings and desires.

In no other film is the issue of female desire and sexuality as explicitly addressed as in KANK. At the same time the significance of the gaze in this film's song and dance sequences is enormous, which becomes clear in the analysis of "Tumhi Dekho Naa". At the beginning of the song there is a series of shots of Maya and Dev marked by frontality, which supports the notion of *darshan* equating embrace with reciprocal gazing. It should be mentioned at this point that the preceding song "Mitwa" extensively displays Dev's desire for her, which will be analysed in more detail in the last chapter. Although Maya seems to notice his desiring gaze on her she does not respond to it until in "Tumhi Dekho Naa". While both of them have already acknowledged that they love each other, they think their situation is hopeless. When they decide to stop seeing each other, Dev takes the active part and decides upon their break-up by saying: "I'm planning to stop travelling by train... Buy myself a new car, a nice new blue car... You like blue? I like blue..." (KANK 2006, 01:36:00). Throughout the film the train station has been their meeting point and retreat. As they now part, Maya's reflections are represented by the cutting in of flashbacks. Finally, while remaining mute and passive the entire time, she decides to act and runs after Dev, calling: "I like blue...". Her active commitment is the basis for their love relationship and also for its representation in the song and dance sequence which immediately follows this scene.[16]

In this way, the realisation and acknowledgment of her desire is again intimately connected to the exchange of gazes as well as darshanic unification. The fundamental condition for *darshan* - that the object of the gaze has to gaze back - is tied here to the condition of female erotic desire. Only the admission of her own feelings and the transformation of the self enable Maya to gaze back. In contrast to the love story, the narrative also presents her lack of desire and her sexual dissatisfaction, for instance in scenes which reveal the problems of her marital relationship in

16 Gopal refers to Maya's action as disruption of the tableau established before by the overhead shot of the lovers departing in the train station. She concludes: "What we diegetically experience as Maya's individual agency is also a cultural transformation" (2011: 88).

Figure. 10: Looking in the mirror: Maya is dancing and exploring her newly discovered feeling of love (KANK)

a conspicuous manner. In "Tumhi Dekho Naa" she explores her newly awakened desire. This transformative aspect of *darshan* might shed new light on parts of the song, such as the mirror scene. The mirror symbolizes a new perspective on the self, which is gained by Maya's gazing back and feeling her own desire. When she dances in front of the mirror and the camera, the pleasure and bliss created by seeing oneself through the eyes of the other are demonstrated. The transformation taking place in *darshan* is a highly liberating experience for Maya. This notion of liberation through desire signified by the gaze can also be found in other films, although hardly ever as explicit as in KANK. Thus, a female subjectivity is established and advocated most strongly in this film.

Direct Gazes and Directing the Spectator's Gaze

As we have seen so far, the shots of the lover's direct gaze are central to the devices used for the representation of *darshan*. As we have seen in the many examples above, the exchange of glances between lovers is usually represented by shot/counter shots often employing frontal, direct address. Most of the time the points of view of the characters are represented like this (Taylor 2003: 316). In addition to this function, it also establishes a distinct relationship of the spectator to the screen. Vasudevan points out that especially in song and dance sequences the frontal, direct address locks the spectator "into a direct auditory relay" (2000b: 138). This is most visible in frontal, direct address without establishing shots. This creates an ambiguous situation, as it is not clear who the gaze is directed at. In the samples, the frequency of such shots with the male star, Shah Rukh

Khan, is striking. The stars are generally one of the main attractions of the film, in addition to the song and dance sequences. Male and female stars are central to the spectacle. Thus, the star's exhibitionism in terms of offering him/herself to the gaze of the audiences is integral to song and dance. It might be interesting to take a closer look at the insertions of frontal, direct address that signify the exhibitionism of the male star in the samples, especially as the song and dance sequences in question otherwise focus on interiority and subjectivity of the characters (in contrast to staged performances, as shown in the next chapter).

In "Tumhi Dekho Naa" the frontal, direct address is staged prominently right after the embrace of Maya and Dev, which marks the beginning of the song and dance sequence. Without any establishing shot, a medium close-up of Dev in outside space follows the embrace of the couple in the train station. He looks directly into the camera before singing the first lines of the song. A cut introduces a medium and a long shot showing him turning around in a match in action. The movement as such draws attention to the body in action and invites the gaze. Interestingly, he is shown standing in an elevated position in relation to the passersby, while he later seems to wait at the bottom of the staircase which Maya is running down. Thus, these shots are slightly demarcated from the following ones showing him in interaction with Maya. The last shot in this series is a close-up offering frontal, direct address, which is then followed by a counter shot of Maya. His gestures in the long shot as well as the close-up emphasize the direct address as he points a finger at the camera and then at himself. Moreover, the lyrics correspond to this as he sings: "I'm yours and you are mine", which further underlines the direct connection to the holder of the gaze. Until the counter shot of Maya, however, this is primarily the spectator. Thus, the relationship between him (the star) and the spectator comes to the fore. Apart from the pleasure of looking at the star as spectacle, this presumably has an effect on how the rest of the song and dance sequence is perceived, which is constituted by very intimate scenes. The direct address makes the spectator aware of his/her presence and the act of gazing. Consequently, he/she might be drawn into the aura of the couple as he/she is included into the intimate space. Thus, the eroticized intimacy is not so much gazed at from an outsider position. Consequently, this could serve to destabilize the voyeuristic gaze on the couple.

Another example of this strategy can be found in "Suraj Hua Madham" in the already mentioned 'wet sari scene'. It is symptomatic that the first shot shows Rahul emerging from the water, again with a gesture underlining the direct address as he splashes water towards the camera. On the one hand, this has a similar effect like to the example from KANK, as it makes the spectator more conscious of the act of looking before being presenting with a series of highly intimate and, here, even more erotic shots. On the other hand, the spectacle of the male star here clearly involves the invitation of the gaze on the male body emphasized by the movements. It is interesting to note that throughout the sequence the atten-

Figure. 11: Extra-SRK: the display of the male star (KKHH)

tion is strongly drawn to the male body. Although there are various similarly ambiguous shots of Anjali with frontal, direct address, they are in strong contrast to those featuring Rahul as they are mostly medium close-up shots. The male body is often viewed in frontal long shots which are ambiguous in terms of who is addressed. In conclusion, the direct address here invites an erotic gaze on the male body as spectacle and at the same time encourages an exchange of glances between spectator and star, as the object on the screen gazes back.

However, it is important to point out that it is not only the male body that is displayed, but also male desire. The staging of emotion and feelings of the male protagonist is often part of spectacle. This is most obvious in "Kuch Kuch Hota Hai", where the frontal, direct address is featured prominently. While the spectator first witnesses Tina's fantasies, an extreme long shot introduces Rahul's part. He turns around and a series of shots, from long shot to close-up with frontal, direct address follows, which gives the impression of a zoom-in on his face. Singing about falling in love, he shyly and impishly hides his face in the close-up shot. He looks back up, again directly into the camera. In the next shot he falls on his back holding the direction of his look, while Tina emerges from behind him and leans over him. Then he turns towards her and their gazes meet. The visual interaction with the camera is quite strong in this case. As the main question in the song is that of whose gaze is returned, Rahul's direct look into the camera emphasizes both that his gaze is not directed decisively at either of the girls yet and that the gaze is the focus of desire. Furthermore, it offers space for the display of male desire and emotion. While the feelings of the girls are represented without the device of the frontal, direct address, it seems to be crucial to the scene representing those of Rahul's. In a queer reading of the film texts this might also been seen as opening up a new space for gazing as well as spectatorship. As the frontal, direct address is reserved for the male character, a gaze on the male star is not determined by feminine subject position as it is construed within the texts. Further meanings and effects shall be treated in detail in the following chapter, which is concerned with staged performances.

Staging the Gaze, Gazing at the Stage: Objects of Desire and the Body as Erotic Spectacle in Staged Performances

Contrary to the song and dance sequences treated in the previous chapter, staged performances are set in social spaces and are usually more integrated into the narrative. Typical settings are the cabaret, the night club or the disco, which are all public locations. Apart from that we can also find staged performances set in the family home on occasions like marriages, for example. Consequently, they differ from other song and dance in that they are supposed to be seen by characters of the film. The characters who are the spectators of such a performance are referred to as the diegetic audience. An important characteristic of the staged performance is that it has conventionally been used to exhibit the female body as erotic spectacle. Thus, the erotic gaze is dominant in the scopic regime at work. However, *darshan* can also play a role in the staged performances. In the following we will compare various sequences to analyse the scopic constellations in more detail. The only example of a staged performance which explicitly stages the female main character according to the conventions displaying the female body as spectacle is „It's The Time To Disco" from the film KHNH. In addition, other song and dance sequences staging the couple give interesting insights into different forms of gazing. Interestingly, the supporting actresses and minor female characters can be found in staged performances which comply more with the conventions of the erotic spectacle, which shall also be investigated.

Staged Performances and the Gaze

To explain the conventions of staged performances, especially in regards to the display of the female body, one type shall be described first: the courtesan's dance. This form has not only been used to display the arts of poetry and dance, but has always involved the fetishization of the female body (Taylor 2003: 309; Tieber 2007: 34). The implication for the staged performance, in general, is clear: nowhere else is the female body so intensively on display and offered as an object of the erotic gaze as in the courtesan's dance. Furthermore, the gaze is emphatically male and the diegetic audience is composed nearly exclusively of men. However, the exchange of glances between the courtesan and her aspiring lover very often constitutes an important element as well, as Taylor points out (2003: 314). Thus, the spectator is offered "a visual participation in the intense exchange of gazes with the courtesan on display from the privileged perspective of a visually-engaged lover" (Ibid.). Consequently, not only the erotic gaze, but also notions of darshan may be activated. In its transference from the deity/devotee relationship to lover/beloved the courtesan can be seen as trying to attract the gaze of the beloved by her beauty, her arts and especially her dance, which complies with the rituals of devotees wooing for the gaze of the deity (Sanzaro 2007: 19). Although there is no immediate relevance of the courtesan's dance for this study as we do not find any examples in the films, it is important to embed staged performances in this tradition and its codes for erotic visual interaction.

Similarly to other song and dance sequences, the staged performance offers a space for transgression. One transgressive pleasure is derived from the woman as erotic spectacle. The display of the female body and its fetishization are central to a great number of staged performances, which poses the question of how the gaze is negotiated in this context. Kasbekar argues that while the mode of dress, body movements and facial expressions all invite the erotic, voyeuristic gaze, there are various strategies to uphold moral claims and disavow voyeurism (2001: 292f): firstly, a strict moral universe is propagated in the narrative, which involves the fetishization of female chastity; secondly, the staged performances justify the voyeuristic gaze of the spectator as it demands the look. This is mostly achieved by the introduction of a diegetic audience. An establishing shot, for example, shows characters as spectators of the performance. In the following, the frontal, direct mode can be deployed to offer the female body even more directly as object of the gaze (Kasbekar 2001: 296). Interestingly, none of the sample films feature an explicit staged performance of the female lead actress, except for KHNH. It seems that the films are generally set apart from this convention, an impression which is reinforced in KKHH by the humorous intertextual reference to a film called RANGEELA (KKHH 1998, 02:24:00). In the course of playing charades, Anjali simulates a staged performance of the film. The erotic content as well as the offering to the voyeuristic gaze in the staged scene is emphasized by Rahul's astonishment and excitation. First his mouth drops open and he stares at Anjali, then he covers the eyes of the boy sitting next to him. While the scene serves to signify Rahul's growing desire and acknowledgement of his feelings for Anjali, it clearly makes reference to staged performances by displaying the direct, frontal mode as well as typical gestures and movements typical thereof.

Many of the sample's song and dance sequences show male and female characters performing together in contexts like club nights, weddings and other festivities. This can also be seen in the context of the increasing integration of song and dance into the narrative, which is a feature all of the films analysed here share. Partly, these scenes display similar characteristics as outlined by Kasbekar and will be analysed accordingly, with a special focus on the erotic gaze. A strik-

Figure. 12: Playing charade: Anjali is imitating a staged performance (KKHH)

ing parallel between KKHH, K3G and KANK is that the female supporting actress can mostly be found in scenes displaying characteristics of the conventional staged performance. I argue that in this way the chastity of the female protagonist is emphasized. Furthermore, the notion of love propagated by the interactions between the main characters is disassociated from this form of the voyeuristic gaze. At the same time, the expectations and voyeuristic desire of cinema spectators are still catered to. This function is also fulfilled by the background dancers, who in some of the song and dance sequences display erotically connoted dancing, like for example in "Say Shava Shava" and "Rock N Roll Soniye". In both songs the dancers are predominantly white and comply with stereotypes of the Western woman. With their short skirts and dresses they stand in stark contrast to the female characters clad mostly in *saris*. Thus, they fulfil a similar function to that of the westernized vamp in earlier Hindi film (Kasbekar 2001: 298). While the diegetic audience in most such staged performances approves and thus legitimizes the transgressive pleasures, there are depreciating spectators in the latter two. In K3G Nandini stops her husband when he dances up against one of the young background dancers together with his son. A general critique of the exhibitionist nature of the performance in "Rock N Roll Soniye" in terms of the erotic display as well as the soliciting of voyeuristic gazing is signalled by the two main characters of KANK. This reflects on basic conflicts in their relationships, but also signifies a renunciation of the erotic spectacle.

Another interesting feature that the films share is the frequency of staged performances that put the male lead character in the foreground. Although they are mostly not set in the typical settings of a night club or the like, they clearly adhere to a certain extent to the conventional characteristics to a certain extent or employ markers like a microphone, for example, to signify the form like a microphone, for example. The songs "Pretty Woman" and "Mehndi Laga Ke Rakhna" are arranged this way. Both cases show the male protagonist singing and dancing for the woman he loves, wooing her. Consequently, his desire and its expression are at the centre of the spectacle. It is clear that this is not a simple reversal of the scopic relationship described before. While the woman as spectacle "solicits and intensifies the voyeuristic gaze" (Kasbekar 2001: 293), the constellation in these songs emphasizes other forms of gazing which might be described in terms of *darshan*.

In general, the renegotiation of the gaze in the staged performances analysed here seems to merge erotic and darshanic gazing. Usually, as Dwyer points out, song and dance presents the body as spectacle and on erotic display, which is reinforced by the lavish costumes, extravagant settings and decoration. In contrast, the narrative invites *darshan*, for example, when the form of the tableau is used (Dwyer 2000: 114), using frontality and iconicity. However, in the analysis of the films, darshanic notions of the gaze turn out to be highly relevant, even concerning the staged performances which conventionally solicit the erotic gaze. Consequently, concepts of *darshan* which can be applied in this specific context are necessary. As suggested by Sanzaro, the staged performances can be seen as analogical to the display of deities in processions (Sanzaro 2007: 9). At festivals the images of deities are richly decorated and carried by the devotees in public spaces (Eck 1985: 57). The characteristics of display and exhibitionism in this context are similar to those of the staged performance. However, the pleasure of looking is not reduced to voyeuristic erotic gazing; on the contrary, scopophilia in this context is enhanced by the layers of meaning inherent in *darshan*:

> Decoration and beauty is secondary to other criterion. Completeness, the deity's presence, and iconographic correctness all take precedence over adornment. All adornment and rituals are secondary in order to serve the primary function – the possibility for meaning, right interpretation, and for a meaningful experience to occur (Ibid.).

Consequently, the notion of spectatorship can change, too. The reciprocity which is achieved in the staged performance sequences and their exhibitionism (Kasbekar 2001: 296) is also established. But various strategies which shall be outlined in the following chapters diminish the voyeuristic elements of the song and dance sequences.

The Couple on Display: Like Deities in a Procession

In contrast to the song and dance sequences treated in the previous chapter, the staged performances present the couple in a social setting, which means that their actions are seen by others and can also drive forward the narrative. However, an intimate space can be opened within the performance, too, as, for example, feelings can be articulated in song lyrics or lovers' interaction can be displayed amidst the diegetic audience, who does not acknowledge the intimacy (Gopal/Sen 2008: 152). The two examples analysed in this chapter, "Yeh Ladka Hai Allah" in K3G and "Mehndi Laga Ke Rakhna" in DDLJ, most strongly display features which can be interpreted in the context of procession and *darshan* mentioned above. Consequently, the lyrics as well as the dancing are fully integrated into the narrative. Nevertheless, intimate spaces are created for the couple, not last by visual interaction.

"Mehndi Laga Ke Rakhna" stages the betrothal festivities which put Simran as bride-to-be in the foreground. Her dress and ornaments make her stand out from the other people attending the festivities. Furthermore, she is seated on a platform, which emphasises the fact that she is supposed to be looked at. This is all shown in a shot staging her frontally at the beginning of the song and dance sequence, which creates an iconic effect. While Simran's eyes are cast down, a counter shot also marked by frontal positioning shows her husband-to-be with his friends, giving the impression they are all gazing at her. This instance emphasizes the erotic gaze more than darshanic notions as the bride is on display, but does not gaze back. Although she is the object of the gaze, she is not the one performing in the sequence, but a group of female and male dancers. In their midst Raj emerges and the focus of attention rests on him for most of the following staged performance. The merging of erotic and darshanic gaze is much stronger in the following segment. On the one hand, he dances for her and woos for her attention as well as her gaze, which recalls of a procession context. This impression is reinforced by the iconic staging of Simran, which evokes the idea of her as a deity. On the other hand, his desire is displayed by his gaze on her and vice versa. The fact that the diegetic audience, as opposed to the cinema audience, does not know of their secret relationship creates an intriguing space for the exchange of intimate glances in the sequence.

Foremost, the intimate space surrounding the couple is created by the spectator's knowledge of the preceding narrative, while at the same time various representations of the exchange of glances contribute to create it. When Raj is revealed in the group of male dancers his back is turned to the camera, which zooms in on him. A cut introduces a frontal shot of Simran glancing at him, although there is no establishing shot affirming the eye match line. Only after two more counter shots is Simran's back framed with the dancing Raj positioned frontally. While there are also several exchanges of glances between Raj and another girl who is

Figure. 13: Iconic staging: Simran at her betrothal party (DDLJ)

leading the female dancers meant to be seen by the diegetic audience, the couple's visual interaction is marked by the iconic series of shot/counter shots of direct gazes. Simran is nearly exclusively shown in close-ups of her face, reinforcing iconicity. The direction of her gaze is represented by several devices. First, there are two establishing shots situating her opposite Raj, once in the mentioned shot which shows him dancing in front of Simran and another time with the camera moving from frontal staging to the profile of her face, establishing the eye match line. Secondly, close-up shots and the zoom-in on Raj place emphasis on the fact that he receives the gaze/is gazed back at. At the same time, he is also the object of her erotic gaze as he is put on display by the performance. In this way, the gaze signifies female desire, too.

In K3G the staged song and dance sequence at the wedding of Anjali's friend primarily provides a public demonstration of Rahul's feelings as well as his courtship. In this case the diegetic audience does not essentially legitimise the transgressive pleasure of erotic display, but the approval of the love relationship is of major concern as the audience is constituted by Anjali's father, family and friends. Thus, it has implications for the following narrative and stands in stark contrast to the scene cut in at the beginning of the song, when Rahul's father is shown arranging his marriage with another girl. The song and dance sequence mainly consists of playful confrontations between Anjali surrounded by a group of girls and Rahul supported by other male dancers. Interestingly, the scene preceding it deludes the spectator into believing that a staged performance with Anjali at the centre will follow, since the camera shows a group of female dancers revealing Anjali behind their colourful cloth, her back facing the camera. In the medium close-up shot she turns around, her eyes squinting in a humorous way. In the following long shot of the women dancing, the camera zooms in on her, but suddenly the music stops and her real voice singing out of tune can be heard. This is a humorous and self-reflexive approach to staged performances as well as song and dance in general. Moreover, it marks Rahul's arrival, which turns the focus of attention from the woman to the couple.

In general, the wedding setting provides opportunity for lavish costumes of the main characters, decorations and spectacle. Furthermore, it evokes association with darshanic notions of the gaze, although in this case it is a Muslim wedding. As mentioned before, in Hindu religion the bridal couple is considered to be able to give *darshan*. Consequently, the procession-like-setting reinforces this notion. In "Yeh Ladka Hai Allah" Anjali is part of the bride's festive procession and is also seated next to her on a platform with other female members of the family first. The entrance of the bride followed by Anjali and others is shown by a shot of male dancers pointing up and the camera tilting up to show the women upstairs from a low angle perspective. However, the focus of attention moves from the bride to Anjali when various close-ups of Rahul looking at her in the form of the direct gaze are cut in. This sequence contains a number of ambiguous shots which blur the notions of who gives/receives *darshan*. For example, at the very beginning of the sequence, the counterpart to Anjali's entrance behind the women's *saris* is Rahul's emergence as the male dancers part to reveal him. He is clad in a glittering *kurta* stressing his to-be-looked-at-ness and the exhibitionist display. A counter shot shows Anjali's gaze also as direct look into the camera while the camera is zooming in on her face. The next cut follows her gaze wandering along the upper part of his body and, with the next cut, to his face, all shots marked by frontality. Her astonishment and intense focus on his body is due to the fact he is wearing a kurta after she has challenged him to wear Indian instead of Western clothes. However, it is also a shot which recalls the conventional representation of the darshanic gaze. The devotee looks at the feet of the deity first and then the gaze wanders upwards. This has frequently been employed as a representation of *darshan* in the filmic context signifying, for example, female desire for a man (Vasudevan 2000b: 140). However, in this scene the relation is reversed as Anjali turns away after a first exchange of glances. With her body posture clearly showing she is acknowledging his gaze on her, she is shown waiting for his efforts to make her return the gaze (or so it seems). The frontal shot shows both of them, with Rahul standing behind her. He then publicly confesses, in the form of a poem, to having fallen in love with her. A cut then shows Anjali turning around, gazing back at him. Thus it may be concluded that there are two varying shot sequences involving darshanic notions of the gaze. The positions of deity/devotee are not fixed. First, Rahul is presented as the object of the darshanic gaze by Anjali's gaze. Then, he woos for her gaze like a devotee for the deity's.

Furthermore, the attraction of glances in this context also expresses erotic desire. For example, Anjali's gaze moving up Rahul's body could be seen as signifying desire. Moreover, it puts the male body on display in the context of the

Figure. 14: Wedding procession: the male performance in the foreground (K3G)

spectacle. In the first part of the song and dance sequence, Rahul is clearly at the centre of attention when he is singing and dancing to woo Anjali. Subsequently, when both of them are dancing, his erotic gaze on her is staged more explicitly. Although there are many shots of the two exchanging glances and of Anjali gazing at him, the frequent close-ups of his face marked by frontality divert the spectator's gaze to his performance. It is clear from the lyrics, the narrative as well as the preceding scenes of the sequence that Anjali is the object of desire at which Rahul's erotic gaze is directed. Two shots showing Anjali's back and Rahul in staged frontally and gazing at her while he is dancing show this. Again this reminds us of *darshan* as shown in a religious context earlier in the film. Interestingly, the object of the erotic gaze is not as central in the spectacle as the gaze itself. This tendency can also be detected in some of the other films, and in a much more explicit way.

The Exhibitionist Display of the Body: Supporting Actresses, Objects and Subjects

In K3G the second love story between Pooja and Rohan (the younger brother and sister of the couple) offers more space for the conventional erotic gaze. As the girl generally displays a rather aggressive sexual attitude that is evident, for example, in the revealing clothes she wears, the song and dance sequences involving them offer her body as spectacle. Although only partly a staged performance, "Deewana Hai Dekho" displays her as object of the gaze. In this case the gaze belongs to Rohan, the male college students as part of the diegetic audience and the cinema spectators. Even in a song and dance which is set in a temple, "Bole Chudyian", Pooja's performance solicits the erotic gaze. At the beginning, there is a medium close-up shot of her body with her face located outside the frame. This focus on the hips, breasts and the naked skin of the belly most clearly reveals that the female body is at the centre of the spectacle.

Similarly, the first love story in KKHH between Rahul and Tina displays more instances of displaying the female body. "Koi Mil Gaya" contains all major characteristics of a staged performance as it is set at a college concert and the diegetic audience includes Tina's father as well as a teacher, both representing adult authorities. While all three main characters perform, the focus of attention is on Tina in the beginning. She enters the stage clad in a short, glittering dress and the spotlight is right on her as she starts to play the bass guitar. There are several young men in the spotlight with her, whose gazes follow her and who literally are at her feet. The enraged audience of students calms down and all eyes are on her. In the course of the song Anjali withdraws more and more from the scene as she realizes that Rahul's attention is almost exclusively focused on Tina. This is emphasized by various shots throughout the sequence showing Rahul and Tina exchanging glances. In contrast to other 'visual foreplays' analysed so far, this is represented here by looking at the 'desirability' of the other, meaning how others desire the beloved. First, Rahul is shown playing the guitar surrounded by girls showing their admiration for him. Then Tina dances in a circle of male students who all gaze at her. In the following shots, they are gradually approaching each other. The fact that the nature of the staged performance is even emphasized here by the intentional and overt invitation of the erotic gaze is intriguing. It seems that the overarching gaze in the public space is dominant as it decides who is 'seen' as desirable and apparently enables the exchange of glances of the couple.

At this point, the way in which Tina as a character is introduced in the college setting must be explained. During a conversation between Rahul and Anjali about girls, shots showing Tina are cut in: a medium close-up of her face, a long shot of her walking down the road followed by gaping men and a shot showing her bottom in a close-up. Consequently, her body appears as object of the male erotic gaze from the very beginning. At the same time, her irreproachable moral character is pointed out by the scenes set in the temple as well as her recital of a prayer at college.

In contrast, the gaze as signifier is deployed differently in the love story between Rahul and Anjali. This is apparent in the song and dance sequence "Ladki Badi Anjaani Hai", which is partly staged performance and partly fantasy sequence. While before at college she did not attract the erotic gaze (neither of Rahul nor of other men) as a tomboy, she now is desired by her beloved. The representation of her body and of the male gaze upon her is very different from that of Tina, which becomes most visible in two scenes of the sequence. In the first of these there is a cut after a performance of children in the holiday camp, and Anjali turns around in a medium close-up performing classical dance. There is no establishing shot, so the frontal, direct mode addresses the cinema spectator without mediation. The next cut shows an extreme long shot of the stage, where she is dancing with some children. Then a counter shot reveals the diegetic audience consisting of Rahul, his mother and children. The following series of shot/counter shots shows another medium close-up of Anjali, again with a frontal, direct address and various long shots. Moreover, Rahul and his mother appear in a medium shot, where he is positioned frontally with his face expressing confu-

Figure. 15: The supporting actress as erotic spectacle: Tina performs on stage with men at her feet (KKHH)

sion and then looking at his mother in astonishment as she applauds Anjali. A long shot of the dancers is followed by a close-up of his face showing a frontal gaze. His elbow slips off, which emphasizes how absorbed he is in the performance. Then he smiles admiringly. Primarily, this scene serves to underline Anjali's transformation from a young tomboy to a desirable woman (complying with the female ideal described before). The mother's approval is a significant contribution to this. However, it also has an effect on the representation of the gaze here. The focus of attention shifts from the object of the gaze – Anjali on stage – to the beholder and, in fact, to the act of gazing itself. In opposition to "Koi Mil Gaya", the mediation of and identification with the male erotic gaze is brought to attention. Consequently, the cinema spectator is made aware of his/her gaze despite the diegetic audience and the setting of the stage performance.

The second scene in the same song that displays this tendency occurs later, when the breeze catches Anjali's sari and parts of her body are revealed. As this exposure is not intentional it is not of the exhibitionist nature that we find in other staged performances. Nevertheless, it is a key scene exposing the male erotic gaze on the female body. First, there is a medium shot, which positions Rahul frontally with sunglasses on, leaning on a fence. The eye match line is established with a cut to a medium shot of Anjali, whose *sari* is caught by the breeze, revealing parts of her body. She is unaware of Rahul's gaze and laughs while she tries to bring the cloth under control. Another shot of Rahul without sunglasses emphasizes that he is gazing at her, especially with the camera slightly zooming in on him. All the shots are marked by frontality. Anjali has now realized he is looking at her. With a facial expression of insecurity, she averts her gaze while the camera zooms in on her face. A cut shows a close-up of her face as she looks back up and returns the gaze. Next Rahul averts his gaze as he hides his face, but then looks at her again. The camera circles around each character with the last shot showing Rahul positioned frontally with Anjali in the background, looking at him. First and foremost, this scene discloses the voyeuristic nature of the erotic gaze. Especially as Anjali is not soliciting the gaze and does not concur to the exhibitionism which is supposedly part of spectacle, her gaze back bestows a different meaning onto the male gaze. It can be seen in terms of the object gazing back as in *darshan*, but in their emotional confusion both characters cannot fully take in the other yet. Furthermore, the attention of the cinema audience might be directed to its own gaze as well. While in the beginning of the scene the spectator easily identifies with the character's perspective (Rahul's), the circling afterwards dissolves this connection to a subject position. Consequently, the spectator's gaze is unbound and the spectator is more conscious of his/her own gaze.

The underlying reason for the disruption of the gaze and the disclosure of voyeurism is manifested most visibly in KANK. It shows in the stark contrast between the two female main characters: Maya and Rhea. From the very beginning the representations of femininity differ widely. The first shot of Rhea shows her backside, and her backless top as well as her short skirt stress physical eroticism. This is reinforced by a medium close-up shot focusing on her bottom. In contrast, Maya is introduced as a character displaying symbols of traditional womanhood: the red wedding *sari*, the *henna* coloured hands and gold ornaments. Her face is shown in a second shot as she looks at herself in a mirror. Later in the staged performance "Rock N Roll Soniye", the contrast between the two female characters becomes even more apparent when Rhea is dancing on stage with Rishi and his father. The song and dance sequence is dominated by the two men performing amidst groups of female background dancers, who are mostly dressed in very sexy clothes and performing erotically connoted dance movements. Although Rishi dances with them and engages in all kinds of philandering, he tries to catch his wife's attention. Maya, however, turns away and vigorously resists when he quite abrasively tries to drag her to the dance floor. Dev also reacts with aversion when Rhea attempts to make him join the dancing, surrounded by a crowd of men, all with their gaze on her. The next shot is a close-up of Dev which establishes the eye match line. Rhea continues to dance, looking at Dev, who averts his eyes. This scene emphasizes the fact that Rhea solicits the male erotic gaze by her exhibitionist performances on stage. Furthermore, by demonstrating other men's desire for her she seeks her beloved's gaze on her, in which, however, she is not successful. At the same time the scene also shows that Dev does not fulfil the masculine gender role ascribed to men in the context of staged performances, as mediator of the erotic gaze on the female bodies on display. On the other hand, Maya resists the female gender role by refusing to perform or to solicit the erotic gaze, especially that of her husband. Rishi is presented as a typical possesor of the male gaze that conveys a sexual desire, which Maya also repulses.

In this case it could be assumed that the female gender roles comply with the binary opposition of western and traditional: Maya as the modest and chaste Indian woman opposing Rhea as the westernized, emancipated and sexually confident woman. One indicator for such an interpretation would be the clothes, as, for example, in the scene mentioned above the latter is wearing a sexy dress, while the former wears a *sari*. However, it is not as simple as that. Maya, for example, cannot have children, which sets her apart from traditional images of womanhood. Of course, her adulterous relationship with Dev furthermore contradicts the prescriptive female role model. The intention behind depicting an extramarital, sexual relationship with a female character not conforming to the stereotype of the westernized, sexually liberal woman might be to represent sexuality and eroticism beyond established binaries. Maya is not an adulteress because of her attitude to sexual liberality, but because she seeks to fulfil her desires and craves self-fulfilment. The stark contrast between her and Rhea serves to establish this in-between position, which renegotiates the issue of female sexual desire.

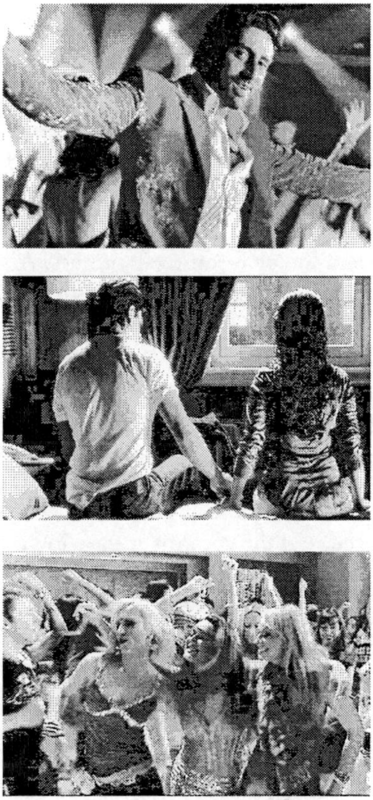

Figure. 16: Switching scopic regimes: a staged performance is mixed with the insights into the intimate space of lovers in a hotel room (KANK)

To underline this, the song and dance sequence "Where's The Party Tonight" represents this issue on a different level. It consists partly of scenes showing Dev and Maya in a hotel room, and partly of a staged performance of their partners in a club, where they are celebrating their professional success as well as their supposedly resolved problems in marriage. The opposition between the erotic pleasures of public display and the private, intimate sexual encounter has interesting implications for the voyeuristic gaze. Let me describe the scene in more detail to explain this further. Dev and Maya meet and finally give in to their erotic feelings for each other. The bodily contact and embraces which have previously been set in a fantasy space in the song and dance "Tumhi Dekho Naa", are now happening in a realist setting. Also, in the following parts of the song and dance sequence there is no indication of narrative arrest. The camera circles around them in their passionate embrace, which is emphasized by rapid cuts. A cut shows a shot of Rishi, joyfully celebrating in the club. The next shot wanders back to the scene of Maya and Dev, revealing Maya's passion with the help of various devices. For example, her hand touching his face is placed in the foreground or a close-up shows her kissing his face. In the following song and dance sequence, the rotational editing of the shots jumping between their intimate encounter and the club setting continues. As already mentioned, the latter is a staged performance which includes a great quantity of shots with frontal, direct address of Rhea and Rishi dancing. This is contrasted with the continuity editing dominating the shots of Dev and Maya, who book a hotel room, take the elevator upstairs and have sex in the room.

This opposition between staged performance and intimate private sphere in the same song and dance forces the spectator to switch between two different scopic regimes. Thus, it is impossible to fully identify with either of the spectator positions, which usually both enable voyeurism. Once again, the act of gazing itself, and the voyeuristic gaze in particular, is constrained. Furthermore, the erotic transgression of the adulterous sexual act is stressed by embedding it in a staged performance. At the same time it is set apart from the erotic spectacle as well as the female body on display, and thus a notion of sexuality based on active female sexual desire is introduced.

The examples so far have shown a dismissal to a certain degree of the male erotic gaze on the female lead role, especially when it is tied to the public gaze. The main love stories of the films do not allow unconstrained gazing at performances. However, staged performances can also offer a space to act out female desire. As Kasbekar points out, powerful and also sexually aggressive identities can be represented (2001: 305), although in the course of the narrative the female desire is often constrained. Sharpe describes this in her analysis of DDLJ, which displays Simran's desire in song and dance sequences like "Mere Khawabon Mein Jo Aaye" and "Zara Sa Jhoom Loon Mai" (2005: 67). Another example of a staged performance in a very typical setting is "It's The Time To Disco" in the film KHNH. The erotic gaze is deployed here in a very conventional way, but is still subject to negotiation. The female main character Naina lives out repressed desires in this scene as she dances on stage in a club. Aman, who has been wooing her in quite a brash manner, provokes her by challenging her sexual attractiveness. Rohit agrees to his comment and they turn to talk about a woman they consider sexy. After some drinks Naina pulls a dancer from the stage. Staged frontally, she is shown taking down her glasses and zipping open her jumper. While her friend Rohit wants to stop her to prevent embarrassment, Aman encourages her to dance. The shot/counter shots establish the two men as part of the diegetic audience and their gaze is clearly focused on her.

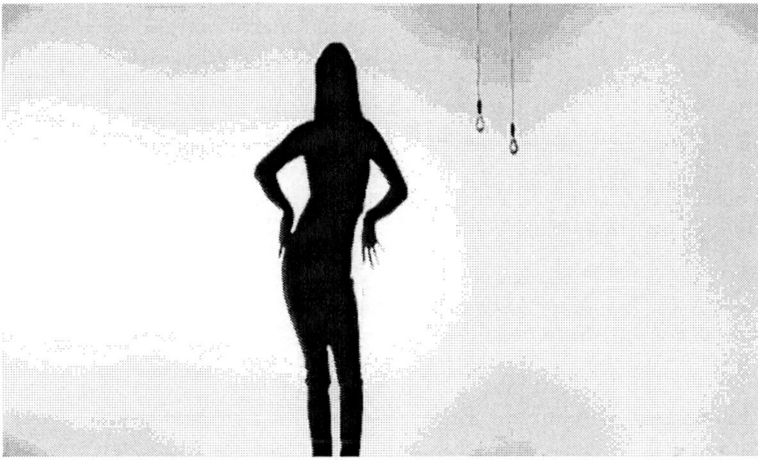

Figure. 17: The display of the female body: Naina in action (KHNH)

In this scene we can find many signifiers of the female body as spectacle and exhibitionist display: Naina is on a real stage, being looked at by many men and women alike in the club, her dancing displaying erotically connoted movements. Her direct gaze into in the camera and various shots of her as a silhouette behind a screen are cut in, which emphasizes the body movements and curves. However, there is an intriguing exchange of glances in the sequence that adds a certain complexity to the otherwise very straightforward relationship of beholder and object of the gaze. Rohit wants Aman to amuse himself, too, and thus convinces some girls to dance with him. This results in some shots of Aman in the middle of a group of them. A medium shot of Naina shows her direct and frontal gaze, followed by a close-up shot of Aman with the girls. This is repeated in a series of shot/counter shots marked by frontality and displaying Naina's gaze on him. In the last shot Aman looks up and meets her gaze, but then she averts her eyes. First of all, these shots emphasise Naina's desire for Aman signified by the gaze on his body in action. Moreover, her desire is also expressed by the wish to be gazed at by him. In this concept of reciprocal erotic gazing, the central issue is 'becoming' or the woman's realisation of her own feelings and desires, similar to various scenes analysed in the previous chapter. Self-recognition and the discovery of erotic as well as romantic desire are integrated here in a staged performance, which undoubtedly caters to the voyeuristic pleasure of the spectator in the first place.

The question arises whether this desire is contained in the following narrative. Although Naina and Aman are not united, as he is fatally ill and 'arranges' her marriage with Rohit, her transformation is still visible. Thus, self-recognition and the realisation of erotic desire are represented as independent from a male character. While in DDLJ, as Sharpe describes, Simran's desire is from the very beginning directed in „Mere Khawabon Mein Jo Aaye" to Raj, whom she has not yet met (2005: 67), Naina can live out her desires in the relationship with Rohit, too, as depicted in the song "Kal Ho Naa Ho". Therefore, the staged performance and its implicit male gaze on the female body are used to represent her discovery of desire and desirability focusing on her personhood rather than on the relationship with a male individual.

Diverting the Gaze to the Male Body: the Male Star, the Display of Emotions and the Rise of a 'New Masculinity'

In all the films discussed here we can find a tendency to move away from the conventional staged performance that presents the female lead character as object of the male gaze in the context of the erotic spectacle. Although minor characters are often used to cater to the voyeuristic pleasures of cinema audiences, a different kind of eroticism is introduced simultaneously. The exhibitionism that is an implicit attribute of song and dance sequences, and especially of staged performances, is renegotiated as the still frequent display of the female body is counterbalanced with the spectacle of the male star. It is obvious that the objectifying gaze cannot simply be reversed and directed to the male body with the same implications that the male erotic gaze possesses. However, in recent times the male body has increasingly become an object of desire and is represented as such in Hindi films (Dwyer 2000: 139). Star actor Salman Khan especially has attracted the gaze to his muscular body and other male stars following this trend take on object positions (Ibid.; Krauß 2007: 57). For a long time, Shah Rukh Khan was an exception as he did not much conform to the muscular hero of the 90s, yet this has gradually changed in recent years with films such as OM SHANTI OM (Farah Khan, 2007). Nevertheless his star image is still based more on persona than on the body (cf. Desphande 2005: 196f).

In reference to song and dance sequences we thus have to look at other modes of spectacle displaying the male lead actor. In Western film studies there are various approaches to the analysis of exhibitionist performances of male actors and the resulting gaze on them. Sturken and Cartwright point out that there are codes of resisting the power of the gaze upon them and mention examples such as the refusal to acknowledge the female gaze or to display male agency by action as well as muscular bodies (2001: 88). Furthermore, Neale concludes that male actors can be part of spectacle but not as objects of erotic display, because of the diegetic audience. The gaze upon the male character is mediated by the looks of other characters that do not show desire but rather emotions such as fear or aggression. He argues that if this is not the case, the spectacle of the male body results in a feminization of the male character (1992: 285f). To understand the role of the gaze on the male character in Hindi films, it is important to investigate how darshanic notions of the gaze influence staged performances.

Indian film studies analyse the effects *darshan* can have on the representation of the male character. Very often, filmic representations of *darshan* have been used to reinforce gender hierarchies. As Vasudevan points out, editing as well as camera movement can entail a sacralisation of the male figure. Iconicity and the form of the tableau are used to establish it as deity-like image which is object of worship. Consequently, although female desire can thus be represented, the authority ascribed to the deity as giver of the gaze is transferred to the male character, which holds an analogy to the hierarchical relationship between wife and husband (Vasudevan 2000c: 390). The approaches of Western as well as Indian scholars cannot wholly be applied to the films analysed here. However, they both lead us to the same issues: to what extent is the female gaze erotic, how is the gaze upon male characters mediated and to what extent are gender hierarchies reinforced or renegotiated?

While these questions will be central to the analysis in the next chapter, I would like to provide first insights into these issues in some of the staged performances of the samples. As already mentioned, the staged performances putting the male character at the focus of attention are frequent. To start with, DDLJ includes two staged performances with Raj on display. While "Mehndi Laga Ke Rakhna" is set as a procession-like performance at Simran's betrothal party, the one earlier in the film, "Rukh Jaa O Dil Deewane", shows Raj performing in a cabaret of a hotel. Actually, it is Simran who challenges his ostentation and calls him on stage to play the piano for the other guests. While Simran believes him to be totally incapable of this, Raj proves her to be wrong and entertains the audience. While he is dancing on stage with a group of sexily-dressed cabaret dancers, several close-up shots of Simran are cut in. As the shots show her frontal gaze, he is constructed as the object of her gaze. At the same time, he is gazing at her, an impression which is reinforced by frontal, direct address that marks the shots of his face. Similarly to "Mehndi Laga Ke Rakhna" he woos her and woos for her gaze. Consequently, both song and dance sequences stage his desire for her. At the same time, Simran is an integral part of the diegetic audience, which is shown by various establishing shots. Thus, the gaze upon him is primarily mediated through her gaze – a gaze signified by female desire. The iconicity and the mise-en-scène of "Mehndi Laga Ke Rakhna" emphasize her position as possessor of the gaze that Raj desires, or the giver of *darshan*, which the worshiper seeks. On the other hand, the spectator can hardly identify with the subject position of the male character, but gazes at the exhibitionist spectacle mediated by the female gaze. In contrast to this, the staged performance that shows Simran dancing in her home at the beginning of the film does not include a diegetic audience. Her direct look into the camera establishes a direct relationship with the spectator and makes disavowal of voyeurism impossible.

Another example where the male desire for the female protagonist is put on display is KHNH. As mentioned in the previous chapter, there is a staged performance in that film which puts the female body on display in quite a conventional way. But the film also contains the song and dance sequences "Pretty Woman" and "Kal Ho Naa Ho". The former is in the first half of the film, which shows Aman wooing Naina and is staged similarly to the performances in a procession context. A remarkable multicultural mix of song and dance is displayed in the sequence, which is set in the streets of their New York neighbourhood. Throughout the song, Aman is at the centre of attention and only a few shots show Naina, whose gaze he is eager to attract. In general, there are some iconic images of him as he dances in front of the US American flag or, together with others, on a car which is shown from low angle perspective. Although this might intensify the procession-like nature of the sequence, more relevant is the ambiguous question of who the object of his gaze is. Apparently, it is Aman who is object of the gaze as it is a staged performance, which is clearly marked, for example, by a microphone which he is singing into. The diegetic audience is mainly represented by Naina, her female relatives and Aman's uncle. Consequently, most of the shots with frontal, direct address that show him dancing amidst the colourful crowd can also be seen as point of view editing. However, some of these shots are not consistent with the eye match line. Aman is dancing along a fence, for example, throwing a direct look into the camera that moves along with him. Only at the end of the shot do we see his mother appear on the other side of the fence, but she is not in eye match line. We have encountered this phenomenon before, but in this song and dance sequence it is more visible than in others. Besides the already discussed effect of a direct relationship to the cinema spectator, it emphasizes Aman's iconic representation. This is most evident in a series of shots showing breakdancers performing in front of the US American flag. Several times Aman's face, sometimes in close-up, sometimes frontal, and sometimes in profile, is shown in the foreground of the shot.

The iconicity and the frontal, direct address continue in the song "Kal Ho Naa Ho". In contrast to "Pretty Woman", Naina is not even aware of the gaze upon her, as scenes of her enjoying herself with Rohit are shown from the subject position of Aman, who is secretly watching them, longing to be in the other man's place. As already mentioned, his arrival in Naina's life is staged in a highly iconic and religiously connoted way. Thus, the sacralisation of the male protagonist is achieved in this case. It is, however, not the gaze of the female devotee that puts him in this position, but that of the cinema spectator. The frontal, direct address and the resulting relationship to the spectator that is established most firmly in "Kal Ho Naa Ho" equate the image on screen to a certain extent with the image of the deity in the context of *darshan*. On the other hand, Aman's gaze is not returned by his beloved and, thus, it seems as if the darshanic relationship is confined to the star-spectator relationship. In a song and dance sequence of the film KANK, "Mitwa", we find a culmination of this when the male protagonist

Figure. 18: Iconic interruptions: Close-up shots of Aman are cut into the song and dance (KHNH)

dances in the middle of an empty football stadium, soliciting the gaze on him without any mediator, but with the clear implication of the spectacle, not least signified by the empty seats surrounding him. What connects all these scenes which stage the male protagonist is that the spectacle for the most part displays not the body as erotic object, but male desire. Consequently, I would argue that the films introduce a new masculinity that does not feminize the male character nor does it adhere to the image of the muscular hero. In terms of the gaze, it is not the *object* of the gaze which is at the centre of attention, but rather the *act* of gazing that signifies desire (male and female). This shall be investigated further in the following chapter.

Reversed Gazes: Masculinity on Display and the Deconstruction of the Gaze

The analyses in the previous two chapters have revealed certain tendencies of masculinity on display, which renegotiate scopic constellations and corresponding scopic regimes. Two song and dance sequences which put the main focus on the male character and the male body shall be considered in this chapter, "Kal Ho Naa Ho" (KHNH) and "Mitwa" (KANK). Furthermore, a short excursion shall put this form of masculinity on display into the context of the narratives and male gender roles represented in the films. Another central issue is how the gaze has been transferred to spaces beyond song and dance in the course of other shifts in representation of the New Bollywood film. The fact that Johar's films put male emotionality and desire in the foreground with the help of the gaze as crucial signifier leads to many interesting questions concerning cinema and spectatorship in general, which can only be touched on briefly in the last subchapters.

The Male Star as Object of Desire? Shah Rukh Khan and New Forms of Spectacle

First of all, it is important to point out that song and dance sequences staging a star the way "Mitwa" and "Kal Ho Naa Ho" do have to be seen in the context of the star text. If we see the star as "structured polysemy" (Dyer 1998: 63) we have to consider the elements which structure the masculinity on display, drawing on previous films and extra filmic discourses. Let us focus on two specific elements in the following. As mentioned before, Shah Rukh Khan could be seen as "mediating signifier" (Dudrah 2006: 85) bridging dichotomies such as tradition and modernity, global and local, as well as in some ways patriarchal/repressive and empowering gender concepts. In the context of hybridity, this is remarkable, as he could be seen as defined by this in-between position. Furthermore, one of the trademarks of the star icon is the emotionality which is incorporated in otherwise very conventional masculine gender roles. Especially in Karan Johar's films we see Shah Rukh Khan frequently displaying emotions in scenes where the male characters cry or experience other emotional breakdowns (we can find examples in all of the films). The representation of the emotional, inner life is, thus, a central component of the star text. Consequently, the song and dance sequencess analysed here interact with and reinforce these signifying elements of Shah Rukh Khan's star persona.

Interestingly, the two songs cannot be classified as either of the categories the two previous chapters referred to. While they represent the inner life and fantasies of the characters, there are also elements of a staged performance when the male character sings about his feelings. Moreover, they are integrated into the narrative as the development of a love relationships is depicted, in the one case between Naina and Rohit (which is observed by Aman) and in the other case between Maya and Dev. Consequently, the two song and dance sequences operate on three different levels: the actual plot, the imagination of characters and an extra-narrative performance. The audience of the latter is the actual cinema audience. Consequently, the gaze in terms of spectatorship is of particular interest. Furthermore, what is on display in the two scenes is not the male body as in other scenes, where, for example, action is emphasized by dance or sports. But rather the focus of attention is on the desire of the male protagonist for the heroine, and thus his gaze on her. This results in a scopic regime different from all analysed so far and is probably the most striking case of an intermixture between erotic and darshanic gazing. Consequently, the underlying structures of spectacle are also negotiated and contrast with the notions of woman as spectacle described by Mulvey ([1973] 2009: 26).

The first step of analysis in this chapter shall focus on the parts of the song and dance sequences which stage the male character in the extra-narrative space. By dispensing with the diegetic audience a direct relay with the cinema audience is established. This relation is marked by frontality and in many cases frontal, di-

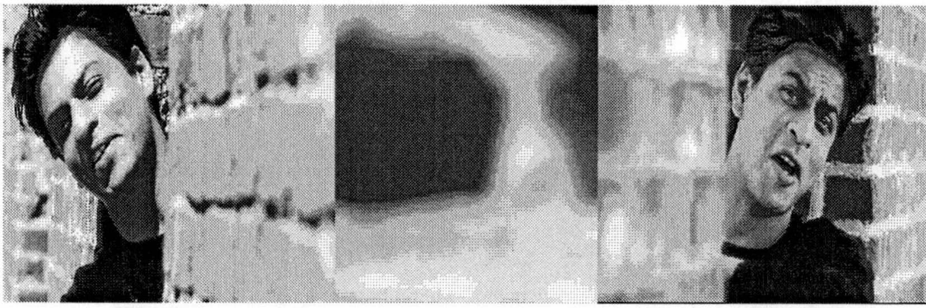

Figure. 19: Playful interaction with the camera: Aman sings about his feelings (KHNH)

rect address. Moreover, the acting is strongly stylized as the star makes gestures which on the one hand invite the spectator's gaze, and on the other hand create a distance by marking the actor as performer. Thus iconicity is reinforced in many examples. In both song and dance sequences the gaze of the spectator is directed towards the male character whose gaze is directed at the female protagonist. The heroine is not as present in the sequences, in general, and hardly at all in the extra-narrative spaces which do not represent character's imagination. By tracing the three characteristics above in the two examples, it becomes clear how the act of erotic gazing is put on display and, thus, at the center of the spectacle. The spectacle as such is predominantly structured by *darshan*.

To give an example, the song "Kal Ho Naa Ho" starts with a shot of Aman staging him frontally as he stands on an elevated floor looking down on Rohit and Naina getting closer to each other. Following this there are various scenes representing Aman's desire, which can be interpreted on different levels. First, he desires Naina as he is in love with her, but because he is fatally ill he wants to ensure her happiness after his death. What he desires, consequently, is her happiness. This is represented by shots of him looking at Naina, who is unaware of the gaze or Aman's presence. Second, he desires to be in Rohit's place as he is a young and healthy man with a promising future. Third, this can also be interpreted as Rohit being the object of desire, as the film includes various subtexts on homosexuality (cf. Krauß 2007: 103f). Although the scenes representing these forms of desire follow the segments of extra-narrative performance, their gradual appearance clearly puts Aman's desire at the centre of the song and dance sequence.

Interestingly, the first shot is followed by a range of extra-narrative scenes addressing the spectator directly. Rohit and Naina are not diegetic spectators, nor are there any indications that any other character is. While the first shots show Aman walking towards the camera or leaning against a lamppost seemingly absorbed in his singing, the direct address of the cinema spectator is more explicit in the following shots. The camera moves towards him sitting in an

Figure. 20: Iconic images: the reenactment of Aman as angel and sacral being (KHNH)

open frame in a red brick wall. In the profile shot he turns to the camera with a direct look, then turns away. The gesture implies an acknowledging of the audience, an impression which is reinforced when a cut shows the opposite side of the wall with another direct look into the camera. From there it moves to the other side again (showing the cross section of the wall) where Aman's face appears again looking directly into the camera in a frontal shot. This playful interaction with the camera establishes a direct relay with the audience, which makes the spectator fully aware of his/her position as the beholder of the gaze and of his/her role in the spectacle.

Furthermore, the extra-narrative space represented in the song and dance sequence is characterized by a considerable degree of iconicity. In terms of the mise-en-scène we find a high density of lines chanelling the focus of attention. The symmetrically composed frames, for example, contribute to this effect when Aman is shown in the middle of a bridge walking towards or away from the camera. Moreover, many gestures display stylized acting and performance, reinforcing the effect of frontal, direct address. Aman is shown spreading his arms or moving his hand in an expressive manner pointing towards the camera, inviting the spectator to look at him. Later in the sequence we find the circling camera as a device to channel the attention. In the last extra-narrative scene an extreme long shot shows Aman walking around a plaza. First, the camera zooms in on him, then a cut introduces a close-up of his back. He turns around, which results in a frontal gaze. The camera begins to circle around him and while he first does not move, he suddenly spins around in the opposite direction of the camera movement. This reinforces the effect the device has in terms of Aman as absolute focus of attention, and the gaze. Consequently, the impression is created that he is watched from all sides and positions, 'all eyes are on him', although the plaza is empty. Obviously, the focused display of Aman is meant for the cinema audience.

Consequently, the techniques of direct relay and iconicity evoke notions of the darshanic gaze. As mentioned before, Aman is introduced as a sacral being in the beginning of the film, which is underlined by iconic images. In "Kal Ho Naa Ho" his appearance as angel is symbolised by his pure white clothes in the first

Figure. 21: The spectacle of male desire and emotions: Dev in the football stadium and amidst New York's skyscrapers (KANK)

couple of shots, his frequently elevated positions in the frame as well as some low angle shots. Moreover, many shots show a great number of lines leading to the centre of the shot, where Aman is placed. However, the position of the devotee is not occupied by his beloved, but by the cinema audience, which effect is structured by the direct relay as well as techniques like the circling camera. Hence, 'we' are the devotees – the cinema audience. Furthermore, the deity we desire is particularly marked by desire. Thus, the implications of the erotic gaze are deeply involved, though heavily modified. Firstly, the focus is redirected from the object to the act of gazing as such. Secondly, the direct relay strips the gaze of all voyeurism. Moreover, the male star thus occupies enormous space in the film, which could be seen in a darshanic tradition of the star/spectator or fan relationship.

The second example, "Mitwa", features this scopic relation even more. This song and dance sequence seeks to mark the transitions from narrative, imagination and extra-narrative space more clearly, seemingly catering to an international audience used to realist modes of representation. Consequently, we can make out a linear development of the elements outlined above. The song starts when Maya and Dev enter a football stadium. While they are first shown enjoying themselves and watching the game, the camera then zooms in on the two when Dev gazes intensively at Maya, who is unaware of it. The connection between looking and touching is established at this point as he bends towards her kissing her cheek. Gazing, as it is made visible in the scene, signifies the desire to touch and is connoted by intimacy. In the following, a cut shows Maya nudging his arm and interrupting what turns out to be a daydream. The realm of imagination is thus demarcated clearly. A next cut introduces the extra-narrative space showing Dev in the middle of the empty stadium stretching his arms in the air and singing about his feelings. As already mentioned the empty seats signify the nature of the performance as spectacle and the intended audience in the cinemas. Gazing, in general, is at the core of the sequence and plays a significant role on all these levels.

Moreover, two characteristics also found in "Kal Ho Naa Ho" are strongly represented. While a sacralization of the male character is never indicated, the iconic representation is achieved similarly. First, the shots set in the football stadium are mostly from a low angle perspective. Also, in the second instance of extra-narrative space, where Dev is displaying similar gestures standing in the midst of New York's skyscrapers, it is used in a steeper angle, which is reinforced by the high buildings in the background. The effect of establishing the male character as the centre of the spectacle as well as the deity-like focus of the gaze is achieved. Second, the circling camera as a device is deployed here excessively. In the football stadium a series of jump cuts introduces different shots, angles and directions of the circling camera, which produces a diffuse and fractured vision on the male actor on display. In the scene set within the skyscrapers this discontinuity is even more pronounced. Thus, we could say that the multiplicity of spectator positions in the cinema audience is stressed and an unmarked or invisible spectatorship disavowed (cf. Coorlawala 1996: 24).

Furthermore, the jump cuts, for example from medium to close-up shots, emphasize the focus on the body. On the one hand, the male body is thus iconized, and on the other hand eroticized. In general, the erotic plays a significant role in these song and dance sequence as well as in the film in general. Desire as the core of the spectacle as well as the trigger for the extra-narrative scenes is shown in various ways. In the first instance, imagining kissing Maya leads to Dev's performance in the middle of the football stadium. The skyscraper scene is initiated by Maya's daydream touching his face. In the third case, an action set in the realist space leads to a display of Dev's emotion. When she incidentally touches his face, both react to the intimate moment in a bashful manner. The next cut shows a long shot of Dev running along the bridge, full of joy. Thus, the spectacle here nearly exclusively is based on the protagonist's desire and emotions.

However, female desire plays a crucial role in this context, too. As mentioned before, Maya's imaginations also trigger spectacle. Towards the end of the song Maya is shown as focus of the spectacle characterized by the circling camera, direct relay as well as iconicity in general. The scene before shows Dev gazing at her intensely, which she supposedly feels and finally admits to herself. In the following shots, we first see her spinning around while the camera is moving. Much like in the shots of Dev before, low angles are deployed here. Moreover, the frontal, direct address which we predominantly have seen with the male star in the

Figure. 22: A different erotic spectacle: the display of Maya's desire and desirability (KANK)

films is reinforced here, for example, with the gesture of throwing her glaring red scarf in the direction of the camera. Her direct gaze into the camera is only later allocated to Dev when he enters the frame and an eye match line is established. Maya first spins around him displaying some more stylized gestures, and then the lovers embrace. What follows is a series of jump cuts like the ones described before, with the camera circling around them. In the end a cut shows a medium frontal shot of Maya, who had apparently been imagining the scene.

In conclusion, female desire can be represented like male desire in the spectacle. The usual objectification of the female body on display built into spectacle, as Mulvey has pointed out, might be disrupted or modified due to the characteristics of these particular song and dance sequences. The reciprocity and interactive nature of the spectacle can be related to darshanic notions of gazing, as opposed to scopophilia as described by Mulvey. Coorlawala states:

> The inner activity of the devotee seeking communion is thus different from that of a voyeur in the darkened theaters of commercial films. Scopophilic pleasure involves anonymity. Invisibility and non-relationship empower the voyeur with the capacity to name and thereby manipulate mentally, what is being projected on the screen, while remaining unmarked, unseen (Coorlawala 1996: 24).

In becoming marked and signified as participant on screen the spectator enters a different relationship to the star on display. Furthermore, as the erotic gaze itself becomes the spectacle, the representation of erotic desire moves away from coercive objectification. While the female character is still object of the male gaze just as the star is object of the spectator's gaze, the subject position is made visible and is considerably destabilized.

Observing the Observer: Gazing at Shah Rukh's Gaze

As has been pointed out various times in this analysis, characters' desire is signified to a large extent by the gaze. Consequently, the activity of gazing as such becomes an essential element not only of the spectacle, but also the star text. This is most obvious in song and dance sequences displaying a scopic relation, which we will call 'observing the observer'. In "Mitwa" as well as "Kal Ho Naa Ho" there are scenes showing the male character gazing at his beloved in a voyeuristic manner typically associated with the erotic gaze as described by Mulvey. However, instead of directing the spectator's gaze to the object of desire, various techniques, which will be discussed in this chapter, lead to the display of male desire and emotions. Furthermore, the direct relay and iconicity emphasize where the gaze should be directed, as the male character effectively invites the spectator's gaze, thus establishing himself and his gaze as object of desire. This results in a paradox between voyeurism and the interactive spectacle described in the previous chapter. On the one hand, gazing at the female character, who is unaware of it and consequently cannot gaze back, is highly voyeuristic and complies to some extent with the male erotic gaze as controlling and objectifying. Moreover, the spectator's gaze here is also one of a voyeur looking at the intimate scene between the characters. On the other hand, the male desire and gaze is subsequently specularized, which is underscored by the direct relay. Let us look in detail at some examples to understand the effect this has on spectatorship as well as the power relations integral to the erotic gaze.

In "Kal Ho Naa Ho" Rohit and Naina are shown getting closer again after a series of emotional entanglements. The beginning of the sequence establishes a voyeuristic relation: the camera tilts up to reveal Aman standing on a balcony against the background of stained-glass windows. Thus, he is established as an omniscient (possibly divine) observer watching the other two characters. In the course of the song and dance sequences various scenes show Rohit and Naina in intimate settings flirting and spending time together. Through the first shots and the already established centrality of Aman's emotions, the impression is evoked that they are shown from his subject position. This is affirmed by a scene following the first series of Naina/Rohit encounters. A cut introduces a medium close-up shot showing Naina's profile. Aman appears from behind her, which results in a shot showing him gazing at her. Naina is apparently unaware of his presence

Figure. 23: Observing the observer: Aman's gaze on Naina at the centre of attention (KHNH)

and when a hand enters the frame tapping her shoulder, the camera zooms out to reveal Rohit. While Aman leaves the frame, the two talk to each other. The next cut shows them walking down a grassy hill, while Aman steps out behind a tree located on the far left of the frame. Again the couple does not acknowledge his presence, and with the next cut showing a medium close-up of Aman, they are rendered part of the blurry background. When he turns in their direction, the couple comes back into focus. The role of Aman as voyeuristic observer of the intimacy between the two is connected to his desire for Naina in the next series of shots. A medium close-up shows her looking to the right off-screen to the right, while Aman walks around her, his gaze placed firmly on his beloved. Another camera movement to the right reveals Rohit and when the two walk away we see Aman following them as the two walk away. Then the couple is again confined to the background while Aman turns to a direct look into the camera while walking away from them. With a zoom-in the scene ends with a close-up shot of Aman.

The insertion of Aman into the realist scenes showing Naina and Rohit, which are integral parts of the narrative, as they show the development of the relationship, first appears to be the ultimate case of voyeurism. His intent gazing and the other characters' unawareness put him in the position of the absolute holder of the gaze, who directs it and thus has the power over it. However, in the scene the gaze itself gradually moves to the foreground until the holder of the gaze is eventually turned into the object of the gaze. Due to the high degree of frontality and frequency of direct relay, the spectator is made aware of his/her voyeuristic activity, too. Consequently, observing is a key element of the male character on display in the spectacle.

This tendency is even stronger in the song and dance "Mitwa", which displays Dev's gaze on Maya in many different ways (some already mentioned in the previous chapter). The significance of this male desiring gaze for the spectacle is most explicitly demonstrated in a short scene after the two major parts in the extra-narrative space. In a realist way, Maya is positioned to the left of the frame, leaning on a column at the train station. Her gaze is directed off-screen left. Dev moves towards her from the right, but does not make his presence known to her and for some seconds just stands there looking at her. Although Maya is in the foreground partly blocking the sight of Dev, the beholder of the gaze is more at the centre of the spectator's gaze, due to his centered position as well as to the movement he introduces to the frame. Gazing as such, thus, becomes the focus of attention.

The second half of the song and dance sequence emphasizes gazing even more. After the third extra-narrative scene displaying Dev's emotions, a cut shows the two characters staged frontally and the shot is marked as realist. The music softens and the dialogue between them can be heard when they talk about planning their wedding anniversaries. Then they are shown in a restaurant preparing the dinner for the event. A long shot first shows Maya talking with a waiter, which is followed by a close-up of Maya's profile. From the shadows behind her Dev emerges with his gaze steadily fixed on her. Her face, although in the foreground first, is blurred very soon after Dev's emergence, emphasizing the holder of the gaze. In the following, not only does he move to a central position as in the scene discussed before, but Maya gradually moves out of the frame, because Dev walks away. Thus, the focus remains on the singing Dev as his close-up continues to be in the frame for a considerable amount of time. The next cut shows a long shot of Maya still talking and Dev moving towards her. Although she acknowledges his presence, she does not look back when Dev continues to gaze at her while walking around her. Consequently, the scene ends with a medium shot of him gazing at her. Interestingly, in this scene the realist narrative space is mixed with the performance, as Dev continues singing and is put on display doing so. The emotions and inner life of the male characters are integrated this way into the realist setting. In contrast to the singing, the gaze seems to be part of the narrative and plot. Moreover, in this scene the object of the gaze even leaves the frame while the holder of the gaze is on display.

In the last medium shot, in which both characters are staged frontally, Maya slightly inclines her head to Dev, who is gazing at her intensely. What follows is the fourth extra-narrative space, which first shows Maya and then the couple in embrace. This could be seen as an attempt to represent the female character in this spectacle, which is not structured by the male erotic gaze. What is on display is female desire, rather than the body as object of desire. Furthermore, objectification is disrupted when Dev joins in and the couple is staged in a similarly iconized way as described previously. However, the male character and star apparently holds a privileged position, while the presence of the female star is diminished in many of the examples analysed.

According to this analysis of the scenes, placing the main focus on the activity of gazing and the role of the observer is a form of representation of male desire. Furthermore, display of emotionality and the male character's inner life is the central attraction of the spectacle. This phenomenon can be found in other contexts, too, and, therefore, I would like to make a short excursion to a film text which, in terms of the gaze, caught my interest before analysing the sample films. Seidl describes scopic constellation very similar to the ones analysed above in a BBC adaptation of Jane Austen's PRIDE AND PREJUDICE (1995). The male protagonist Darcy is represented through various ways of putting "masculine emotionality on display" (Seidl 2006: 89). The gaze is a crucial device in this context: "Man as spectacle is further highlighted by scopic regimes having Darcy at the centre of attraction" (Ibid.). The main point is that Darcy is not only constructed as an object to be looked at and that his gaze constantly rests on the female protagonist Elizabeth, but it is obvious that the shots showing him gazing at her hold a prominent position. The most symptomatic is a close-up shot showing Darcy watching Elizabeth playing the piano. Although there is an exchange of looks represented by various shot/counter shots, the camera lingers on Darcy's face for a considerable amount of time. This partly iconized shot gives spectators the opportunity to observe the observer. This apparently appeals most to the fans (Ibid.: 93) and these scopic relations have been an integral part of the star text. Similarly, Shah Rukh Khan's gazing has become one of his trademarks as, for example, fans often use screen shots which offer room to gaze at him gazing at the female protagonist (Mader 2008). This short excursion to reception context emphasizes parallels between the effects of a Colin Firth/Mr.Darcy as "a compulsive on-looker" (Seidl 2006: 85) and Shah Rukh Khan in various roles. Likewise the song and dance sequences analysed in this chapter contain elements of feminization, as does to the spectacle centering on male desire which Seidl identifies in PRIDE AND PREJUDICE (Ibid.: 93f). In both cases masculinity is reaffirmed in the narrative which displays activities complying with predominating patriarchal gender roles. However, I would argue that 'feminization' in the context of Shah Rukh Khan as spectacle falls short in explaining the effects of the scenes in question. Rather we will see below that the majority of the characters he plays in the films analysed are marked by lack, thus, deviating from masculinity in the patriarchal discourse. But it cannot be reduced to feminization as suggested by Neale concerning the spectacle of the man in the context of Hollywood films (1992: 285). Generally, Hindi cinema offers the space of song and dance to represent male emotions. Moreover, it is a specific form of spectatorship that is highly significant for the understanding of spectacle. Consequently, we have to take a closer look at to the effects of 'observing the observer'.

Silverman discusses a technique in Fassbinder's films that leads to a reversal of the objectifying gaze. Instead of zooming in on the object of the gaze the technique of zooming in on a gazing character is frequently used (1994: 278). Reversed gazes can thus destabilize patriarchal scopic regimes as the conventions of subject and object positions are subverted. She argues that the look built into spectacle is turned back upon itself, which can result in disabling the look in reaching and subjugating the object (Ibid.). Also, Metz describes the emphasis of the looker's presence as one of the scopic relations able to disturb the order of scopophilia (Metz 2000: 428). *Darshan* essentially reflects on the act of gazing, too. Sanzaro states that "[darshan] gives people the perceptive ability to gaze at perception itself" (2007: 17) by deconstructing the object status. In the case of the scenes analysed here we can observe the reversal of gazes as well as the reflection on gazing as such. The spectator, who observes the observer, engages in the act of gazing he/she is him/herself involved with. Furthermore, when the gazer on screen turns to the audience in frontal, direct address, the desire is turned back upon itself. Consequently, it is not the desire to be or to have the object which is stimulated, but desire in a mediated way. This could be seen in the context of *rasa* theory, as the effect of emotionality on display here is the experience of the emotion as such. 'Observing the observer', thus, might be a device to evoke the rasa of love in separation in contrast to the love in union more related to the scenes described previously. In this context the erotic gaze serves as signifier of desire, but is largely detached from objectification. Specifically, this can have great influence on female spectatorship. As Vasudevan points, darshanic notions of the gaze make possible that the one being looked at is the powerholder. In this case, he describes the sacralization of the male character and the female subject position of the devotee (2000c: 389). However, darshan can also enable turning the female object position into an active subject position. As Coorlawala points out, shifts of "the locus of the power to construct the love object" can open up new ways for male and female audiences to enter narrative (1996: 23). The female characters in songs analysed here might enter as the object of desire/the gaze, but in the course of the scenes they occupy a different position, which could be described as "seeing-constructing subject". Coorlawala identifies this element in Indian folk dance: "His presence and actions are constructed by her gaze and actions" (Ibid.). Consequently, the pleasure of looking is not structured by the split of active/male and passive/female as described by Mulvey ([1975] 2009: 19). Furthermore, female desire can be represented in a new form as it is fit into the kind of spectacle introduced in "Mitwa". In conclusion, a female subject position is introduced, which bestows agency to the female character. Moreover, identification as such is negotiated. The next chapter investigates more closely how female agency is represented in the narrative, which is also important for an understanding of the scopic relations in song and dance.

Transferring the Gaze Outside Song and Dance: Negotiating Internal Hierarchies of Erotic and Darshanic Gazing

As song and dance becomes more integrated into the narrative, so do its predominating scopic regimes. For example, "Mitwa" and "Kal Ho Naa Ho" exhibit increasingly blurry boundaries between extra-narrative, imaginative and narrative space. Consequently, new ways of negotiating the gaze are explored. Moreover, we can find a range of scenes in the films which are set in the realist, narrative space, but display features of song and dance. The analysis of this chapter shall focus mostly on those with an emphasis on the renegotiation of inherent hierarchical relations in the gaze. However, it is important in this context to look at some elements of the films' plots, which so far have been largely excluded. Consequently, scopic relations shall be put in the context of representations of power relations in the narrative.

Of all films discussed here the one which displays most elements of *darshan* in the narrative is KHNH. Although a Christian context is affiliated with the deity-like status of the male protagonist, various forms of representation drawing on *darshan* are employed. As mentioned before, the character of Aman is introduced in a highly iconic style and is symbolically represented as an angel. However, despite the tendencies of sacralization there are no shots to be found in which the relationship between Naina and Aman is structured by *darshan*, which displays the traditional hierarchy between deity and devotee. Rather the spectator is put in the position of devotee in the various scenes of iconic representation. As Aman constantly tries to attract Naina's gaze, it is highly ambiguous as to who holds which position. Moreover, the homoerotic subtext in the film adds to this uncertainty through the ambiguous desire of Aman as well as Rohit.

When looking at the integration of the darshanic gaze into the narrative, it is important to note that music and some other elements of song and dance play a significant role in the representation of intimacy, be it in imaginative or narrative space. As previously mentioned, song and dance sequences have served as space where repressed desire can be expressed and transgressions may take place. Thus, the union of lovers related to *darshan* is marked by music (Sanzaro 2007: 20). In the films we find various strategies for using this marker in the context of gazing in the narrative. On the other hand, song and dance has sometimes been seen as a narrative arrest. This is similar to similarly to Mulvey's description of how spectacle freezes "the flow of action in moments of erotic contemplation" ([1975] 2009: 19f). This has changed considerably, as crucial events for the diegesis happen in the space of song and dance. The most striking example is probably found in KANK, when the two adulterers finally take a hotel room and have sex.

The probably most overtly erotic scene in KKHH takes place when Anjali and Rahul are dancing in a pavilion on the grounds of the summer camp after they have been surprised by rain shower. Markers such as rain and the wet sari signify the erotic desire represented in the scene. While Anjali wrings out her hair, Rahul kneels down in front of her and beckons her to come closer. In a series of shot/counter shots, Anjali first shrugs her shoulders in an inquiring way. Rahul responds by miming movements of ball room dancing, which she counters with a mute, then whispered allusion to the lack of music. Next, he gets up from his knees, and while the camera slowly zooms out, his hand starts to imitate the playing of a piano. At the same time the basic melody of the lead song resounds and Anjali looks around in confusion as if she is trying to locate the source of the sound. After an approving smile from her, a close-up of their hands joining marks the beginning of the dance, which is erotically connoted. This eroticism marked by the first three shots, which first show a medium long shot of him turning her towards him. The second is a medium shot of their faces when she falls into his arms, the third one, interestingly, is a medium shot from hips to breasts. The focus lies on his hand at the centre of the frame, which firmly grips her waist. This is followed by various embraces and caresses. Consequently, the scene shows how essential music is for establishing a space of intimacy. Furthermore, the pavilion and the setting of the dance scene recall the staging of song and dance. However, it is clearly marked as narrative event (meaning that the dance moves are actually happening, and are not imagined by the characters) by the preceding shot/counter shot series. The re-evoking of the song and dance setting can be seen as a strategy to activate darshanic spectatorship, which strips the erotic gaze of its voyeuristic nature.

In the song and dance sequences as well as the narrative space of KANK, gazing plays a conspicuously prominent role. Similarly to the scene of KKHH, the most intense gazing in KANK takes place in a narrative space where music is an essential element. After the song and dance sequences which signify the lover's feelings and union, their desire is more closely represented in the narrative. When Maya and Dev visit the ballet, each with their partner, they first try to make their respective lovers jealous by exhibiting intimacy (KANK 2006, 02:05:00). The entering of the theatre hall is shown from Maya's perspective, which becomes clear when the blurred back of her head is framed, positioned in the foreground. In the background, which is in focus, Dev and Rhea take their places on the balcony opposite. A shot follows where Maya and Rishi are positioned frontally, and she is casting down her eyes. This indicates that her gaze was on the other couple, while Rishi looks straight at where the stage is. Next we cut to a shot of Dev and Rhea with him looking directly into the camera, towards Maya, while Rhea looks towards the stage. The next shot shows the curtains opening on the stage and the beginning of the show. Dev is shown again looking into Maya's direction, who is seen linking arms with Rishi. What follows is a series of shot/counter shots showing Maya and Dev gazing at each other while gradually heightening the intensity of intimacies exchanged with their partners. The turning point is when Dev's gaucheness makes Maya laugh out loud, which makes Rishi turn towards her and intensify his response to the caresses. As is made clear earlier in the narrative, Maya is not sexually attracted to her husband and is repulsed by his constant approaches. In rapid cuts, we see alternate shots of three events happening simultaneously: Maya displaying displeasure and distress due to Rishi's intrusive touching, the ballet on stage and Dev in eye match line gazing at the couple opposite. Maya is clearly aware of Dev's gaze on her and looks back various times. Once again a moment of intense gazing is marked by music as well as a stage setting, which alludes to the conventions of song and dance. Moreover, the ballet dance on stage displays the actions between the characters on a symbolic level, as, for example, when Dev watches Rishi touching Maya, a female dancer is pulled between two men. The music itself intensifies or diminishes with the feelings on display; for example, the moment Maya laughs, it softens noticeably.

Figure. 24: The pavillion scene: Music as marker of a space for intimacy and the erotic (KKHH)

Interestingly, this scene takes place after (darshanic) union was represented in "Tumhi Dekho Naa". While before the representation of desire was still mainly confined to the space of the imaginary (the song and dance), the film now breaks with this convention. The gaze in this scene is clearly linked to sexual desire and actuates in the narrative space. Although the male gaze is on the female character, it differs in so much from the objectifying, erotic gaze that the holder has no power position in the situation. Consequently, the spectator cannot feel omnipotence in identifying with the male protagonist as it is not the case that "the power of the male protagonist as he controls events coincides with the active power of the erotic look" (Mulvey [1975] 2009: 21). Nevertheless, the gaze signifies sexual desire, which is thus declared as an essential part of darshanic union. Various shots of Maya and Dev establish the eyeline match, but she always averts her eyes quickly. This could be interpreted as the foreclosure of darshanic union in the narrative or rather the necessity of transferring it from the imaginary to the symbolic (the narrative).

The next scene shows Maya and Dev meeting the next day. While the extreme long shot shows Dev's back, Maya approaches him. In the next medium shot the two are staged frontally as they discuss their feelings: the shame of using their partners and their desire for each other. Dev is acting extremely jealous and claims his right to be with Maya, because she loves him. The dialogue in this scene thus also reflects the patriarchal possessive claim on the female body, even if is is grounded here in mutual desire and love. What follows is an intense embrace accompanied by the lead song of the film. Scenes appear in turns of Rhea and Rishi in a club talking to their groups of friends appear in turns, which are contrasted with the passionate embrace of their respective spouses. It is important to note that in the first half of this scene Dev is depicted as active, through speech but also through how he touches Maya, sometimes verging on being rough. Furthermore, he is the one who initiates the embrace, while she murmurs: "Dev, what are you doing …". His hand is depicted in the centre of the frame, and all his fingers spread and draw her closer. But then the following shots showing the couple put her movements into the focus of attention. After the scene showing Rishi in the club, a close-up shot of the lovers' shoulders appears, in which Maya's hands and her arm around his neck are pronounced against the background of Dev's black jacket. When the camera moves to their faces, her hands are still in the frame and remain highly visible in their movements throughout the scene. Moreover, she is seen kissing his face passionately all over. Consequently, her desire for him is represented in the narrative space.

This intimate encounter is part of the narrative and advances it significantly. Nevertheless, we can find techniques and markers used before in the film in the space of the song and dance. For example, later in the scene the joints of the shots are dissolves, resulting in double exposures of the frame. Thus, the effect of dissolves emphasizing darshanic union as used in "Tumhi Dekho Naa" as discussed in the chapter "*Darshan* as unficiation" is reactivated in this context, inside the narrative. Furthermore, shortly after they start to embrace, the camera begins to circle around them, which is another technique extensively used in the preceding song and dance sequences, especially "Mitwa". Consequently, two central devices which have been used to represent the couple, and which evoke a spectatorship based on mediation between erotic and darshanic gazing, are transferred to the narrative space.

The next scene is the highly complex song and dance sequence "Where's the party tonight" showing Maya and Dev in a hotel room having sex. Before analyzing it in more detail, it is necessary to look detail at how female agency is represented in the film. In the scene the male character is the driving force as he commits several actions which push the event forward: he rents the hotel room at the counter, he takes off his shirt and touches her naked skin first. Together with the almost pushy gestures in the preceding embrace scene as well as his words such as "You are mine", this gives the impression that he is in control and Maya just gives in. At the

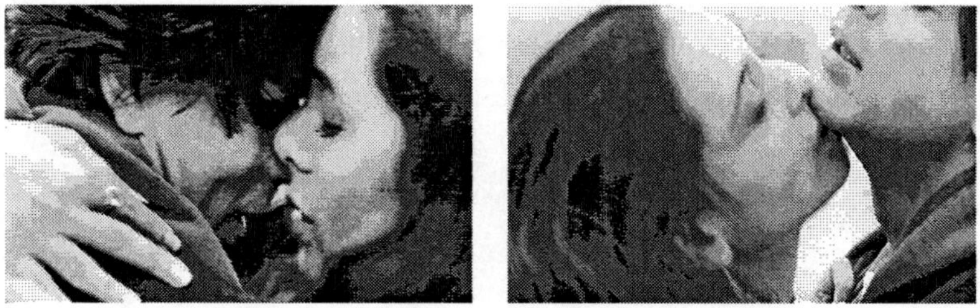

Figure. 25: Putting female desire in the foreground: Maya kissing Dev (KANK)

same time we have the already mentioned indicators of her agency such as the active movements in the embrace, or the decision to run back and commit to the relationship, symbolized in the words "I like blue". Once more it should be pointed out that KANK depicts adultery in a highly unusual way as the love outside marriage finally becomes a marriage, and is thus, legitimized in the moral universe the narrative upholds. However, this is only possible after a long time of separation and suffering as well as the blessings of their former partners. What is deconstructed by the storyline is the otherwise "totally uncompromising stance on the subject of female chastity" (Kasbekar 2001: 293).Without markers of female agency as well as sexual desire, the male gaze would turn out to be nothing else than an objectifying, possessive force. In this context, however, the emphasis on Maya's actions reveals a female subject position in the narrative. She is not a damsel in distress who is saved by the hero out of the villain's arms, but she chooses according to her feelings and desires to be with a man. This is marked by actions such as expressing her wishes ("I like blue"), meeting Dev the day after the ballet (she is the one moving towards him in the scene) or taking his hand on the way to the hotel room. Consequently, the heroine is not just representing (vs. acting) or making the hero act the way he does (Mulvey [1975] 2009: 20). She herself is a maker and not simply a bearer of meaning, thus obtaining for herself a subject position.

Furthermore, the blurring of boundaries between narrative and song and dance in "Where's the party tonight" is most extreme. A r ealist scene in private space is embedded within the highly conventionalized form of a staged performance including frontality, diegetic audience and the display of the female body as spectacle. An erotic scene of this kind which is embedded in the narrative would normally correspond with the conventions we can find in Western films. However, as the erotic scene takes turns with the staged performance, once again, the act of gazing is reflected upon and the spectator reminded of his/her presence. This is especially due to the frequency of direct frontal address in shots showing either Rhea or Rishi. Consequently, identification with the erotic gazing happening in the hotel room setting is not easy for the spectator, because the voyeuristic perspective is constantly disrupted.

Let us now look in detail at how the erotic gaze is deployed in the shots of Maya and Dev in the hotel room. The gaze plays a significant role in the first part, while the actual sex act is dominated by other forms of representations. In the first shot Maya and Dev sit on the bed with their backs turned to the camera. He puts his hand on hers and then a medium close-up shot shows his face, his eyes moving up to look into hers. While first it is only Maya's back in the frame establishing the eyeline match, the counter shot shows her gazing back. In the next is a profile shot of the two looking at each other. In the following we mainly see close-ups of Maya looking at Dev, in contrast, his body and movement is clearly at the centre of attention, especially when he pulls off his shirt and reveals naked skin. Most of the time Maya's back is in the frame, too, which indicates her gaze on him as well as the identification of the spectator's gaze with hers. However, when he takes off his shirt, a counter shot shows Maya with averted eyes when confronted with the naked skin. His gaze, on the other hand, steadily rests on her throughout the shots. As he tenderly undresses her (which is only indicated by pulling her shirt down her shoulders), his gaze wanders from her face to the revealed shoulders, moving downwards. This is shown in a close-up shot of his face, which is followed by a counter shot of Maya with bare shoulders, who looks up the first time since Dev has undressed. This marks the beginning of the shots depicting the sex act as such, in which we can still find some intense gazing, but other forms to represent union are more significant.

Gazing, therefore, fulfills the purpose of a visual foreplay (Taylor 2003: 308), this time literally. In the series of shots outlined here, the fusion of erotic and darshanic gazing as described by Taylor are most apparent. Moreover, the gaze here contributes to a renegotiation of gender relations by the way it signifies male and female desire. Firstly, the conventional shot/counter shots show both characters as holder of the gaze and in most shots its object (the other character) is present in the frame. But the spectator's gaze lingers on the male character' body, which is shown more extensively. Thus, the female sexual desire and attraction is emphasized. Secondly, Maya's averted gaze not only marks her virtuousness, but in the following also serves to stage a darshanic union. As she finally gazes back at Dev, this act strongly emphasizes the reciprocity and mutuality of the sexual encounter. Consequently, erotic as well as darshanic notions of the gaze are negotiated here in order to represent female desire.

After unification in the gaze, we find other modes of representation of their union in the scene. For example, there are various extreme close-ups of the character's faces in horizontal position, seeming to merge completely. Moreover, towards the end of the scene a profile shot shows Maya's face and a tear running down her cheek, which is kissed away by Dev. In my interpretation, the tear is used here as a symbol for ultimate symbiosis: orgasm. However, it is a sign which allows a wide range of interpretations. In this scene, the erotic gaze signifies Dev's desire with an emphasis on the physical, corporal elements of desire that

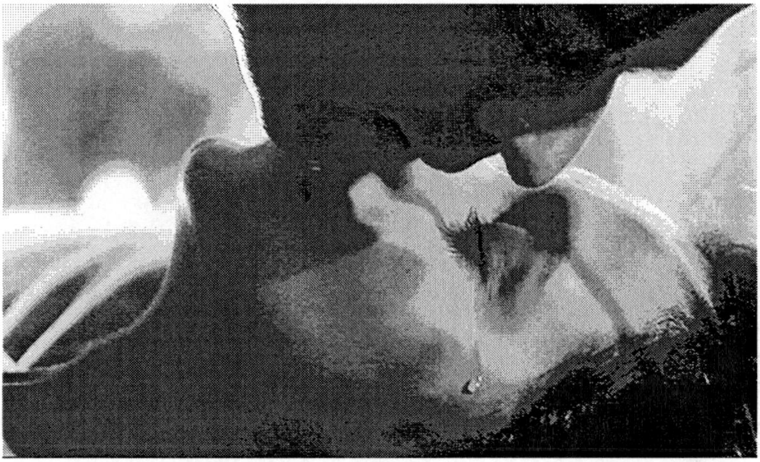

Figure. 26: The climax of unification: Dev and Maya have sex in a hotel room (KANK)

he feels for Maya. At the same time her gaze is given a considerable amount of space in the first couple of shots, which is emphasized with more close-ups and the central positing of her face in the frame. Furthermore, her desire and her gaze are ascribed more to the spectator's position, with the many shots showing her back blurred in the foreground and the focus on Dev as object of her/the spectator's gaze, even more so by the exhibition of his body. Consequently, the holder of the male gaze becomes at the same time the object. Although it is clear that he is marked by action and movement, making the initiating first steps. Furthermore, through this representation, his desire as well as desirability come to the fore, which partly superimposes female desire. On the one hand, this weakens the female subject position as maker of meaning; on the other hand, the woman does not appear here as sexual object or image, but is mostly defined through the gaze. Furthermore, it is important to note that the adulterous act (strongly condemnable in the moral universe the film is set in) is more imputed to Dev than to Maya, thus, partly maintaining the image of the heroine as virtuous, which is emphasized by acts such as averting her eyes at first.

In this context, the shots of Rhea and Rishi which continuously disrupt the intimate scene have the effect of reminding the spectator of the injustice inflicted on the partners. This is underlined by the last shot, which is a close-up of Maya and Dev's entwined hands with their shining wedding rings. Another effect of the cross-cutting is the already mentioned disruption of the voyeuristic space. While intimate scenes such as these are set in a private space, where the spectator gazes in from the outside, the song and dance context hinders the illusion of an enclosed space. Consequently, the erotic is represented here in a way neither fully adhering to exhibitionism nor voyeurism. Thus, the mixing of codes is very visible in this example.

As Mulvey points out, the erotic in mainstream Hollywood films has been codified into the language of the dominant patriarchal order. What is needed is a "new language of desire", which represents the erotic differently ([1975] 2009: 16). Similarly, French feminists concerned with literature have postulated a new language which can represent female desire and sexuality (Robbins 2000: 117). In the example treated here the voyeuristic nature of the erotic gaze, which is inherent in the realist style of Hollywood, is negotiated. On the other hand, the inhibition of the representation of the private in mainstream Hindi cinema as described by Prasad, which is also apparent in the kissing prohibition, is overcome. Similarly to the kiss, the intimate encounter in the scene represents the emotional and the erotic together, which threatens the institutions of patriarchy. *Darshan*, which has often been associated with the overarching patriarchal gaze (cf. Prasad 1998: 103), is renegotiated and used to create an aura of the couple which is not necessarily linked to an "inauguration of the history of realist voyeurism" (Ibid.: 97). The elements of the darshanic gaze which activate communal relations, in contrast to the "atomistic individualism" engendered by the realist, voyeuristic cinema (cf. Ibid.: 102f), are thus set into a new context. Similarly to Vasudevan, I would argue that the representation of the private does not have to go along with atomistic forms of spectatorship. Like direct address, this form of representation "constitutes a narration of desire in which the relationship between zones of intimacy and socio-political arrangements need not follow a model of opposition and separation of public and private experience" (Vasudevan 2000b: 152). By avoiding kissing scenes, the films by Karan Johar affirm a refusal to take over conventions of Western cinema unconditionally, nonetheless, the films do not cease to investigate representations of the erotic intrinsically connected to the emotional. Thus, in contrast to many other Hindi films that seek to enter a globalized space of cinema, in Johar's films the realist norm of Hollywood is not simply incorporated or juxtaposed with other forms of representation, but is negotiated intensively. Consequently, processes of hybridization are more profound and complex here.

In conclusion, KANK is the film in which representations of desire most obviously merge erotic and darshanic gazing. The establishment of a female subject position is a significant point in assuring the basic principle of giving space to the object to gaze back. Moreover, in terms of spectatorship, this has similar effects, as Coorlawala describes, referring to dance performances: "the tendency of the observer to identify with a singularly male or female orientation" is fractured, which results in a "darshan-rasa model" which "has less hegemonic implications for both viewer and performer" (1996: 26). The power positions shift as the subject/object relations are destabilized.

Escaping the Phallus? Patriarchal Authority, Masculinity and Lack

Looking at the male characters in the samples, they seem on first sight to comply with the typical hero of the 90s family films (except for Dev in KANK). However, it is striking that three of them display features which make them deviate from the norm in some way: Rahul in K3G is adopted, Aman in KHNH is fatally ill and Dev in KANK is crippled. Although the other two, Raj in DDLJ and Rahul in KKHH, represent the norm, it is interesting to see that in the course of the storyline they are in situations untypical of masculine gender roles. Rahul, for example, is a single parent when he meets Anjali again. Consequently, this deviation is a decisive element of the film text which influences scopic relations, too. Generally, the hero of the 90s is described as mediating between tradition and modernity, especially concerning gender issues. As Tieber points out, Shah Rukh Khan has been playing many roles which could be described as 'a patriarch to fall in love with' (Tieber 2007: 140). Furthermore, we have already identified an example where the male star is partly identified with a divine being, namely KHNH. Aman is referred to as an angel not least through the visual constellations accompanying the introduction of the character. Interestingly, when he woos for Naina's love (and her gaze) he displays characteristics of what could be called the "Krishna-lover" (Kakar 1990: 36f). Generally, the Krishna lover encounters his beloved with importunate, teasing and annoying behavior, sometimes verging on harassment. The psychoanalyst Kakar argues that he is striving to reassure his phallic power by "melting [the woman's] indifference and unconcern into submission and longing" (Ibid.: 37). Although this is only one side of Krishna, mostly going back to the stories surrounding his years as a young man running after the cow-herdesses, it is still a characteristic associated with the god. Moreover, we can find this behavior in most of the male characters in the samples: Raj in DDLJ, Rahul in KKHH wooing Tina as well as Rahul courting Anjali in K3G. Even Dev in KANK, who generally does not have many similarities with the young and playful god, teases Maya when they meet again. Therefore, the excessive display of masculinity and male emotionality could be seen in the light of the deified male star giving *darshan*. To a certain degree this might reinforce the power of the star image and also establish a link to *bhakti* traditions of worship focusing on Krishna. However, in the context of the characteristics outlined above which display lack, a paradoxical situation evolves.

In Johar's films we find a complex relation between the patriarchal order and the male protagonist. In some instances we find an identification with a feminine subject position in the patriarchal order. Even in DDLJ, which features a male main character largely conforming with predominating male gender roles, Raj is set apart from the masculine hero figure as he, for example, fasts with Simran during the traditional festival of Karwa Chauth, which is undertaken by women praying for their husband's well-being. Furthermore, he spends his time with many of Simran's female relatives and, thus, with the family of the bride instead of the groom, whose guest he is officially (DDLJ 1995, 02:38:00). On top of that, in the song "Mehndi Laga Ke Rakhna" Raj joins Simran's mother and other women dancing at the betrothal party. He is wearing a veil when suddenly her father enters (which makes everyone stop dancing) and stares at the young man. Although the patriarch then joins the singing and dancing, it is clear that the controlling gaze does not approve of transgressions like this.

In KHNH we also find transgressions, most of them in the depiction of Aman and Rohit's friendship. Various scenes show the two male characters in ambiguous situations implying a homosexual relationship between them, which is mostly treated in a humorous way in the film. This quite explicit homoerotic subtext runs like a thread through KHNH. As Florian Krauß points out, various markers of and allusions to homosexual subcultures as well as stereotypes open up the film to queer readings (2007: 103f). In the final wedding scene, for example, not only the bridal couple is at the focus of attention, but also the two friends Aman and Rohit (Ibid.: 105). Krauß argues that the romantic family film could also be seen as mocking and satirizing heteronormative institutions such as marriage, as well as patriarchal structures in general, by exaggeration (Ibid.: 106). As Krauß also points out, the intention of the filmmakers to broach the issue of homosexuality and insert it into mainstream popular culture, as well as to open up the film for queer readings, became even more apparent in the marketing of the film with the male co-stars alluding to the homosexual subtext in various dance performances and promotion gigs (Ibid.: 105). The intentions of the director are relevant in this context. Through these transgressional elements in KHNH, the patriarchal laws with which the gaze as phallic gaze is ultimately connected are at least partly subverted. Similarly as in DDLJ, we can find transgressions in KHNH which do not offer an explicit criticism of the patriarchal order, but which question the norms and insert alternatives into an otherwise rigidly patriarchal discourse represented in the films.

According to the general tendency of the 90s Hindi family films, none of the samples display any open rebellion against patriarchal authority but they certainly all present criticism of it. Very often it is voiced not by the young hero and heroine, but by the older generation of women. For example, in DDLJ Simran's mother disparages the repression of women in patriarchal society and later prompts the young lovers to run away. In KHNH Aman pushes Naina's mother to stand up against her mother-in-law, who in this case more or less represents the patriarchal order. Most explicit is the critique of the patriarch in K3G, which also contains a challenge to the hierarchical inequality in the Hindu religion. In contrast to the song and dance number "Kabhi Khushi Kabhie Gham" in the beginning of the film, the underlying idea of worship is deconstructed by the challenge to the patriarch's authority in the end. His wife states: "You are not god, you are just a husband; a husband who has made a mistake" (K3G 2001, 3:14:00).

Thus, the hierarchical gender relations as well as the concept of worship are negotiated in the film. This has implications for *darshan* and the gaze in general, especially as the film prominently features the gaze of the patriarch.

When Yash Raichand enters the first song and dance sequence of the film "Kabhi Khushi Kabhi Gham", his appearance in many ways resembles a setting evoking *darshan* as Vasudevan describes it in older films (2000b: 139f). As the patriarch he is worshipped similar to the deities by his wife, as has been described in detail before. However, his gaze can also represent the male erotic gaze. Especially, in the song "Say Shava Shava" we can observe his male erotic gaze on Naina, whom he intends to marry to his son. Although he dedicates the song to his son Rahul and Naina, from the beginning the song, which is highly sexually-connoted as the reactions of the diegetic audience show and which is underlined through the attractive female background dancers, he directs his words to her. Interestingly, a shot of him positioned frontally and pointing directly into the camera is followed by a counter shot of Naina with her father. Then the stage is shown again, but in the foreground the blurred image of the young girl's dancing body from hip to neck remains in the frame. The patriarch's gaze could be seen as representing the overarching phallic gaze here. In the course of the story he actually arranges the marriage of his son, who elopes with his beloved Anjali. Thus, the male erotic gaze is shown here as more than just portraying mere desire, but also as representing the patriarchal power structure and maintaining boundaries of class as well as caste.

Again the young hero does not overtly rebel against the patriarchal law. He ends up marrying the woman he loves because her father dies and leaves behind Anjali and her younger sister quite unprotected. Subsequently, Rahul's father not only banishes him from the family, but states that this act showed that Rahul was not his son. As the male protagonist is adopted, the scene shows his vulnerability in the patriarchal order. Only after long years of separation from his family does Rahul finally utter an emotional reproach, telling his wife that his parents have no right to hurt him so much. Shortly after, the patriarch himself confesses to his son that he needs his love. The melodramatic mode partially hides the critique here as not only the women (Anjali, Nandini) suffer due to the patriarchal law, but also the men (Rahul, Rohan and even Yash). Nevertheless, in all the films the blessings of the patriarchal authority are of immense importance. Even in KANK, which differs greatly from the 90s family film but still moves in the same moral universe, Maya's father-in-law, who has also raised her, tells her on his death bed:

> I am a father. I can't punish … I can only advise … Leave Rishi! You don't love him. By being with him like this you are keeping him away from his true love. And yourself too … These incomplete relationships will bring happiness to no one. [Maya: Dad!] It's not your fault, Maya. Love and death, both come uninvited. No one has any control over them (KANK 2006, 02:31:00).

However, the challenge Dev as the adulterer poses to the patriarch has already been made evident in a preceding scene. An intense exchange of gazes takes place when the two couples, Sam and Dev's mother meet for dinner. Seated at the ends of the table, Sam stares extensively at Dev, who had been joking before about having an affair with Maya, which is actually true. As her lover, he is a threat to the patriarchal law, as he puts into question the possessive claim on the woman by her husband and her father-in-law. The confrontation is reinforced here, as Amitabh Bachchan and Shah Rukh Khan as stars can be seen as rivals in some regards, since the one represents the older generation, the other the younger.

In general, the lack displayed by the male characters has a profound effect on the gaze. Taking a term by Silverman, we could speak of "dephallicized men" (1994: 284), although they might not be "stripped off masculinity" completely. Rather, they hold subject positions which turn out to be vulnerable in the patriarchal society. For example, Aman cannot fulfill the role of a husband because he is fatally ill. According to the predominating gender roles it is essential to Naina's happiness to be married and provided for. The most extreme example of lack can be found in KANK, where both main characters are marked by it. Maya cannot have children, which clearly hinders her from living up to expectations of womanhood in patriarchal society. Dev, on the other hand, used to be a professional soccer player but is crippled and, therefore, filled with bitterness. Furthermore, his wife Rhea is a highly successful business woman, which poses a grave problem to their relationship, as he feels inferior due to not being able to fulfil the predominating masculine role in patriarchal society as head of the family and breadwinner. When Dev and Maya meet again years after their first meeting, he says: "[Y]our life is empty … incomplete … It shows in your eyes … just like in mine". It becomes clear that the effect of lack in male characters enables identification with the repressed woman in patriarchal society. The gaze of the male characters is thus differentiated from the phallic gaze, which determines the subject as lacking (cf. Ibid.: 275).

Due to the usual compliance of the camera with this patriarchal, overarching gaze, feminist film theory has gone as far as to decribe cameras "as weapons of phallic power" (Sturken/Cartwright 2001: 78). In contrast, the films analysed here display many characteristics deviating from this, especially in the context of eroticized *darshan*. As pointed out by Flitterman-Lewis, a gaze that makes it possible to 'desire differently' is also empowered by a certain subjectivity of the director. She mentions the "desiring position" of the director as a key element in authorship, which is generally not seen here as an entirely conscious act (2000: 18). Of course the idea that certain filmmakers use specific forms of the gaze in their films is nothing new. Laura Mulvey takes Sternberg's staging of the female figure and in particular Marlene Dietrich producing "the ultimate fetish"([1975] 2009: 23) as an example. The desiring position of a director becomes most clear in Mishra's description of Raj Kapoor as "auteur as voyeur" (2002: 98): "there is something illicit, almost pornographic, in his use of the camera as voyeur"(Ibid.: 99). In his collaboration with Nargis as lead actress in a series of films, many of the characteristics of the male erotic gaze outlined by Mulvey can be identified and the female body is objectified and fetishized. The auteur's male desire as driving principle of the staging of Nargis as actress is reinforced here by the real-life relationship between the two at the time, which is reenacted in the film. Consequently, the spectator participates in this relationship by identifying with Kapoor's gaze on the female body (Ibid.: 110).

In opposition to this, Karan Johar is an interesting example of how a director can encourage a gaze that makes it possible to desire differently. The subjectivity that enables this might partly derive from Johar's own deviant position in terms of masculine gender roles. His performances in media as well as social contexts have often led to assumptions about his sexual orientation. Independent of his assumed homosexuality, he clearly seeks alternative forms of representation in his films. In terms of the gaze he employs devices which enable non-normative points of view and deconstruct the implicit male erotic gaze on the female body. As mentioned before, a crucial marker of his films is the exuberant staging of the male characters. Especially Shah Rukh Khan is staged by the director in ways that solicit the spectator's gaze and in this case the desire is not defined either as male or female. Furthermore, in some films an explicit invitation to queer readings of the texts amplifies the diversity of potential spectator positions. Along with this deconstruction of conventional forms of representation comes the questioning of the patriarchal order and its norms, which also results in the establishment of female subject positions. Not only do the filmic texts show alternative forms to represent female desire, but they also enable a desiring position of female spectatorship. In conclusion, the desire that the gaze here signifies is beyond heteronormative patriarchal discourses, mostly due to the director's sensitivity towards and reflection on the various repressive sides of patriarchy.

Conclusion

The negotiations of the gaze in the film corpus offer great insights into recent processes of hybridization in Hindi cinema. In the analysis it has become clear that the forms of representations and scopic relations are not a mere mixture of existing cultural forms, but rather constitute 'a new gaze'. The hybridization processes are located in what Homi Bhabha calls the third space: cultural symbols are renegotiated, new meanings are ascribed to them and thus they are reinterpreted (Bhabha 1994: 36). Generally, Karan Johar's films are characterized by startling contrasts between conservative and innovative forms of representation as well as Hollywood and Hindi cinema conventions. For example, the strict adherence to the kissing prohibition is contrasted with scenes displaying deep intimacy, most explicitly in KANK. Interestingly, the analysis of 'the new gaze' in the films reveals tendencies of destabilizing the male and objectifying erotic gaze as described by Laura Mulvey. Indeed, some forms of representation partly respond to the demands of feminists for alternatives, or as Mulvey calls it, "a new language of desire" (2009 [1975]: 16). In feminism such tendencies have typically been looked for in art house films. Surprisingly, we encounter them here in mainstream blockbuster films by Johar. Their success is probably due to the combination of alternative forms within a narrative dominated by a conservative, patriarchal discourse.

With an emphasis on these destabilizing techniques, this last part of the book seeks to point out the potential the 'new gaze' has to negotiate inherent power structures of scopic relations in Western as well as Indian culture. Let us first sum up the most important conclusions of the analysis, especially in regards to the devices deployed in the films. In the first chapter, frontality and iconicity are identified as key characteristics of representations of *darshan*. The references to darshanic gazing in religious contexts are discussed briefly in order to show how its markers are transferred to the realm of love. It becomes clear that devices such as shot/counter shot and close-ups of frontal gazes are commonly applied to evoke darshanic gazing. Furthermore, the mise-en-scène and framing contribute strongly to darshanic settings. For example, when Anjali and Rahul meet again in KKHH, the female character is identified with the position of the deity, since in the series of shot/counter shots she is staged frontally, directly in front of the deity's image for which she has just been performing a *puja*. In Johar's later film

KHNH, the male character Aman is referred to as an angel, which is reinforced by techniques such as low angle shots and jump cuts. The resulting iconic images of an often static stature can be found in other films, too, employing the same devices. Consequently, the iconic mode plays a fundamental role in evoking darshanic gazing. This is of great significance, particularly in connection with female characters on display, this is of great significance as the iconicity creates a certain distance, thereby resisting objectification.

In general, darshanic unification involving eroticism is established in the song and dance sequences of the samples by various forms of representation. The film corpus shows intense exchanges of glances marked by "prolonged close-up shots of the beloved's intense frontal gaze" (Taylor 2003: 313), often followed by physical contact. Thus, the relation between seeing and touching as incorporated in the concept of *darshan* is established. Significantly, the representation of visual exchanges employing shot/counter shot series demonstrates the necessity of the reciprocity of the gaze and, consequently, of mutual desire. The act of gazing back in this context often emerges as the right of the female character to choose a partner to whom she feels attracted to. Moreover, the fundamental basis of darshanic unification as the desire to look at and be looked at is reflected upon and negotiated in the context of gender relations. The most striking example is a scene in KANK showing the female character dancing playfully in front of a mirror. In this case the display of the body emphasizes the pleasure she experiences in being looked at and, in the context of the representations of desire, draws on the transformative aspect of *darshan* marked by self-recognition.

Inevitably, these exchanges of glances, which we have also referred to as visual foreplay, result in the physical union of the characters. As there is no kissing in the films, this mostly occurs in the form of passionate embraces. Certain devices are predominant in these representations of unification. For example, the frontal staging of the couple with one of the lovers appearing behind the other I refer to as *Radha&Krishna shot*. Another very common technique is the circling camera, which is frequently used after profile shots of the couple in embrace have been shown. In both cases the intimate moment between the characters is set in the iconic mode, which creates a distance that does not allow the spectator to identify with a voyeurist position. The circling camera movement in particular invites the spectator to participate in the sphere of the couple. This device is also frequently used in the spectacle of the male star in the film corpus marking his to-be-looked-at-ness. Similarly, the staging of the couple here invites the spectator's gaze, favouring a spectatorship connected to darshanic identification. The circling camera also appears in combination with other devices such as the editing techniques in the song and dance sequence "Tumhi Dekho Naa" in KANK. Camera movement and jump cuts are combined here with dissolves that reinforce the signfiying of unification.

The analysis of the second chapter focuses on staged performances, which are conventionally closest to the erotic spectacle of the female body described by Mulvey. Similarly to other conventional forms that solicit the male erotic gaze and put the female body on display, such as the wet sari scene, staged performances of this kind are rare in the film corpus. Most of them stage minor female characters such as Tina in KKHH or Pooja in K3G. Furthermore, many of the staged performances in the samples play with codes and conventions associated with *darshan*. For example, single characters or the couple are put on display, recalling deities' images in processions. Iconicity plays a decisive role in evoking this effect. The majority of the song and dance sequences in question put the male character in the foreground, as he is shown, for example, wooing the female character. These scenes are marked by frontality and address the spectator in direct relay. Thus, this display of the male star results in a spectacle that is marked by hybrid forms of the gaze.

Even in song and dance sequences representing the interiority of characters, the spectacle of the male star emerges. One device used frequently in this context is a frontal, direct address without preceding establishing shots. The ambiguity of the situation that is usually resolved shortly after by a counter shot showing the female character amplifies the effect of frontality. In staged performances centered on the male protagonist we also find many such scenes. Furthermore, iconic images of the male star in these sequences diminish the role the diegetic audience usually plays. For example, in KHNH's song and dance "Pretty Woman", close-up shots of Shah Rukh Khan in front of a US American flag are cut rapidly into the scenes. In combination with the frequent direct relay and highly stylized performances, this results in the establishment of a scopic relation between star and spectator that can also be seen in the context of *darshan*. The self-awareness of the spectacle of the male star enables a spectatorship based on the desire to be gazed back on by the object on the screen.

All these devices and techniques are employed frequently in the song and dance sequences analysed in the third chapter. Here, the spectacle of the male star clearly dominates the sequences. In "Kal Ho Naa Ho" the direct interaction of Shah Rukh Khan with the camera reaches a climax with the help of camera movement, direct relay and stylized acting. Moreover, the song and dance "Mitwa" offers an abundance of circling camera movements as well as jump cuts reinforcing their effect. The setting of an empty football stadium even alludes to the focus of attention on the male body by displaying thousands and thousands of empty seats in the background. The fractured, but almost 360 degree view of the star as object of the gaze, which signifies the multiplicity of spectatorship, tears down all reliance on an enclosed space typical of the realist mode. Other devices, such as low angle shots of the stylized performance of Shah Rukh Khan in the stadium as well as admidst New York's skyscrapers, also contribute to the establishment of an object position of the star that recalls a deity giving *darshan*.

The spectacle thus renders a spectatorship based on voyeurism impossible. This is of particular relevance as the spectacle still centers around desire, which is conventionally encoded by the display of the object.

The focus of attention in these scenes is on the desire of the male protagonist for the heroine, which is predominantly signified by the gaze. Generally, the gaze is modified strongly by the masculinity ascribed to the male characters. In all of the films of the corpus they display lack in the patriarchal order, which shall be discussed in more detail below. Interestingly, the spectacle also does not display male strength or action, but emotionality. In fact, the gaze itself and, thus, desire are on display, which offers an interesting perspective on the erotic. While desire still is at the core of the spectacle, the erotic gaze is redirected from the object of the act of gazing as such. In fact, scopophilia can be redefined in this context, since the pleasure of the spectacle lies in gazing at the holder of the gaze. This has also been referred to in the analysis as 'observing the observer' and, indeed, there is evidence that also in other film texts this phenomenon and its effects can also be found in other film texts, in Hindi cinema and beyond. Furthermore, the spectacle of male emotionality and desire is also transferred to the representation of the female figure in "Mitwa". As the desiring position presupposes subjectivity, female desire can be represented in the spectacle. Thus, it resists the display of the female body as erotic spectacle. Here, the pleasure of gazing at the object on screen is created by a complex mixture of codes of erotic and darshanic gazing.

Moreover, it becomes clear that the hybridized forms of the gaze correspond with a renegotiation of the relationship between narrative space and song and dance. The examples analysed in the last chapter are sequences that operate on different levels: the actual plot, the imagination of characters and an extra-narrative performance. Furthermore, elements of song and dance find their way into the narrative space mostly marked by music such as in the pavilion scene of KKHH or the ballet in KANK. This kind of integration also includes the scopic regimes predominating in song and dance sequences. Thus, erotic encounters such as the one between Anjali and Rahul in the pavilion evade representations that merely draw on the realist mode and put the spectator in the position of the voyeur. Similarly, in KANK, one scene refers to a song and dance sequence earlier in the film to evoke darshanic notions of unification. In this case it is not achieved by referring to the song, as in KKHH, but to the editing technique. As the dissolves and double-exposures of the frame are distinct markers of the representation of Maya and Dev's love relationship, it is used again shortly before the sequence depicting their sexual unification starts. The re-evoking of the song and dance settings in the narrative space can be seen as a strategy to activate representations of the erotic that do not rely on voyeurism.

The most fascinating example in this context is the song and dance sequence "Where's The Party Tonight". It shows an unusually explicit erotic scene in a film corpus that does not include any kissing at all. Although the forms of representation used in this scene strongly draw on the realist mode maintaining a private, intimate space of the couple, the voyeuristic gaze is destabilized by the interruption of recurring cuts to a staged performance. There is a stark contrast between the narrative turning point of the adulterous act and the spectacle displaying its conventional pleasures. On the one hand, the 'visual foreplay' between Dev and Maya strictly adheres to the rules of continuity editing through the insertion of many establishing shots and an unmistakable series of shot/counter shots. On the other hand, in the scenes showing Rhea and Rishi, frontal, direct address is frequently used to mark the public space and the spectacle's invitation of the gaze. Consequently, it is necessary for the spectator to switch between two entirely different scopic regimes, which can result in self-awareness and reflection on the act of gazing. The embedding of the sex scene in a staged performance results in the disruption and destabilization of the voyeuristic gaze. Thus, the erotic is not constrained to the private, enclosed space.

This contrast also sheds light on the contrast between narrative space and song and dance. While the plot of the samples usually strongly adheres to the patriarchal order and norms, song and dance sequences offer space for the renegotiation of the gender relations. As the analysis shows, the gaze as signifier plays a crucial role in representing female desire and subjectivity. Johar's oeuvre shows a gradual reconciliation of the patriarchal discourse in the narrative and the potentially liberating one in song and dance. The gaze and related scopic regimes are highly significant in this process. Since KANK is probably the film that overall adheres most to Western cinematic style, it is interesting to see that the interplay and mixing of codes in the film go far beyond the borders of narrative space and song and dance. Moreover, the gaze is most frequently deployed in KANK out of all films of the corpus, which speaks for the significance of the gaze in the hybridization processes as well as signifier of 'different desire'. To understand this better we have to consider the philosophical underpinnings of the erotic as well as darshanic gaze.

As we have already seen, *darshan* can be viewed as a mode of perception as well as a critique of perception, as Sanzaro points out (2007: 1). Thus, it goes far beyond religious meanings and their renegotiations of the erotic in the filmic context. In fact, it adresses deeply-rooted philosophical concepts of the self and other, opening up new perspectives on desire. In the filmic context this allows a reconsideration of what pleasure in seeing is – or what scopophilia can mean. This reflection on the gaze affects all three levels that have been focused on in the analysis. The representation of desire of characters in the film texts offers a renegotiation of gender roles, which becomes evident when looking at female subject positions and deviant masculinity on display. Consequently, this renegotiation affects the star image and has had a particular influence on Shah Rukh Khan's onscreen persona. Furthermore, the reconsideration of scopophilia can be traced on the level of spectatorship. Spectatorship is of particular interest to me, because the mixing of codes is very prominent in this regard. Alternative forms of spectatorship in the samples have had a powerful effect on me as a recipient socialized in Western cinema culture. Strategies such as the continuous switching between different sopic regimes within the same song and dance sequence not only draw attention to the moment of hybridization, but also serve as mediating bridge. *Darshan* reinforces the exhibitionist character marked by spectacle in Hindi cinema, but the gaze in the film corpus goes beyond that: it can raise self-awareness in the spectator and stimulate a critical reflection on the gaze.

Furthermore, voyeurism has been identified as a crucial component of the erotic gaze as well as the realist mode, which is renegotiated through the mixing of codes. The representation of the couple and intimacy is closely related to this, as we have seen in the analysis. For example, the kiss can be seen as a symbol of the autonomy of the couple, because it is intimate and erotic (cf. Dwyer 2000). In the film corpus, although there is no kissing, the intimacies in the song and dance sequences and partly in the narrative refer exactly to this notion of the erotic. Elements and symbols conventionally associated with other forms of eroticism, such as the wet sari or rain scenes, are deployed, evoking contracted voyeurism in their public, exhibitionist display, are deployed. Moreover, such scenes feature scopic relations that invite the voyeuristic gaze so typical of the private, hermetically sealed world evoked by the realist mode. But the context they are set in partly inhibits their usual voyeuristic effect. The autonomous space for the couple is created within otherwise restrictive patriarchal surroundings, but at the same time is not confined entirely to the private. This stands in opposition to Prasad's approach, which states that the couple is either subjected to the private that is linked either to the claims of authority of the state or to the patriarchal institution of the traditional family. While the autonomous space of the couple guaranteed by the state conveys realist voyeurism, the latter is associated with *darshan* and communal viewing (Prasad 1998: 96f). However, it is interesting to note that Prasad refers to the "shamefaced" voyeurism as connected to the "subject's solitude" in capitalist society (Ibid.: 103). In the analysis, various strategies to avoid voyeurism by making the spectator aware of his/her own gaze have been identified, which is often achieved by activating darshanic notions of the gaze. Such strategies do not comply with the ones Prasad describes and which he ascribes to the patriarchal family authority. Rather, *darshan* as lover's union emerges as spectacle dissolving the boundaries of private and public. Direct relay, for example, is used in the song and dance sequences to transform spectatorship and create a more "expansive communitas" (Vasudevan 2000b: 152), but at the same time the space of the couple is maintained. Consequently, the spectator is involved in the aura of the couple without voyeuristically gazing into a private world. This is highly relevant in the context of Western society as well as consumer culture in general, which shall be discussed in detail below.

When analysing this representation of the couple and their intimacy it is necessary to differentiate between the overarching patriarchal or the phallic gaze and the gaze/look of the male character. As Silverman points out, the gaze signifies what "constitutes the subject as lacking within the field of vision" (Silverman 1994: 275). As we have seen in the last chapter, the fact that men are subjected to that gaze, too, is emphasized by the male lead characters, displaying lack. Moreover, these characters are set apart from the patriarch's gaze as in KANK or K3G. The patriarch's gaze is criticized, not overtly but through subtle words and the capitulation of the patriarch in the narrative ending. In Silverman's terms, what is achieved here is that the male look does not "transfer its own lack to the female subject" nor does it "[attempt] to pass itself off as the gaze" (1994: 286). This renounces the controlling power ascribed to the phallic gaze. Consequently, the overarching gaze always threatening to catch the voyeur loses this power and shame, since the effective means of control is detached from the representation of the intimate. Another effect of this is a different perspective on male and female desire as well as the construction of the object.

As Silverman states "[t]he problem, in other words, is not that men direct desire toward women in Hollywood films but that male desire is so consistently and systematically imbricated with projection and control" (Ibid.). In contrast, the film corpus displays examples of how the erotic gaze can be liberated from the voyeuristic and controlling power imposed on the object, if space is created for the object to gaze back in the sense of *darshan*. Apart from the negotiations of masculinity and lack, the representation of female desire contributes to a gaze as signifier of desire beyond dominance. An essential part of *darshan* as lover's union, which also dissipates the inherent hierarchy between devotee and deity, is the establishment of female subject positions. The established link between "intimacy, liberation and perception" (Sanzaro 2007: 5) in *darshan*, which we can find on the level of filmic representations of love, is the fundamental basis for the subject positions. The process of self-recognition fundamental to darshanic union is not only constituted by the act of looking or by a female gaze that signifies desire, but also in being looked at, being desired and seeing oneself as the object in the other's eyes. For the transformation of the self it is essential to see oneself (Babb 1981: 399). This is reinforced by the extensive display of the male body as object of the gaze, in many cases in the iconic mode. Moreover, the spectacle of man as beholder can be seen as displaying male desire as seen through the eyes of the other. Sanzaro states that *darshan* reveals "the truth that the object is an object only in so far as it is framed and ritualized" (2007: 17). Once more we encounter the reflectivity *darshan* entails. In this context darshanic representations of the gaze renounce fixed positions of subject and object as well as an ascription of female or male to these positions. The relativity of the object status is most visible in scopic constellations such as 'observing the observer'.

The element of self-recognition in *darshan* is thus renegotiated in the context of modern Western concepts of love, which put knowing the self in the foreground (cf. Dwyer 2000: 9). Furthermore, director and screenwriter Karan Johar puts forward the basic idea of a love relationship which is constituted by the mutual desire of the partners. The filmic texts speak for the necessity of female desire and agency for a relationship fulfilling personal happiness. But the negotiations of gender concepts through filmic representations go even further. As the norms in patriarchal society are deconstructed, the filmic texts also invite queer readings. This becomes not only obvious in subtexts as in KHNH, but also in the structure of spectacle and the diversity of potential spectator positions it invites. The use of frontal, direct address with indefinite addressee is one way of achieving this effect, since the gaze on the male or female body is not gendered. As mentioned before, this is an indicator of Johar's own alternative desiring position, which establishes the possibility of desiring differently (cf. Flitterman-Lewis 2000). Furthermore, these deviations from the norm are juxtaposed with elements complying so clearly with the predominating patriarchal discourse. Thus, topics like homosexuality, representations of female desire or queer spectator positions are not pushed asides as niche agendas as in art house cinema. Rather, they are integrated into mainstream popular cinema.

Another issue which arises in the context of self-recognition and seeing oneself as object is that of identification. The connection between being seen as object and the constitution of the subject position recalls of one of the basic assumptions of psychoanalysis. Drawing on Lacan, this means that only when the subject realizes itself as object in the mirror phase, is the self constituted. However, the subject/object relationship of Western philosophy contradicts that of *darshan* in several ways. As mentioned previously, Hinduism trancends the dualistic nature of Western discourse. This means that unification and identification in *darshan* are also based on a totally different conception of self and other. Sanzaro puts it as follows: "To use Western philosophical concepts (…) subject becomes object and object becomes subject" and "[t]here is no distinction between the two, each is subsumed into the other – a lack of duality characterizing the highest form of Hindu religious consciousness" (2007: 6). Consequently, in terms of cinema and spectatorship, we also have to revisit the dichotomy between scopophilia and identification described by Mulvey ([1975] 2009: 19).

In psychoanalytic theory scopophilia as the pleasure of looking at something demands an object (the Other), while identification, on the other hand, is based on the refusal of difference. As Friedberg states, identification "refuses and recuperates the separation between self and other" (1990: 36). In terms of spectatorship this means it leaves the spectator with the choice between denying one's identity or constructing an identity opposing the other: "This leaves us, as viewing subjects, caught in the bind between specular cannibalism and scopic bulimia, between the introjection of an imposed other and the rejection of what the eye has taken in"(Ibid.: 45). In contrast, *darshan* does not deny difference as it refuses the dichotomy of self and other. It rather invites one to understand and familiarize oneself with the Other (cf. Chatterjee 2005: 103), which does not comply either with scopophilia or identification in Mulvey's sense. In fact, *darshan* in the filmic contexts can turn the gaze back onto the spectator him/herself, as in the experience of the devotee in union with the deity (cf. Sanzaro 2007: 6). This results in reflection on the act of gazing itself as described above. When the object on the screen gazes back, the spectator may gain a different perspective on or a new vision of him/herself. This means that identification is not determined by the object but by the subject/the spectator. Consequently, pleasure in seeing cannot only be created by the act of gazing at the object on the screen, but also by the feeling of identification evoked by representations of and scopic relations alluding to darshanic union.

The conceptions of self and other predominating in Western thought can, consequently, be deconstructed with *darshan* as a critique of perception. Moreover, it offers alternatives to the established systems of representation, which have also been much sought after in feminism. In this conceptual framework the binaries can be dissolved, as it is not "founded on the dialectic logic of opposition" (De Lauretis 2001: 108). Interestingly, feminist film theorist De Lauretis sees the necessity of conceptually bridging "perception and signification", which "suggests a complex interaction and mutual implication rather than opposition, between the spheres of subjectivity and sociality" (Ibid.). As we have seen in the analysis, *darshan* establishes a form of spectatorship that moves between subjectivity and sociality. In this context, Coorlawala argues that a model of the gaze which is based on *darshan* and *rasa* evokes "reciprocal activity involving mutual recognition" (1996: 26). This perspective on cinema does not present the screen as signified by absence. On the contrary, through the self-awareness of the spectator, his/her own presence becomes the decisive factor. Can it thus be possible that the pleasure evoked by *darshan* lies in feeling oneself to be rejoicing in spectacle?

What is clear is that the concept of the screen does not comply with the split subject and the mirror concept described in psychoanalytic theory. It is important to see the darshanic gaze and identification beyond the boundaries of the imaginary and symbolic order. By no means shall another dichotomy be introduced that presents *darshan* as located in the space of the imaginary identifying it with song and dance, in contrast to the symbolic in the narrative space. Neither is difference rejected nor defined by lack. By taking in the other in darshanic union, the other/'Other' is not devoured, but an instance of being both is created: separate and one. Spectatorship is, thus, neither cannibalistic nor bulimic as suggested by Friedberg, but is continually assuring the self in its autonomous existence as well as in the communitas of the cinema. This is even more significant in the context of the contemporary global consumer culture as well as in capitalist society. Consumerism produces an endless circle of desires and, thus, of lack (what we do not have and, therefore, need), leaving the subject with a constant longing to 'have' something and be someone else. In addition, globalization processes such as the excess of mass media offer innumerable identity choices, causing fractures and disjunctions, but also enabling alternative and hybrid cultural forms.

In this context the effect of darshanic union of encompassing self and other along with subject and object is extremely appealing. The desire of receiving *darshan* is not bound by the notion of having something or being someone else. Consequently, lack is not inherent to identification. Moreover, this involves an experience of wholeness that can potentially bridge the fractures and disjunctions of identity encountered in daily life in consumer culture. This notion of wholeness, however, is not marked by an oceanic feeling of being one with the Other often associated with the imaginary as constructed in psychoanalytic theory. While the latter describes the dissolution of the self, in *darshan* the self is present as object as well as subject. This is probably one of the major reasons for the success of Johar's films, since they display both the needs of contemporary global consumer culture and the contrasting desires which can overcome the predominating notion of 'ego' in exactly this same kind of culture.

Furthermore, the star image of Shah Rukh Khan fits perfectly into these disparate desires. As has been pointed out previously, it signifies the bridging of contradictions and differences in multiple ways. Although Shah Rukh Khan has been a leading representative of capitalist consumer society, presenting brands and leisure activities in the filmic texts accordingly, he has managed at the same time to address the void produced by the feeling of lack. Consequently, we might say he addresses today's collective needs and desires, representing fragmentation and wholeness at the same time (Dudrah/Desai 2008: 87). In the context of Western audiences he could also be seen as bridging the split imposed on the subject by the hegemonic concept of binaries. As with the 'surrender' to the divine resulting in bliss (Babb 1981: 195) the spectator can release the ego's strenuous desires by partaking in the darshanic spectacle Shah Rukh Khan offers on screen. As *darshan* is primarily renegotiated in the realms of love and eroticism, these emerge as the spaces to give in and let go. At the same time the desire for the star is fuelled by presenting the actor more than ever as a commodity.

In conclusion, can we speak of a new form of scopophilia as the gaze is negotiated in the context of *darshan*? Is it possible to "acknowledge the ways in which reciprocal relationships of looking can be sources of pleasure" (Sturken/Cartwright 2001: 76)? It is clear that the analysis has not touched enough on the question of how far *darshan* in the filmic context can deconstruct the hierarchical inequality rooted in Hinduism, nor of how far the over-presence of the male star contributes to discriminating, gendered representations. However, the approach to *darshan* can contribute to a concept of the gaze which discards the objectifying effect of erotic gazing in Western culture.

Finally, rejecting this objectifying effect of the erotic gaze opens up the possibility for new interpretations of the gaze; I shall conclude my arguments by presenting on more concpetion of the erotic, darshanic gaze. Irigaray states:

> More than the other senses, the eye objectifies and masters. It sets at a distance, maintains the distance. In our culture, the predominance of the look over smell, taste, touch, hearing has brought an impoverishment of bodily relations. It has contributed to disembodying sexuality. The moment the look dominates, the body loses in materiality (Irigaray in Heath 1992: 47).

In contrast to this Western way of 'looking at something/someone', *darshan* is based on a very different conception: "Not only is seeing a form of 'touching', it is a form of knowing" (Eck 1985: 9). This conception is especially evident in the representation of love and intimacy in the samples. KANK in particular establishes the meaning of the gaze: first in the signification of desire, second in darshanic union and at last in the context of physical, sexual union. All three require self-recognition in terms of knowing one's own desires as well as desirability. Similar to *darshan* in the religious context, sexual union is represented in the film as ideal merging. For this ideal merging to occur, the preceding construction of darshanic union in the representation of the couple is of essential importance. Only then can orgasm, the ultimate symbiosis of human beings, mean both: being oneself and being one with the other.

List of Figures

References

Babb, Lawrence A.

1981 "Glancing: Visual Interaction in Hinduism". *Journal of Anthropological Research* Vol. 37 No. 4, pp. 387–401.

Barnard, Malcolm

2001 *Approaches to Understanding Visual Culture.* Hampshire: Palgrave.

Bhabha, Homi

1994 *The Location of Culture.* London: Routledge.

Bordwell, David

1996a "Contemporary Film Studies and the Vicissitudes of Grand Theory". In: David Bordwell and Noel Carroll (Eds): *Post-Theory: Reconstructing Film Studies,* p. 3–36. Madison: University of Wisconsin Press.

1996b "Convention, Construction and Cinematic Vision". In: David Bordwell and Noel Carroll (Eds): *Post-Theory: Reconstructing Film Studies,* p. 87–107. Madison: University of Wisconsin Press.

Bordwell, David and Kristin Thompson

2001 *Film Art: An Introduction.* New York: McGraw-Hill.

Buscombe, Edward and Christine Gledhill, Alan Lovell, Christopher Williams

1992 "Psychoanalysis and Film". In: John Caughie and Annette Kuhn (Eds): *The Sexual Subject:* A Screen Reader in Sexuality, p. 35–46. London: Routledge.

Chakravarty, Sumita

2008 "The national-heroic image: masculinity and masquerade". In: Jigna Desai and Rajinder Kumar Dudrah (Eds): *The Bollywood Reader,* p. 84–94. Maidenhead: Open University Press.

Chatterjee, Gayatri

2005 "Icons and Events: Reinventing Visual Construction in Cinema in India". In: Raminder Kaur and Ajay J. Sinha (Eds.): *Bollyworld: Popular Indian Cinema through a Transnational Lens,* p. 90–117. New Delhi: Sage.

Coorlawala, Uttara A.

1996 "Darshan and Abhinaya: An Alternative to the Male Gaze". *Dance Research Journal* Vol. 28 No. 1, pp. 19–27.

Coward, Rosalind

2001 "The Look". In: Julia Thomas (Ed.): *Reading Images,* p. 33–39. Hampshire: Palgrave.

Creekmur, Corey K.

2005 "Bombay Boys: Dissolving the Male Child in Popular Hindi Cinema". In: Murray Pomerance and Frances Gateward (Eds.): *Where the boys are: Cinemas of Masculinity and Youth,* p. 350–376. Detroit: Wayne State University Press.

De Lauretis, Teresa

2001 "Imaging". In: Julia Thomas (Ed.): *Reading Images*, p. 102–108. Hampshire: Palgrave.

Derné, Steve

2000 *Movies, Masculinity, and Modernity: an ethnography of men's film-going in India.* Westport: Greenwood.

Desai, Jigna

2008 "'Ever since you've discovered the video, I've had no peace': diasporic spectators talk back to Bollywood Masala". In: Jigna Desai and Rajinder Kumar Dudrah (Eds): *The Bollywood Reader*, p. 229–242. Maidenhead: Open University Press.

Desai, Jigna and Rajinder Kumar Dudrah (Eds)

2008 *The Bollywood Reader.* Maidenhead: Open University Press.

Deshpande, Sudhanva

2005 "The Consumable Hero of Globalised India". In: Raminder Kaur and Ajay J. Sinha (Eds.): *Bollyworld: Popular Indian Cinema through a Transnational Lens*, p. 186–206. New Delhi: Sage.

Dudrah, Rajinder Kumar

2006 *Bollywood: Sociology goes to the movies.* New Delhi: Sage.

2008 "Queer as Desis: secret politics of gender and sexuality in Bollywood films in diasporic urban ethnoscapes". In: Jigna Desai and Rajinder Kumar Dudrah (Eds): *The Bollywood Reader*, p. 21–31. Maidenhead: Open University Press.

2010 *Unthinking SRK and Global Bollywood: from Film Studies to Rasa Theory to New Media Assemblages.* Paper at the "Shah Rukh and Global Bollywood" Conference , Universität Wien, 30.9 – 2.10.2010

Dwyer, Rachel

2000 *All you want is money, all you need is love: sexuality and romance in modern India.* London: Cassell.

2006a "Kiss or tell? Declaring love in Hindi films". In: Francesca Orsini (Ed.): *Love in South Asia: A Cultural History*, p. 1–39. New York: Cambridge University Press.

2006b *Filming the Gods: Religion and Indian Cinema.* Abingdon: Oxon.

2009 "Ich mag es, wenn du zornig wirst: Amitabh Bachchan als nationaler Held in Krisenzeiten". In: Claus Tieber (Ed.): *Fokus Bollywood: Das indische Kino in wissenschaftlichen Diskursen*, pp. 99–116. Wien: Lit.

Dwyer, Rachel and Divia Patel

2002 *Cinema India: The visual culture of Hindi film.* London: Reaktion Books.

Dyer, Richard

1998 [1979] Stars. *London: British Film Institute.*

Eck, Diana L.

1985 *Darsan:Seeing the Divine Image in India.* Chambersburg: Anima Books.

Flitterman-Lewis, Sandy

2000 "To Desire Differently: Feminism and the French Cinema". In: Robert Stam and Toby Miller (Eds): Film and Theory: An Anthology, pp. 16–20. Malden: Blackwell.

Friedberg, Anne

1990 "A Denial of Difference: Theories of Cinematic Identification". In: E. Ann Kaplan (Ed.): *Psychoanalysis and Cinema*, p. 36–45. New York: Routledge.

Fuchs, Bernhard

2009 "Schaufenster Bollywood: Kleidungsdiskurse im Film". In: Claus Tieber (Ed.): *Fokus Bollywood: Das indische Kino in wissenschaftlichen Diskursen*, p. 30–49. Wien: LIT Verlag.

Fuller, Christopher J.

1992 *The Camphor Flame: Popular Hinduism and Society in India*. Princeton: Princeton University Press.

Gaenszle, Martin

2009 "Pop und Poesie: Sprachformen in Bollywood Love Songs". In: Claus Tieber (Ed.): *Fokus Bollywood: Das indische Kino in wissenschaftlichen Diskursen*, p. 50–67. Wien: LIT Verlag.

Gopal, Sangita

2011 *Conjugations: Marriage and Form in New Bollywood Cinema*. Chicago: University of Chicago Press.

Gopal, Sangita and Sujata Moorti (Eds.)

2008 *Global Bollywood: Travels of the Hindi Song and Dance*. Minneapolis: University of Minnesota Press.

Gopal, Sangita and Biswarup Sen

2008 "Inside and Out. Song and Dance in Bollywood Cinema". In: Jigna Desai and Rajinder Kumar Dudrah (Eds): *The Bollywood Reader*, p. 147–157. Maidenhead: Open University Press.

Govil, Nitin

2008 "Bollywood and the frictions of global mobility". In: Jigna Desai and Rajinder Kumar Dudrah (Eds): *The Bollywood Reader*, p. 201–215. Maidenhead: Open University Press.

Govindan, Padma P. And Bisakha Dutta

2008 "'From Villain to Traditional Housewife!' The Politics of Globalization and Women's Sexuality in the 'New' Indian Media". In: Anandam P. Kavoori and Aswin Punathambekar (Eds.): *Global Bollywood*, S. 180–202. New York: New York University Press.

Gunning, Tom

1989 "'Primitive' Cinema: A Frame-up? Or the Trick's on Us". *Cinema Journal*, Vol. 28 No. 2, pp. 3–12.

1990 "The Cinema of Attraction: Early Film, Its Specator and the Avant-Garde". In: Thomas Elsaesser (Ed.): *Early Cinema: Space, Frame, Narrative*, pp. 63–70. London: BFI Publ.

Hall, Stuart

2005]1973] "Encoding/Decoding". In: Meenakshi Gigi Durham and Douglas M. Kellner (Eds.): *Media and Cultural Studies: Keyworks*, pp. 163–173. Oxford: Blackwell.

Heath, Stephen

1992 "Difference". In: John Caughie and Annette Kuhn (Eds): *The Sexual Subject:* A Screen Reader in Sexuality, p. 47–106. London: Routledge.

Herrman-Pfandt, Adelheid

2010 *"And I love Hinduism Also". Shah Rukh Khan: A Muslim Voice for Interreligious Peace in India*. Paper at the "Shah Rukh and Global Bollywood" Conference , Universität Wien, 30.9 – 2.10.2010

Hirzer, Petra und Elke Mader

2011 "Peruanisches Masala. Hybridisierungsprozess in der lateinamerikanischen Bollywood-Fankultur". In: Eva Gugenberger und Kathrin Sartingen (Eds): *Hybridität – Transkulturalität – Kreolisierung: Innovation und Wandel in Kultur, Sprache und Literatur Lateinamerikas,* p. 73–100. Wien: Lit Verlag.

Iriagray, Luce

1985 "The Oppositional Gaze: Black Female Spectators". In: Julia Thomas (Ed.): *Reading Images*, p. 123–138. Hampshire: Palgrave.

hooks, bell

2001 *The sex which is not one*. Ithaca: Cornell University Press.

Kabir, Nasreen Munni

2010 *The Worlds of Shah Rukh Khan*. Paper at the "Shah Rukh and Global Bollywood" Conference , Universität Wien, 30.9 – 2.10.2010

Kakar, Sudhir

1990 *Intimate Relations: Exploring Indian Sexuality.* New Delhi: Penguin.

Kaplan, E. Ann

1990 "Introduction: From Plato's Cave to Freud's Screen". In: E. Ann Kaplan (Ed.):*Psychoanalysis and Cinema*, p. 1–23. New York: Routledge.

Kasbekar, Asha

2001 "Hidden Pleasures: Negotiating the Myth of the Female Ideal in Popular Hindi Cinema". In: Rachel Dwyer and Christopher Pinney (Eds.): *Pleasure and the Nation: The History, Politics and Consumption of Public Culture in India*, p. 286–308. New Delhi: Oxford University Press.

Kaur, Raminder and Ajay J. Sinha

2005 *Bollyworld: Popular Indian Cinema through a Transnational Lens.* New Delhi: Sage.

King, Anna S.

2005 "Introduction". In: Anna S. King and John Brockington (Eds.): *The Intimate Other: Love Divine in Indic Religions,* p. 9–30. Hyderabad: Orient Longman.

Krauß, Florian

2007 *Männerbilder im Bollywood-Film: Konstruktionen von Männlichkeit im Hindi-Kino.* Berlin: Wissenschaftlicher Verlag Berlin.

Larkin, Brian

2008 *Signal and Noise: Meida, Infrastructure, and Urban Culture in Nigeria.* London: Duke University Press.

Mader, Elke and Philipp Budka

2008 *'I cannot stop looking at him ...' Reflexionen zum erotischen Blick im indischen Kino und seinen Fankulturen.* Paper at the 4. Tage der KSA, Universität Wien, 11.4.2008

2009 "Shah Rukh Khan @ Berlinale: Bollywood Fans im Kontext medienanthropologischer Forschung". In: Claus Tieber (Ed.): *Fokus Bollywood: Das indische Kino in wissenschaftlichen Diskursen*, p. 117–133. Wien: LIT Verlag.

2010 *Shah Rukh Khan, Participatory Audiences, and the Internet.* Paper at the "Shah Rukh and Global Bollywood" Conference , Universität Wien, 30.9 – 2.10.2010

Majumder, Sonja

2009 "Hindunationalismus, Identität und Hindi Blockbuster". In: Claus Tieber (Ed.): *Fokus Bollywood: Das indische Kino in wissenschaftlichen Diskursen*, p.145–160. Wien: LIT Verlag.

Metz, Christian

2000 "The Imaginary Signifier". In: Robert Stam and Toby Miller (Eds): Film and Theory: An Anthology, pp. 408–436. Malden: Blackwell.

Mikos, Lothar

2008 *Film- und Fernsehanalyse.* Konstanz: UVK Verlagsgesellschaft.

Mirzoeff, Nicholas

1999 *An introduction to visual culture.* London: Routledge.

Mishra, Vijay

2008 "Towards a theoretical critique of Bombay Cinema". In: Jigna Desai and Rajinder Kumar Dudrah (Eds): *The Bollywood Reader*, p. 32–44. Maidenhead: Open University Press.

Mulvey, Laura

2009 *Visual and other pleasures.* Hampshire: Palgrave Macmillan.

2009 [1975] "Visual Pleasure and Narrative Cinema". In: Laura Mulvey (Ed.): *Visual and other pleasures*, pp. 14–30. Hampshire: Palgrave Macmillan.

Nandy, Ashis

2008 "Introduction: Indian popular cinema as a slum's eye view of politics". In: Jigna Desai and Rajinder Kumar Dudrah (Eds): *The Bollywood Reader*, p. 73–83. Maidenhead: Open University Press.

Neale, Steve

1992 "Masculinity as Spectacle". In: John Caughie and Annette Kuhn (Eds): *The Sexual Subject:* A Screen Reader in Sexuality, p. 277–287. London: Routledge.

Orsini, Francesca

2006 "Introduction". In: Francesca Orsini (Ed.): *Love in South Asia: A Cultural History*, p. 1–39. New York: Cambridge University Press.

Pagel, Gerda

2007 *Jacques Lacan zur Einführung.* Hamburg: Junius.

Pauwels, Heidi R. M.

2008 *The Goddess as Role Model: Sita and Radha in Scripture and on Screen.* New York: Oxford University Press.

Pendakur, Manhjunath

2008 "In the thrones of change. Exhibition, production and distribution". In: Jigna Desai and Rajinder Kumar Dudrah (Eds): *The Bollywood Reader*, p. 57–71. Maidenhead: Open University Press.

Peterson, Mark Allen

2003 *Anthropology & Mass Communication: Media and Myth in the New Millenium.* New York: Berghahn Books.

Prasad, Madhava

1998 *Ideology of the Hindi Film: A Historical Construction.* Delhi: Oxford Univ. Press.

2008 "The economics of ideology: popular film form and mode of production". In: Jigna Desai and Rajinder Kumar Dudrah (Eds): *The Bollywood Reader*, p. 45–56. Maidenhead: Open University Press.

Prince, Stephen

1993 "The Discourse of Pictures: Iconicity and Film Studies". *Film Quaterly,* Vol. 47 No. 1, pp. 16–28.

Rajadhyaksha, Ashish

2000 "Who's Looking? Viewership and Democracy in the Cinema". In: Ravi Vasudevan (Ed.): *Making Meaning in Indian Cinema,* pp. 267–296. New Delhi: Oxford University Press.

2008 "The 'Bollywoodization' of the Indian cinema: cultural nationalism in a global arena". In: Jigna Desai and Rajinder Kumar Dudrah (Eds): *The Bollywood Reader*, p. 190–200. Maidenhead: Open University Press.

Roy, Parama

2008 "Figuring Mother India: the case of Nargis". In: Jigna Desai and Rajinder Kumar Dudrah (Eds): *The Bollywood Reader*, p. 109–121. Maidenhead: Open University Press.

Robbins, Ruth

2000 *Literary Feminisms.* Basingstoke: Macmillan.

Sanzaro, Francis J.

2007 "Darshan as Mode and Critique of Perception: Hinduism's Liberatory Model of Visuality". *Axis Mundi 2007–2008* , p. 1–24.

Seidl, Monika

2006 "Medialising Mr Darcy: Colin Firth as Extra Darcy in Pride and Prejudice 81995)". In: Juergen Kamm (Ed.): *Medialising Britain*, p. 81–97. Passau: Stutz.

Sen, Biswarup

2008 "The Sounds of Modernity: The Evolution of Bollywood Film Song". In: Sangita Gopal and Sujata Moorti (Eds): *Global Bollywood: Travels of Hindi Song and Dance*, p. 85–104. Minneapolis: Minnesota University Press.

Silverman, Kaja

1994 "Fassbinder and Lacan: A reconsideration of Gaze, Lack, and Image". In: N. Bryson, M.A. Holly and K. Moxly (Eds.): *Images and Interpretation*, p. 272–301. Hanover: Wesleyan University Press.

Sharpe, Jenny

2005 "Gender, Nation, and Globalization in Monsoon Wedding and Dilwale Dulhania Le Jayenge". *Meridians: feminism, race, transnationalism* Vol. 6 No. 1, pp. 58–81.

Stacey, Jackie

2001 "Desperately Seeking Difference: Jackie Stacey Considers Desire Between Women in Narrative Cinema". In: Julia Thomas (Ed.): *Reading Images*, p.109–122. Hampshire: Palgrave.

Sturken, Marita and Lisa Cartwright (Eds)

2001 *Practices of Looking: An Introduction to Visual Culture*. New York: Oxford University Press.

Taylor, Woodman

2003 "Penetrating gazes: The poetics of sight and visual display in popular cinema". In: Sumathi Ramaswamy (Ed.): *Beyond Appearances? Visual Practices and Ideologies in Modern India*, p. 297–322. New Delhi: Sage.

Thomas, Rosie

2008 "Indian Cinema: Pleasures and Popularity". In: Jigna Desai and Rajinder Kumar Dudrah (Eds): *The Bollywood Reader*, p. 21–31. Maidenhead: Open University Press.

Tieber, Claus (Ed.)

2007 *Passages to Bollywood*. Wien: LIT Verlag.

2009 *Fokus Bollywood: Das indische Kino in wissenschaftlichen Diskursen*. Wien: LIT Verlag

Uberoi, Patricia

2008 "Imagining the family: an ethnography of viewing Hum Aapke Hain Koun ...!". In: Jigna Desai and Rajinder Kumar Dudrah (Eds): *The Bollywood Reader*, p. 172–187. Maidenhead: Open University Press.

Vajdovich, Györgyi

2010 *Shah Rukh Khan's pioneer role in introducing new production, distribution and marketing techniques in globalized Bollywood*. Paper at the "Shah Rukh and Global Bollywood" Conference , Universität Wien, 30.9 – 2.10.2010

Vasudevan, Ravi S.

2000a "Introduction". In: Ravi s. Vasudevan (Ed.): *Making Meaning in Indian Cinema*, p. 1–32. New Delhi: Oxford University Press.

2000b "The politics of cultural address in a 'transitional' cinema: a case study of Indian popular cinema. In: Christine Gledhill and Linda Williams (Eds): *Reinventing Film Studies*, pp. 130–164. London: Arnold.

2000c "Addressing the Spectator of a 'Third World' National Cinema: the Bombay 'Social' Film of the 1940s and 1950s". In: Robert Stam and Toby Miller (Eds): Film and Theory: An Anthology, pp. 381–402. Malden: Blackwell.

Films

Dilwale Dulhania Le Jayenge. DVD. Directed by Aditya Chopra. 1995; Yash Raj Films 2001.

Kuch Kuch Hota Hai. DVD. Directed by Karan Johar. 1998; Rapid Eye Movies 2009.

Kabhi Khushi Kabhie Gham. DVD. Directed by Karan Johar. 2001; Rapid Eye Movies 2006.

Kal Ho Naa Ho.DVD. Directed by Nikhil Advani. 2003; Rapid Eye Movies, 2009.

Kabhi Alvida Naa Kehna. DVD. Directed by Karan Johar. 2006; Dharma Productions 2006.

Song and dance sequences:

Mere Khwabon (DDLJ: 00:08:20–00:12:15), *Ruk Jaa O Dil* (DDLJ: 00:38:10–00:43:15), *Zara Sa Jhoom* (DDLJ: 00:58:00–01:02:20), *Tujhe Dekha* (01:45:00–01:50:40), *Mehndi Laga Ke* (DDLJ: 02:17:10–02:23:30), *Yeh Laaka Hai Deewana* (KKHH: 00:22:40–00:29:10), *Koi Mil Gaya* (KKHH: 00:51:20–00:59:00), *Kuch Kuch Hota Hai* (KKHH: 01:06:30–01:11:30), *Ladki Badi Anjani Jai* (KKHH 02:12:20–02:18:00), *Kabhi Kushi Kabhie Gham I* (K3G: 00:13:00–00:20:30), *"Suraj Hua Madham"* (K3G: 01:03:20–01:10:00), *Say "Shava Shava"*(K3G: 00:43:20–00:50:00), *Yeh Ladka Hai Allah* (K3G: 01:15:00–01:20:40), *Deewana Hai Dekho* (K3G: 01:56:40–02:02:30), *Bole Chudiyan* (K3G: 02:40:00–02:47:00), *Pretty Woman* (KHNH: 00:25:30–00:31:00), *"It's The Time To Disco"* (KHNH: 00:51:30–00:56:30), *Kal Ho Naa Ho* (01:58:00–02:02:30), *Tumhi Dekho Naa* (KANK: 01:41:00–01:45:50), *Rock 'N' Roll Soniye* (KANK: 00:51:20–00:57:00), *Mitwa* (KANK: 01:15:30–01:22:00), *Where's The Party Tonight* (KANK: 02:10:00–02:16:00)

Index

O

P

Q

R

S

V

W

Appendix

DDLJ film plot:

Raj and Simran are brought up in the Indian diaspora in Great Britain. While he is the son of a rich widower and leads a reckless, hedonistic life, the girl lives in a sheltered home dominated by a patriarch who is a hardworking, rather conservative shop owner aiming to return to his homeland. Raj has a memorable encounter with her father when he tricks him into giving him beer at his convenience store. The two young people meet on a trip through Europe. At this point in time Simran's marriage to the son of her father's friend in Punjab has already been arranged. However, Raj and Simran fall in love after various events and adventures with their friends including a night they spend together in Switzerland. Although both of them are drunk, they do not get intimate. Back home her father finds out about her secret love and decides to take his family to India immediately. Raj follows her there, determined to win the hearts of all her family members and, ultimately, the consent of Simran's father to marry her. By supposedly befriending Simran's husband-to-be, who is a selfish and ruthless person who disregards his fiancée's feelings, he gains entrance to the marriage festivities. When Simran's mother finds out his true identity, she urges the young lovers to elope. But Raj insists on staying and winning over the patriarch's heart. Her father finds out at last and expels him. Raj and his father, who has arrived in India in the meantime, head to the train station, disheartened. There the husband-to-be waits for them with a group of friends to take revenge and beat up Raj as well as his father. The respective families of Simran and her fiancé arrive at the station, too, and stop the fight. When Raj enters the train with his father, Simran tries to run after him. Although her father stops her first, he finally lets her go as he realizes no one could love his daughter more than Raj.

KKHH film plot:

Rahul and Anjali(1) are best friends at college, when a new girl, who is the principal's daughter and has grown up in London, arrives. While Anjali(1) is a tomboy, Tina is a very feminine young woman. Rahul feels very attracted to Tina, but his best friend Anjali(1) also discovers her feelings for him. When she realizes that Rahul is in love with the other girl, Anjali(1) is broken-hearted and leaves college. Rahul and Tina get married. The couple have a daughter, who is named after her father's best friend by Tina, who was aware of Anjali's true feelings. Shortly after childbirth the young mother dies. Rahul brings up his daughter with the help of his mother, but is lonesome. On each birthday the young girl gets one letter of a series her mother wrote before her death. The eighth one tells her about her namesake and instructs her to find Anjali(1) and make her father realise they belong together. In the meantime Anjali(1) has got engaged, but she is still uncertain about the marriage as she is not truly in love with her fiancé. The young Anjali(2) and her grandmother, who knows about her plans, manage to visit a summer camp, where Anjali(1) works. The little girl not only grows to love Anjali(1) and regard her as a future stepmother, but also manages to arrange a meeting of her father with his former best friend. When Rahul and Anjali(1) meet again their feelings are revived. They even share some very intimate moments, but when her fiancé arrives at the camp Rahul does not want to interfere. When Rahul wishes her luck in her marriage, Anjali decides it is best to leave and prepare for her wedding. At last, Rahul takes the initiative and confesses his love for her on her wedding day. However, it is her fiancé who finally joins their hands together and gives his consent to their union, thus fulfilling the little girl's greatest wish.

K3G film plot:

Rahul is adopted as a child by the rich Raichands, who also have a younger biological son, Rohan. When Rahul returns from university in England he is supposed to take over the family business. However, he falls in love with Anjali, who lives in Chandni Chowk and is poor compared to his family. While his father arranges Rahul's marriage with another girl, Rahul makes his intentions very clear to Anjali in public. Although his wife-to-be Naina accepts that Rahul is in love with someone else, his father rejects the relationship with Anjali due to her social status and expresses great disappointment about his son's, as well. The young man decides to give up his love, but Anjali's father dies and leaves his two daughters behind, quite destitute. Rahul marries her spontaneously. When his father finds out he not only expels him from his home, but also denounces him as his son. Rahul and Anjali leave for England with her younger sister Pooja. Years later Rohan finds out the truth about his brother's disappearance and also his mother's grief. Vowing to reunite the family he goes to London to study. At university he meets Pooja and she agrees to help him. She persuades Rahul to let Rohan stay at their place as a guest, not telling him who he really is. Although Rahul and Anjali have a son and live comfortably, the family conflict casts a shadow on their happiness. Slowly the family finds out who Rohan is and the brothers are reunited.

However, the attempts at reconciliation between the patriarch and his adopted son fail. The parents visit London, which gives the mother an opportunity to see her son again. In the end, Rahul returns to India with his family when his grandmother dies. Her last wish was that her son together with her two grandsons would light the funeral pyre. It is the mother who finally criticizes her husband for hurting everyone and not giving in. The patriarch admits his mistake and the family reunite, which culminates in the marriage of Rohan and Pooja.

KHNH film plot:

Naina is young woman living in the diaspora in New York with her family. They have a lot of problems as her father committed suicide and her mother struggles to run a restaurant independently and raise the two younger siblings of Naina. The grandmother criticizes her daughter-in-law a lot, most of all for adopting the youngest child, Gia. When Aman moves into the neighborhood he changes everything by cheering up her family and supporting them in various ways. Although she first expresses a dislike for the lively young man, she ends up falling in love with him. At the same time Aman encourages her best friend Rohit, who is the son of a rich man, to acknowledge that he is love with her. Before he can confess his love to Naina, she tells him about her feelings for Aman. Shortly after that she finds out that Aman is married. However, this is a lie her beloved tells her because he is fatally ill and wants her to be happy with Rohit. Next, the two men plan Rohit's courtship, which is finally successful as Naina agrees to marry him. In the meantime Aman also finds out the truth about the adopted child. She turns out to be the illegitimate child of the dead father, which brings about a reconciliation of Naina's mother and grandmother. The preparations for the marriage start, while Aman's health deteriorates. At the engagement party he breaks down and nearly dies. While he is in hospital Naina finds out the truth, because she gets to know his doctor (who Aman pretended was his wife). Naina meets him again knowing now that he returns her feelings. Yet she marries Rohit and fulfils her promise to Aman to be happy. On his deathbed his family members and friends are by his side, but it is Rohit who stays with him till the end, promising him that in every other life Naina will be his. The last scene shows Naina and Rohit many years after as a happy couple, telling the story to her daughter.

KANK film plot:

The paths of two couples cross when Dev meets Maya on her wedding day and persuades her not to be afraid and to marry Rishi, whom she has known since childhood, as his father raised her. Right after leaving her behind, Dev is crippled in a car accident, which ruins his career as a professional football player. As a result, his marital relationship with Rhea suffers under the new circumstances, because while she becomes a very successful business woman, while he looks after their son and is filled with bitterness. Years later Dev and Maya meet again and as both of them are frustrated and feel lonely, they become friends. Together they plan to repair their marriages, but fail as they end up falling in love with each other. Maya, who not only feels guilty for not being able to bear children, but also for failing to feel any sexual attraction to her husband, experiences romantic fulfilment in the extramarital relationship. Dev also enjoys the love and understanding missing in his marriage. However, his mother and Maya's father-in-law find out about the lovers' secret. Shortly after, the latter dies of a heart attack, but on his deathbed gives advice to Maya to leave his son, as neither of them can be happy in this marriage. Dev and Naina both confess their infidelity to their partners, who leave and divorce them. However, they do not tell each other as both want the other one to be happy in marriage. Years after, Maya is invited to Rishi's second wedding and meets Rhea there. Both ex-partners convince her to meet Dev, who is leaving town for a new job. At the train station they finally reunite and agree to get married.